ARCANA VI

ARCANA VI
MUSICIANS ON MUSIC

EDITED BY
JOHN ZORN

HIPS ROAD 2012

Book design by Heung-Heung Chin.

First published in 2012
ISBN 978-0-9788337-5-6
ISBN 0-9788337-5-9
Printed on acid-free paper
Printed and bound in the United States of America

Hips Road
200 East 10th Street #126
New York, NY 10003
http://www.tzadik.com

Distributed to the trade by D.A.P. / Distributed Art Publishers
155 Avenue of the Americas, Second Floor
New York, NY 10013

Orders: (800) 338-2665   Tel: (212) 627-1999
Fax: (212) 627-9484

CONTENTS

Preface
John Zorn   *v*

11   **Chapter 1**
Rants
Richard "Duck" Baker

Chapter 2
The Outcome is Unforeseen:
Some Preliminary Notes
Eve Beglarian   *18*

23   **Chapter 3**
Music Mind at
The Stone and Beyond
Karl Berger

Chapter 4
In Search of the New Density
Claire Chase   *32*

41   **Chapter 5**
Blank Screen
Anna Clyne & Elizabeth Tasker

Chapter 6
Building Music
John Corigliano   *46*

50   **Chapter 7**
Life Preserver/In the Wilderness
Jeremiah Cymerman

Chapter 8
To [re]think of Milton Babbitt
David Fulmer   *60*

63   **Chapter 9**
Behind The Mask
or
I Didn't Know What Time It Was
Jeff Gauthier

Chapter 10
Performance and Interpretation
Alan Gilbert   *71*

89   **Chapter 11**
We Are All Beethoven
Judd Greenstein

i

Chapter 12
Troubadours' Dilemmas
Hilary Hahn 97

102 **Chapter 13**
The Invented Horizon is Free
Mary Halvorson

Chapter 14
How I Came to Write a Few Songs
Jesse Harris 109

113 **Chapter 15**
Death Speaks
David Lang

Chapter 16
Why Do I Write Music
the Way I Do?
Mary Jane Leach 119

124 **Chapter 17**
Spectral Music as a Framework
for Improvisation
Stephen Lehman

Chapter 18
Righting Wrong Notes
Steven Mackey 136

145 **Chapter 19**
"He Said What?"
Rudresh Mahanthappa

Chapter 20
China Diary
Denman Maroney 154

168 **Chapter 21**
Rock Hemiolas
Brad Mehldau

Chapter 22
Process, Creativity and
Planetary Returns
Jessica Pavone 173

180 **Chapter 23**
Old and Lost Muses
Tobias Picker

Chapter 24
Dreamy Bits
Gyan Riley 183

188 Chapter 25
Lines in Red Sand
Jon Rose

Chapter 26
To a Gathering of Percussionists
Steven Schick *207*

222 Chapter 27
Lelewå: Memoirs of a
Bone and Voice Tracer
Jen Shyu

Chapter 28
Flukey Concatenations
David Taylor *238*

248 Chapter 29
Some Memories of John Cage
Richard Teitelbaum

Chapter 30
John Henry
Julia Wolfe *256*

261 Chapter 31
Wollesonics
Kenny Wollesen

Chapter 32
Small, Still Voice
Nate Wooley *275*

281 Chapter 33
A Note on BBM
Charles Wuorinen

About the Musicians *283*

300 *Recommended Listening*

PREFACE

In Defense of Difficulty

JOHN ZORN

"Do not follow where the path may lead. Go, instead, where there is no path and leave a trail."

—Ralph Waldo Emerson

We are living at a time of revolution: politically, intellectually, emotionally, artistically, spiritually and technologically. History has shown us that times of crisis are also very exciting times for the Arts, and accordingly there is a great deal of amazing music being made today. Unfortunately the best of it remains obscure, overshadowed by work that is more easily grasped on first hearing. Backed by promotion and hype, lesser work is championed while more profound, difficult, challenging work is being quite unceremoniously ignored. Although this is not a particularly new phenomenon, there is something disturbing about today's version of it. With advertising more oppressive and ubiquitous than ever, the techniques involved in manipulating popular opinion have taken a sinister turn. Propaganda is one word for it, brainwashing is perhaps closer to the truth. The push toward conformity has rarely been stronger, leading some social critics, cultural analysts (and conspiracy theorists) to make comparisons to neo-fascist fear tactics.

Accessibility has become the new mantra. Blogs and tweets proliferate with reductionist sound bites and advertising tells us daily to "be stupid",—encouraging our basest desires and most primitive emotions. Much has happened in this first decade of the new millennium, and there is of course more to come. For an artist to survive in this fast changing world one must learn to adapt. But in adapting one must be careful that one's basic nature and value system does not alter in the process. This is one of the challenges that a creative artist faces in this modern world: how to adapt without giving in to society's pressures, without losing one's *essence*.

Distractions and opinions of every conceivable (and inconceivable) variety surround us, attacking our perceptions of reality with a growing vehemence, making it more and more difficult to establish a base of operations from which to launch pure creative vision. In today's overwhelmingly market-driven society success has become synonymous with popularity and monetary gain,—films are rated by their weekly gross, CDs by their unit sales, artists by their fan base and pay scale. People's need for familiarity and preference for uniformity is being exploited, and the result is a proliferation of the trite, the easy, the familiar, the vulgar and the mediocre. What we hear in most concert halls, clubs and venues is largely driven by compromise, self-serving agendas or the narrow restrictions of the comfort zone. Educational institutions are suspicious (if not downright afraid) of new and challenging ideas, of courting controversy or of introducing radical curricula and modern views. We are living in a state of emergency,—a spreading disease of playing it safe, fashion over content, popularity over education, face recognition over integrity is robbing us of a depth, challenge and spirituality that we, as humans living in an increasingly conformist and digitized world need *more than ever*.

For centuries music was at the center of life,—a special event, a mystical experience, a spiritual endeavor, a way of communing with the angels, with the eternal, with each other, and with ourselves. In centuries past one had to enter temples and churches to encounter it. Music was performed at seasonal festivals, in regal courts, lavish homes and spectacular theatres. To hear it was a privilege, to appreciate it a sign of breeding, integrity, culture. Before the 20th century music was exclusively a live event,—to hear it you either went to a concert, hired musicians, or learned to play it yourself. This took time, money, effort, thought and feeling. Many families owned musical instruments and would play music together, bonding in a way that is sadly rare these days. Now all you have to do is flip a switch and you have all the music you want, and unlike water, gas and electricity you don't even have to pay for it! In losing this aspect of ritual in music and art making, not only is the importance and integrity of art withering away, our minds are withering along with it, suggesting a magical connection between human essence and Art itself.

The Internet has presented us with some new challenges. In making music more available than ever before, the power of the Net has also propagated the idea that music is free for the taking. Today we find music everywhere, but more often than not it is relegated to the background. The threat of music being reduced to *Muzak* (a faceless, nameless sound with little or no information accompanying it to allow a deeper appreciation of the who-what-where-when-why) poses a real danger. As the context in which music is presented changes, people's perceptions of the nature of music itself changes as well.

We need to reclaim the importance that real Music plays in our lives. Music has inspired poets, saints, scientists and artists. It was at the center of magical rituals, a bridge to the beyond, a way of transcending the mundane, the commonplace and was a magic carpet to the unknown. It also fed the everyday hunger for knowledge, humanity, compassion, spirituality, beauty and truth. New music that aspires to these values is being more and more marginalized, and survives only through the tenacity and persistence of a small group of dedicated believers who refuse to give in to the pressures that surround them every moment of every day. Although one can't help but worry about how great work will be treated by future generations,—to whom music has become anonymous, disposable, a mere accessory, not much more than a fashion statement,—it still remains prescient and at the center of a small group of creative people's lives. The artists contributing to the *Arcana* series are all members of an inner council who are carrying the torch of truth through the Dark Ages.

Now is a time when we should join hands as a community and take seriously the responsibility of protecting and nurturing the Art we love and believe in, of upholding the values we hold dear,—values that enrich our lives and make life worth living. This can only happen through education. To return to a place where challenge and adventure in Art again becomes something to be treasured and sought after we need guidance from reliable, intelligent sources who place integrity above personal gain and who will not compromise their vision or values for fame or financial rewards. The *Arcana* series is a small step toward educating the interested listener about the inner workings of the artistic process, at creating a resource one can reference in reaching under the surface,—towards a deeper understanding and appreciation of the magical properties and future possibilities of music. This volume contains a wide range of voices from diverse backgrounds and disciplines. Each musician has something unique and personal to say and all are taking the necessary steps to protect the integrity of their vision, and of this most sacred of all art forms.

Music is one of humankind's greatest accomplishments, and one of its greatest treasures. It must be nurtured to survive. May these few insights prove inspiring, and lead you all on the even more exciting adventure of exploring the music itself.

—John Zorn, *NYC 2012*

ARCANA VI

THOUGHTS ON FOLK MUSIC, JAZZ, AND CONTEMPORARY MUSIC

RICHARD "DUCK" BAKER

Sometime in the late 1990s when I was living near San Francisco, I went into town to meet John Zorn for a meal before his gig that night, and wound up at an amazing sushi restaurant in the Richmond district along with John, Willie Winant and Mike Patton. It gave Zorn a chance to speak Japanese with the proprietors (a good way to get the best house has to offer), and during the ensuing conversation it came out that we were all musicians. This lead, naturally enough, to the question, "What kind of music do you play?" Usually, this is an easy question, but in this case, John hesitated a moment before replying "We all play different styles; I play jazz, he (Patton) plays rock, he (Winant) is classical and he (indicating me) plays folk."

It was an interesting moment. I'm sure all four of us work in enough different situations that we don't always answer this question with a one-word answer, but John's reply reflected the fields with which each of us is usually associated, while the fact that we were all there together demonstrates that boundaries between musical categories are anything but rigid. In fact, one could engage in some fairly serious polemics about the extent to which the terms jazz, rock, classical and folk each have meanings that change according to who's using them, and I think this is particularly true of the last. And this is why, when John asked me to write something for this collection, it seemed natural for me to talk about connections between traditional and contemporary music. Many people see such connections easily enough when the folk music in question is from Africa, Turkey, or Tuva, but less readily when it's from their own culture.

A classic definition of folk music would be music that is played in folk communities, free to whatever extent is possible from outside influences and passed on orally from generation to generation, often by family members. In most traditional African village societies, the whole population would participate in singing, dancing, and playing instruments, and the music would never have been notated or recorded. European folk communities might not have all taken part in the music making, though most would certainly have danced, and everyone would have known the songs and dance tunes; they were basic facts of the shared culture. As long as we are talking about traditional rural communities with little exposure to other kinds of music, all is well and the folklorist's job is straightforward. But, of course, it has been a long time since such isolated communities have existed at all in western countries, and so the meaning of the term "folk" has had to be stretched to try and accommodate the modern situation. Ultimately, the big folk revival that came to a head in America in the '50s and '60s produced its own community, of urban college kids who sang old songs while picking guitars and banjos, or wrote new songs, often of a topical nature. Nowadays, most people who use the term "folk music" are more likely to be thinking of Bob Dylan than of the people Dylan listened to as a young man. And even when we use a term like "traditional folk" when we refer to contemporary musicians, it is with the understanding that the social contexts that used to define such music are gone forever.

I'd like to examine some ways that a folk approach might be applied to modern musical styles, but first let's look at the more obvious question of how folk music has interacted with pop, country and rock. In the most basic way, all pop music (or indeed, all music of any kind, as Louis Armstrong famously noted) is folk music. You don't need a degree to trace how American folk styles lead directly to C&W and rock & roll, when you have Johnny Cash singing Leadbelly songs and Elvis singing Bill Monroe and Big Boy Crudup. The addition of electric guitars and drums is not really a big deal; guitars themselves were relative newcomers to country music when it began to be recorded. For the folkies who reacted negatively to Dylan's much-discussed appearance with an electric band at the 1965 Newport Folk Festival, it wasn't really a matter of him doing something new and heretical. It was more that they saw themselves as having turned their backs on the world of commercial pop music, and viewed Dylan's new sound as a betrayal of their *Weltanschauung*. Whether he was betraying his own muse was quite another question, but once this reaction had been discredited, it left the folk world free to embrace all kinds of middle-of-the-road pop performers, as long as they strummed acoustic guitars; one could certainly argue that they were better off being overly purist. The whole thing underlines how hopeless it is to try and figure out what is "authentic" at this point.

We can also note, in passing, connections between folk and western classical traditions, which are mostly a matter of individual composers drawing inspiration from what used to be called national music (viz Dvorak, Grieg, Vaughan Williams, Copland). The relationship becomes more complex when we consider Eastern Europe, where the presence of Bartók looms over everything. Here the great composer is also the great father of modern folk musicology and collecting, and traditional music informs and even interacts with classical to a far greater degree. Among many reasons for this we can note the very challenging nature of Eastern European folk music, full of odd-meter rhythms and dissonant harmonies.

Jazz developed from the same folk traditions that produced rock, country, rhythm and blues, and other vernacular forms. To a large extent, American music is a matter of African rhythms combining with an English-Scottish-Irish melodic sense and European harmony. Anything else that's in it (German, French or Spanish melodic tendencies, a very few specific borrowings from indigenous Americans) can be seen as flavoring, but to begin with, you have the spirituals, and Appalachian fiddle tunes. In the first case, the sense of Anglo-Scots melody was absorbed and adopted by African Americans, and in the second, African syncopation and a rhythmic propulsion that would later be called "swing" were applied to Scots and Irish fiddle tunes. Soon after the civil war, the spirituals were subjected to harmonizations and at this point things start to get very interesting. WC Handy would write about "a groping sense of racial harmony" and it's impossible not to hear what he means if we listen to the early recordings of black vocal groups. This style of harmony singing reflects several things besides basic tonal thinking. One can, I believe, detect the influence of the odd and somewhat archaic system that spread through America from New England, known as shape-note singing. But there's something else going on, something to do with blue notes and the way the flatted 3rd and 7th are superimposed on the major scale, so that the minor 3rd can be sung over a major chord. This is generally assumed to be African in origin, but in fact one does encounter the same melodic tendency in Scottish and especially in Irish melody; the difference is that African Americans began to harmonize these melodies.

It's hard to see how African American music could have developed the way that it did in a society that wasn't racially segregated. Segregation meant that, no matter what sophisticated musical ideas were introduced to black music, it was going to remain directly connected to its community; unless of course an individual managed to acquire classical training and devoted himself or herself to that music, as a few significant composers did manage to do. As long as African Americans were forced to live in their own part of town, they were constrained to be folk musicians in many senses of the term, and this held true right into the time that even the most modern jazz styles were in gestation. Talented youngsters often began to play instruments in their schools (many of which provided instruments), often under the influence of dedicated teachers who knew that music represented important career opportunities for African Americans. Jazz musicians were not only given much of the technical instruction they would need in high school, but were introduced to whatever jazz community there might be in their home towns, all without access to higher education. One can assume that the atmosphere in such classrooms was markedly less competitive than it is in today's jazz schools, and that there was a lot less emphasis on the purely technical side of things (even allowing for the fact that the technical side has evolved terrifically in recent years). Since integration, the more successful African American families are not constrained to live in ghettos, and those who are left in the inner city don't have access to instruments, making rap music almost a cultural necessity. Can anyone doubt that the world in which jazz developed simply doesn't exist any more? And can anyone doubt that something has been lost for the music because of this? (I do hope no one supposes for a moment that the author is arguing for segregation, but in these confused times it's probably just as well to specify that I certainly am not.)

If jazz in many ways was forced to remain a folk music, its sheer complexity is far removed from traditional folk styles, at least apparently. But we need to tread lightly here; if we accept this premise at face value, we risk buying into a fundamental misapprehension about traditional African music, in which counterpoint was elevated to such a high degree that the first Europeans exposed to it really couldn't hear what was going on. They dismissed music that was actually much more complex than their own as "primitive." Moreover, the idea that folk melody is not as advanced as classical melody is very questionable. Even without any real harmony going on, Irish melody is enormously complex and sophisticated. So when we encounter something like Gunther Schuller's suggestion that, with the improvisations of Louis Armstrong, jazz ceased to be a mere folk art, we can agree that something enormously important was added, but it would be wise to be wary of that word "mere." The distinction conjures up a bourgeois European notion of what constitutes "high art." The idea that the sounds that ensue when a conductor raises his baton in a concert hall is, ipso facto, going to be more meaningful than what an uneducated Negro pianist might have been doing in a whorehouse a hundred years ago—that's the kind of thinking we don't need. It just ain't necessarily so.

My own feeling, is that neither Louis Armstrong, Charlie Parker, Thelonious Monk, or John Coltrane ever gave us music that was deeper or more beautiful than that left to us by people like Skip James, Robert Johnson, or the Soul Stirrers. In many ways, modern jazz isn't even any more complex. Find a modern jazz guitarist who can do what Blind Lemon Jefferson did with his voice and one instrument, then we can talk about who's doing something complex. Of course we do celebrate the evolution of the improvised jazz line, the melodic extension of bebop, the harmonic detail of modern jazz. But many of the greatest modernists, from Monk and Mingus to Ornette Coleman and Albert Ayler, are great precisely because they retain something raw and organic, something that's found in great folk art but not in western classical music. And I should note that I don't mean to limit the discussion at this point to African American folk artists. I hear the same intense cry and almost existential yearning in the music of Appalachian musicians like Roscoe Holcomb, Dock Boggs and Edden Hammons.

I'd like to focus on a particular tragicomic quality we can hear on recordings by Gus Cannon's Jug Stompers, but not in the works of Johannes Chrysostomus Wolfgangus Theophilus Mozart. Listen to Mr. Cannon sing a song like *I'm Going to Germany*, accompanied by the homeliest ensemble imaginable; banjo, guitar, harmonica, and a jug into which bass notes are blown. The music of this jug band has a comic veneer, but when the listener actually focuses on the SOUND of it, it is intensely beautiful in a way that a symphony orchestra cannot be. This owes to a self-deprecating quality, an awareness of being a subject of mockery and of having to play the clown in order to be able to sing at all, that imbues the music with raw, existential sadness that somehow enhances a feeling that's ultimately joyful. It's as if to say, you can force me to act the clown, and you can give me next to nothing to work with, but I am still a man, I am still here, I still have a voice! Polish and sophistication can help put across many things, but not this.

15

Besides the ragtime-blues of Cannon and similar stylists, we can hear this quality in some Cajun and hillbilly music, in almost all early klezmer, and even in modern jazz, especially the music of Monk and Mingus. I also think it was an important component of early ragtime, as the recordings of Brun Campbell demonstrate. Can avant-garde musicians put this across? In the case of Marc Ribot and Ben Goldberg, I hear them doing this with klezmer material much more successfully than the straight revivalists usually do.

It is dangerous to succumb to the temptation of confusing what's "new" with what's innovative in our approach, and equally dangerous to think that only innovative music is meaningful. Our societal tendency for wanting what's "new" is in large measure a response to the pressures of the market, where those who don't want to be left out have to buy this year's shirt, this month's bestseller, this week's pop star. In the context of jazz, the arriviste on the cover of a jazz glossy is very unlikely to be putting out music as challenging as what Ornette Coleman was doing fifty years ago. On the other hand, the fact that Ornette showed us that we don't have to follow chord progressions doesn't mean we can't. Nor does this particular even have to be viewed as innovation; it's just as easy to see the jettisoning of preset harmonic schemes as a reactionary step. We can also note other folky qualities in Ornette's playing, like his bluesy sound and feeling, or his penchant for Mexican melodic turns. One might say that Coleman's step "forward" to free jazz has more to do with down-home Texas than uptown New York. But what's important is that Ornette reached back into the music's core, and his own, and the change came out of that. He broke some rules, and he followed others, but in each case he was doing what he needed to to get the job done.

My own feeling is that one doesn't have to innovate to play great music. I've been transported by too many Irish fiddlers and pipers to believe otherwise. Musicians like Tommy Peoples and Liam O'Flynn are neither innovators nor improvisers, but they certainly have more soul than a lot of contemporary jazzers. For that matter, a trad jazzman like Kenny Davern could lay out some beautifully improvised solos, and had lots of soul, too. The important thing is being real, and for some people the way to do that will be in a musical context that has already been laid out, be it Irish dance music, Texas fiddle tunes, ragtime, or bebop. For others it will be to study modern classical composition, or Carnatic music. For others it may be combining influences from various sources.

I want to emphasize once more that traditional music is often more complex than it might appear. Irish pipers will drone a low D while playing in A minor and fiddlers often do the same thing when they bow a low G when returning to the tonic in D minor, but modern listeners tend to internally edit things like this when they listen to records; it's easy to fall into the trap of thinking that this happens because these folk musicians didn't "know what they were doing." Well, they did it every time. They learned it that way, they heard what it sounded like, they dug it, and they thought it was right. The fact that classical musicians wouldn't have done it until the 20th century wasn't their problem. But it is ours, unless we understand that all the things in the old music that don't conform to our preconceptions are not just "mistakes." This is an easy example, but I could say much the same about instrumental tone, pitch, voicings and structure. Where in classical music would we find something like the "ride" in a gospel vocal performance, like what Ira Tucker would do with the Dixie Hummingbirds? Nowhere—but you'll sure find it in John Coltrane. That's practically what later Coltrane is: gospel rides with a lot of added harmonic information.

We all need to draw inspiration from whatever sources are available to us. I personally love to listen to modern classical composers, the more because I don't have a clue about the systems they use. This enables me to hear the music without trying to track everything, which can be hard for me when listening to jazz. However, I don't hear this music as being more immediate or even more contemporary than a lot of folk music. If a youngster listening to Boulez or Ferneyhough senses the need to get inside these systems, he or she certainly should, but the rest of us can just enjoy it as music. The same is true of George Russell's Lydian Chromatic theory, Hindustani ragas, or the blues. But really, the great advance of 20th century music wasn't serial composition, the 32-bar pop song, or the introduction of electrically amplified instruments; it was the simple fact of recorded music. Now, you can sit in your living room and hear music from all over the world. You can dig all kinds of approaches, and I can't help thinking that the more you take in and really digest in this manner, the more ways you can find to deal with things that come up in your own musical adventures.

THE OUTCOME IS UNFORESEEN: SOME PRELIMINARY NOTES

EVE BEGLARIAN

I am resistant to writing about my own music. I had never spent much time thinking about it, but being asked by John Zorn to write something, anything, about music has made it abundantly clear to me. Writing about what I'm doing when I actually do my work? Annie Gosfield is great at it, I have loved reading her essays. But most descriptions of musical procedures, music theory, and musical technique are of absolutely no interest to me. Perhaps it's a leftover reaction to those blindingly dull quasi-mathematical theory articles I tried to read in *Perspectives of New Music* as an undergraduate.

I am not interested in program notes either. I can't remember ever reading much of anything in a program note that wasn't either obvious or beside the point. The only music criticism I have really loved is Lester Bangs': the collection *Psychotic Reactions and Carburetor Dung* is a masterpiece, for sure. And *Silence*, of course: John Cage is a delight, even when I disagree with him. Every now and then I run across something by Alex Ross or Kyle Gann that interests me, but I don't make a point of reading their work regularly.

I guess I'm not sure it's actually interesting to write about music. It's so much better to listen to it. And to make it.

But on the other hand, I recognize and appreciate that what Zorn is doing with this *Arcana* series is attempting to foster a community. For a community to thrive, there needs to be a shared conversation that works towards knitting us together.

So I offer this provisional attempt to participate in the conversation. (Thanks to Corey Dargel and Frank Brickle and Linda Norton for conversations that helped shape these notes.)

*　　*　　*

I like John Cage's definition of experimental music: music about which the outcome is unforeseen, or something like that. I am not interested in writing music if I know how it's going to turn out before I start writing. That's hack work to me. When I start making a piece, I don't know how it's going to turn out, but the piece isn't finished until it's turned out somehow. So the finished work doesn't necessarily reflect the uncertainty and confusion and risk-taking that I went through to make it. If I've made the piece well, then it's the result of my experimental process rather than an illustration of it.

My pieces often tell stories, and sometimes I get irritated, because I'd like to write something that goes one way, but I can't do it because it needs to go another way. So I can't do what I feel like doing, I have to do what the piece is telling me it needs to do. There are tensions that have to be resolved, and that's where the story is. Actually, that's *what* a story is. Underneath the facts and the plot and stuff we call story, the point of narrative is that there are tensions that need to be resolved.

I experience writing a piece of music as a narrative process whether there are words present in the piece or not. To structure time is in some way to tell a story; it's embedded in how we deal with unfolding time. Also, perhaps because I worked as an audio book producer for years, the sonic qualities of text and the narrative qualities of music are things I think about. I'll often write a piece of music responding to a text in order to make that text available in some deeper way, because music does certain things a whole lot better than words do. You can do really complicated things emotionally with music, which is why everybody loves music, I think. And music is much more nuanced than words, which after all, have semantic qualities that limit your experience in a funny kind of way, even though they're really good carriers of meaning, because that's what they're for.

I think there are composers who think purely in music, and they may also end up with a set of tensions that get resolved as happens in stories, but they're thinking directly about those musical elements, and I don't start there. There are composers who are totally engaged with notes and rhythms *as* notes and rhythms. While I love using those tools—they are my tools, after all—they're not what inspire me. For me, to write music is to investigate some set of issues that I'm struggling with as a human being, issues that I can only resolve by writing music. What I'm really trying to do is figure out how to live, and playing with notes and rhythms is how I'm working it out.

19

*   *   *

I'm really resistant to letting externally determined notions of success, how you're supposed to do things, influence how I do things. I've worked to remain independent of the pressures of conformity that exist in every social domain. It's part of why I didn't become a professor of music. I worry that participating in the academic world creates certain habits of thought that are almost invisible to you when you're in that world, but that can prevent you from following your own path in the richest and deepest ways. But the commercial world can be a similar trap. If you consciously aim for success, you can end up doing things that warp your own path. So I'm pretty insistent on staying untethered from what the outside world sets up as goals and guidelines.

Of course we have to survive in the world. We have to come up with a way of living, of eating, and paying rent, but it's important to me that I do things on my own terms, which means it's probably taken longer for me to get recognition than if I'd been more responsive to the establishment around me, if I had tried harder to fit in. I would suggest that if you're having a lot of success right away, it might be wise to be very suspicious. Some of the most promising artists get too much reinforcement right away, and it can prevent them from going deeper into the sources of their own obsessions and interests and gifts.

*   *   *

Lately I've begun to re-think my relationship to the words *radical* and *conservative* as they are commonly applied. I have been called a radical, an experimentalist, for most of my career, and I can understand how that's true, but I also wonder at it. In my work, I'm responding to, finding kinship with, collaborating with things that already exist in the world. I'm interacting with a line, a lineage, of art-making that's been going on for five thousand years. I'm not setting out to break new ground as I'm making something, I'm making connections among things that are already right here. If that's not conservative, I don't know what is.

In 2007, I was commissioned to write a piece using a Persian text and working with traditional Persian musicians, and I spent about a year reading various Persian classics. One of the writers I found was a 12th century Sufi mystic named Al-Ghazzali. He has interesting things to say about the tension between the intellectual and the mystical, and I was considering using one of his texts. I spoke with a very sophisticated Persian woman about it and she said, "Oh no, you can't do that, because the Muslim fundamentalists have him. They own him. He belongs to them."

It was distressing. It was as if, in order to be a progressive person, you have to close the door on really compelling ideas and materials. It would be as if we didn't read St. Bernard because right-wing Catholics own him. Right-wing Catholics don't own St. Bernard, and it's important for me to assert my right to engage with those texts on my own terms. Just because nightmare right-wing people engage with a text doesn't mean we have to cede it to them. I think it means just the opposite, actually, that it's really important for us to find all the different facets that are in these texts, so they don't get owned by the fundamentalists.

I think Al-Ghazzali and St. Bernard have something really important in common, which can be summed up best not by any religious writer, but by Wittgenstein: "Whereof one cannot speak, thereof one must be silent."

Or make music.

❊   ❊   ❊

> "And sometimes, even music
> Cannot substitute for tears."
> —Paul Simon, *Cool, Cool River*

I think the role of an artist is to be completely engaged in the world as it is and also to stand outside it and give voice to things that people who are in the midst of it either can't see or say or don't want to see or are afraid of seeing. You need to be a stranger in the midst of the world. And it's a dangerous place to be. In a certain way you have a kinship and an intimacy with people on a very deep level, but in another way you're untethered from the ties of life that others use to stay connected and comfortable and safe. I think it makes you spiritually vulnerable, and you have to be careful, you have to protect yourself while remaining open. Making music is a spiritual practice, a psychological process, I don't really know where the line between those things is. And I think listening is a spiritual practice as well, and that's why we do it. Music *does* make something happen, despite John Cage's claims to the contrary.

Going down the Mississippi River during my *River Project*, I took solo journeys during the day, but then in the evening I would gather with my fellow travelers and we would set up camp and make dinner and hang out together. You need to be alone when you're traveling in order to be fully available to the experience. When you're a stranger traveling alone, people talk to you, confide in you, confess to you. It doesn't work if you're traveling with another person. But you don't have to be alone all the time, and you shouldn't be. I found that when I was alone on the river without company for any length of time I went to a very dark place, and that isn't useful. It isn't useful to get too far over the edge, and it doesn't make me a better artist or a better person. So I was conscious of flirting with the edge and working hard to make sure I protected myself from falling off the edge.

One of the things I experienced on the river, and maybe it's something about the Mississippi River in particular, is this strong sense of life and death being right next to each other all the time. You can hardly find where the line is, because everything living is growing out of things that have died. And the river, even early on, is muddy and fetid and full of organic stuff, and it feels both full of life and full of death. My relation to it is complicated. It was beautiful and fun and totally wonderful to do the journey, but also I began to see remnants of the development of this country that are horrifying. And I *lived into them* in a way that is not like reading a book or watching a documentary. It's absolutely present and immediate. The whole story of the Native Americans, the whole story of North vs. South and slavery, those things are growing right out of the ground somehow, and the pain of that and the loss associated with that—the combination of promise and abundance that this country represents and that the river basin embodies, on the one hand, and the repeated horrors of human relations along that same river—they're married to one another, you can't separate them. That's how it felt to me. The things I love most about this country are shot through with the things that I grieve over the most, the things that can't be undone.

I do think that making something is a hopeful thing to do. Always. And even if I'm composing a piece about loss, the act of making something always has hope at its center, and it inspires faith and engenders faith.

And I believe that maybe we really can do that for one another.

MUSIC MIND AT THE STONE
AND BEYOND

KARL BERGER

Recently I had the pleasure of conducting and playing with what we called "Karl Berger's Stone Workshop Orchestra" weekly for eight months (April to December 2011) at The Stone in New York. We were invited to The Stone by John Zorn, of course, who sensed that this would become something very special. And indeed it did; for me it was like going to heaven every Monday.

Each week, we came together for an open workshop/rehearsal at 7:15, followed by a performance at 9 PM. I invited young (and young at heart) professionals to join and kept an ongoing invitation on the Internet. Within a few weeks we had more than forty players of all instruments on a constantly growing roster. We typically crammed sixteen to twenty players into the narrow space each Monday.

It is quite amazing to note how many high-level improvising players of all instruments are now in the New York City area. And actually everywhere I visit, the number of players and the levels of expertise has increased exponentially.

My aim with this orchestra was to explore the "Music Mind" topics that I developed at the Creative Music Studio in the '70s and '80s. Music Mind was—and still is—developed with student participants at CMS and in residencies worldwide. Music Mind addresses issues that concern every style and form of music-making, aiming to maximize and intensify individual and collective performance, as well as listening skills.

The participants in the The Stone Workshop Orchestra were highly skilled professional players. Yet it turned out that Music Mind topics found an eager audience with them. Although Music Mind addresses the most fundamental issues affecting any kind of dedicated music-making, these issues are not in the foreground of traditional musical training, which is mostly codified to emphasize instrumental/vocal techniques and conventions in a specific stylistic environment.

This article doesn't afford us the opportunity to spread out the complete palette of issues that we address in this Music Mind approach. Yet, we can touch upon four of them—the ones that are paramount to the orchestra's uniqueness of character: personal touch; feeling vs. impulse; infinite dynamics/space; and what I call "harmonic tuning."

Personal Touch

It is my goal to maximize the quality of the music by having everyone in the orchestra express their unique ideas and personal sound. It is an orchestra of strong individual improvisers and the collective orchestral passages provide the framework for extraordinary solo, duet, trio sections. So personal touch is the first issue to address.

It amazes me every time, how many shades of sound come from the same category of instruments, depending on who is playing them. These differences seem to be directly linked to our voices, which are entirely unique, so much so, that "voice prints" are supposed to be even more accurate than fingerprints to identify a person!

Our voice is so unique that when we hear it for the first time on a audio recorder, we think there must be something wrong with the recorder itself. Right? It is hard to get used to one's own voice, because it doesn't sound like anyone else's. And many people never get used to it, ending up trying to imitate other people's voices. I heard that famous singers like Frank Sinatra or Jimi Hendrix were never quite happy with their voices even though most everyone else was.

Improvisers (and interpreters of written music as well) make a choice right there, consciously or not. Am I going to stick to my original sound, or I am going to try to sound like somebody else?

Usually, we end up with a mixture of the two. Yet our original sound, even the way of phrasing and intonation, is unavoidably present, no matter how hard we would try to suppress it. But the sound of our peers is also there, loud and clear, and unavoidable as well. It takes a rather strong character to ignore the prevalent sound ideals, trends or zeitgeist and push forward with a sound, phrasing, intonation, that remains entirely original.

Musical styles develop codified idioms of sound, intonation and approaches to phrasing. The "classical" sound, the "jazz" sound, the "folk" sound, the "rock" sound, etc. There are uniform sound ideals prevalent in all styles of music. Although jazz, for example, is, supposedly, more geared towards individual expression of sound than "classical" styles, there are only a few players that lead the way with entirely new approaches and personal voices, setting examples for the majority of players to orient their choices accordingly. However, there is a larger group of jazz players, who develop identifiable approaches without leaving the parameters of a prevalent style. To realize one's personal voice does not necessarily mean to leave or even expand the boundaries of a given style of playing.

To my mind, for one's sound, phrasing, intonation to be personal and recognizable means to simply get used to what wants to come out naturally when we play. When I started out improvising with seasoned jazz musicians from the U.S., jamming at a club in my hometown Heidelberg/ Germany, I used to record some sessions on my Uher tape recorder. Listening to those tapes, I can see that I was trying to emulate players like Bud Powell and Thelonious Monk on the piano, or Milt Jackson on the vibes. But now I notice that the mistakes I made in emulating their sound and phrasing, clearly show the beginnings of the kind of sound and phrasing that make up my own sound and playing now. It's uncanny; our personal way with sound, rhythm, phrasing is right there, ready to come out. One could say, we just have to get out of the way of our fixed, less-flexible ideas that we picked up listening to others.

As we develop technically on our instruments, we usually also pick up habits from our teachers, our idols, our peers. It is an unavoidable paradox; we learn mostly by imitating others, but then, finally, we need to learn to trust what wants to come directly and naturally. Our innermost feeling for sound, phrasing, and intonation that we bring with us into this world is uniquely ours—our personal voice, sound and style—and it's something we must learn to trust and encourage.

When I first came to New York in 1965 I went to see two concerts that I will never forget. The first one was a double bill at the Village Vanguard of the Bill Evans Trio and the Thelonious Monk Quartet. It was not only an experience of a complete switch of sound and style between the two: it sounded as if a different piano had been rolled in between the sets! That's how extreme the difference was. When Monk played I thought he had finally managed to ruin the tuning of the piano. Then Bill came on and the piano was perfectly in tune.

The other was a marathon concert at the Fillmore East with three saxophonists and their groups: Archie Shepp, Albert Ayler, and John Coltrane with Pharoah Sanders. One would, of course, appreciate the utter differences of approach between these musicians on their recordings. But hearing them in sequence, **live** was an ear- and mind-opening experience of the deepest nature.

The kind of individualism that is encouraged and expected in original approaches to jazz and all improvised music, doesn't appear to be encouraged and prevalent in classical music. Yet, when one listens closely, while the range of differentiation might not be as broad as we'll find in improvised music, there is definitely a personal touch detectable in the sound of every player. It is, of course, more sharply pronounced with solo players, than with orchestra members. Soloists like Pablo Casals and Glenn Gould, for example, are instantly recognizable by their sound.

I remember being in a concert hall in the afternoon for an interview. On stage was a piano tuner preparing the piano for a concert by Rudolf Serkin, pounding out intervals and single notes. As I was being interviewed I realized that all of the sudden, the sound of the piano changed distinctly. I looked up and instead of the piano tuner, there was Serkin on the stage playing intervals. One might think, a piano has a certain sound, and pianos certainly have distinctively different sounds between them, but the person playing it brings his/her own touch to it, their own sound.

We come into this world with unique features, with minute details of sound and rhythm, all our own. Nobody sounds the same way, nobody walks and talks the same way. That is our spirit, our very special edition. We can go for it, whatever that means, or we can blend in with the prevalent styles and trends and just hope our individuality shines through that. Or we can just adapt some elements of styles we like and incorporate them into our own approach, which slowly but surely wants to develop, all by itself. There are endless variations to this theme. The point is: whatever we choose to do, our own personal sound and feel is there. It is not changeable or even accessible by our rational mind, but we can trust it, believe in it, and nurture it.

Feeling vs. Impulse

During our Music Mind Orchestra's rehearsal/workshop part I brought up a story that a member of Ornette Coleman's Prime Time once told me. In a rehearsal, one of the musicians asked Ornette about a particular piece and how to deal with an open-ended section, "What do you want me to do here?" Ornette's answer couldn't have been simpler or more profound: "Play what you feel." The musician started playing and Ornette interrupted him, saying: "That's not what you feel."

So what is Ornette saying? Feeling is a word that has become overused in so many ways and contexts, often in quite sentimental settings. Musical feeling, as it is meant here, defies descriptions of any kind because it emanates from a place that is utterly empty of purpose. Impulse is often confused with feeling, but impulsive action does not come from that empty place. We hear a lot of impulsive playing in improvised music. There is a purpose of filling the space. Often it brings with it a lot of routine playing.

Just as we are each uniquely set in our ways of sound and rhythm, so is the music that we truly "feel." It comes from nowhere, seemingly, and we are not really creating anything. Instead, we are more like radio stations that receive and pass on what we play. We cannot force the issue. But there are ways to tune in, so to speak, to prepare ourselves for the music to come through directly and naturally. Again, no aspect of the rational mind can help this. Rather we have to let the impulses pass through, waiting for the music to happen, coming from a completely non-conceptual point of view. We need to wait for the music to surface, ideally surprising us as much as anyone else. It is not a long wait, however. It is more the state of waiting, of not forcing the issue, that is crucial here.

It is a feeling like no other when the music, sound and silence, flows like water in a stream. When listeners talk about an "unforgettable" performance, they are tuning into the music's completely non-conceptual, spontaneous space. And curiously, what is unforgettable for the listener might well remain subconscious for the performer. Indeed, the greatest performances are often the ones where the player does not remember too clearly what happened. They were in the zone, locked and tuned in to something larger.

A listener can have a similar experience, receiving the magic of music directly in the present moment, being locked in and tuned in, too. This level of meetings of minds (and hearts) can happen between players, and between players and listeners. It happens between players in ensembles or in orchestras every day. And it has the capacity to reach the level of unforgettable performance, whether the music is originally written or improvised. Here lies the key to the question of what it is that makes the difference between a solid performance and a magical, unforgettable one.

An experience comes to mind that I had as a student, listening to the Parennin String Quartet from Paris. They specialized in the music of Arnold Schoenberg, Alban Berg and Anton von Webern, a canon of music that could be described as a pinnacle of cerebral composition, and mostly considered to be difficult to access by the average listener. The Parennin Quartet played this music by heart and was obviously married to it. The result was an unforgettable performance from start to finish. Each and every note was played from the heart, which is another way of describing musical feeling.

Infinite Dynamics/Space

Each week at The Stone, the orchestra workshop started by spending 20 minutes or so on creating long-tone sounds together. The idea here is to create a sense of "harmony" without determining pitches beforehand: that the harmonic partials of all these pitches begin to melt into a consonant whole rather than remaining a dissonant sound. The secret here is, of course, mostly dynamics. I call it *infinite dynamics*.

Twenty-four bit recording recognizes millions of shades of dynamics and 16-bit recording still reacts to more than 800,000 shades. We must be able to recognize, again consciously or not, many more shades of dynamics than we typically do. If the recorders can do it, so can we! There are minute differences of dynamics that blend a tone with every other tone. Obviously, this is nothing to figure out. But we can feel it, distinctively feel it, when that blending is happening.

The theory behind this is, of course, the law of overtones and undertones, where every tone contains every other one, although in an inaudible way, stretched in distances from the fundamental and in dynamic shades that reach way beyond the conscious capacity of hearing. We "hear" it as colorations or timbres.

The fact that no instrument sounds quite like another, simply means that we are hearing not one tone at a time, but thousands of "partials", called overtones/undertones, forming a distinct sound. The way the instrument is built favors a specific preference of how these partial combine to form a distinct sound. Adding the player's unique inclination and preference of sound and we'll arrive at an even more pronounced character of the sound. Using subtle dynamic shades in playing together allows the individual sounds to melt into a "harmonious" whole.

After several rehearsals, practicing long-tones started to pay off in a major way. Our Music Mind Orchestra created what a reviewer referred to as "luscious harmonies." They were achieved without any written music or other preconceptions, but simply by dynamically fine-tuning what could be called the meeting of the minds of the players, creating a sound together.

One could also refer to this process as developing an infinitely detailed sense of space, whereby we feel an increasing amount of silence in the sound. To me, sensing space is a more intuitive and expansive way to feel the differentiations of dynamic qualities, to think of them as increasing and decreasing amounts of silence in the sounds.

In 1977, Kalu Rinpoche, a Tibetan meditation master and one of my teachers at the time, came to the Creative Music Studio in Woodstock, NY, and presented us with a poem he had written. In this poem he described CMS as the "Joyous Grove of Liberation through Sound." Liberation through Sound, that was too big a concept for me to embrace without asking for detailed instructions about what was expected of anyone to practice and work towards such a lofty goal. Kalu Rinpoche replied: "Listen to the sounds disappearing."

It made sense to me to add that practice to our daily practice at CMS. At the time we called it Basic Practice, meaning basic to all kinds and forms of music, such as rhythmic-dynamic training and harmonic/overtone practices. At CMS we used cymbals and other long-sounding objects, or just listened to whatever occurred in nature or in our practice rooms. There, my understanding of sense of space, as well of the infinite steps of sounds disappearing constantly became very clear: infinite shades of dynamics disappearing continuously, while a sense of widening and deepening spaces develops in the process. Talk about basic practice! It doesn't get more basic than that. And it can be done any time one remembers to do it. An instant switch, total switch of perception takes place.

Years later, the Karmapa, head of Kalu Rinpoche's lineage came to Woodstock, and we had the opportunity to dine with him one evening. In typical western fashion I thought, this would be the opportunity to ask him about the next steps concerning Liberation through Sound. The Karmapa smiled and said, "That is quite enough."

It is quite enough. We can always get more attuned, practicing with the same detailed approach to sound and dynamics. There is no end to the details of sound in silence that we can hear, as every tone contains so many partials of tones that no sound we'll produce can ever be repeated exactly the same way. The images of sounds on a recording screen show this in vivid detail. All sounds are new and every tone played now is new, never to be repeated.

Harmonic Tuning

There is no such thing as an A could be the name of the other part of the orchestra's practice of blending long-tones. I also call it "harmonic tuning." There we hold a long-tone pitch while changing the harmonic foundation of that pitch. For example, it could be D A in D minor changing to A in F♯ minor, F major, B7, etc. There are incremental yet tangible changes in the actual pitch as you hold it through the changing chords. This is true when you use your voice to hold a pitch and close off one of your ears so that you can hear the sound inside your head. When changing the harmonic context on a piano or guitar, the need for adjusting the pitch becomes quite obvious. Yet it is the same pitch; te change is very incremental and the actual tone is changing ever so slightly.

When I first started playing with Don Cherry's group in 1965 in Paris at the "Chat-Qui-Peche" Club (we played every day, except Mondays, for months on end), he pointed this out to me; a trumpet note for example, even as it is a single tone, should indicate the harmony that it belongs to. It should indicate what fundamental tone it belongs to. The player should have the fundamental tone in mind, in order to give his tone the feel of the particular harmony of that moment. In other words, there is no such thing as a single note. There are no tones without a harmonic context.

Don Cherry also told me time and again, that all there is to know about music theoretically, we can hear and feel ourselves. I was at the time still in a stage of bewildered development, trying to make theoretical sense of things. As one can see, I am still interested in putting my finger on the ultimate secret of musical energy. Yet, in the final analysis, one cannot really put one's finger on it. It's as personal and mysterious as each of us are. But we can fine-tune our abilities to transmit and receive. The beauty is that "Music Mind" addresses abilities that are right there. They don't need to be manufactured. They are the abilities of our natural state of mind, unobstructed by concepts and plans. The fine-tuning consists of letting all the concepts, plans, all the thinking processes go and letting the music, sound and silence, come through purely, honestly, directly.

Today I conclude that we should, of course, know as much as possible about the endless styles and ways of playing music, but I feel that it is all-important for improvisers and interpreters aiming for the highest levels of personal expression and communication to continue trusting and relying on what wants to come through naturally and spontaneously. And to trust and rely on the meeting of the minds that wants to happen. There is ultimately nothing to aim for. The spontaneous state of mind that we can rely on here is our natural state of mind. We just have to get out of the way.

IN SEARCH OF THE NEW DENSITY:

Claire Chase on Varèse's Density 21.5

CLAIRE CHASE

I first encountered the work of Edgard Varèse at the awkward, hopelessly melodramatic age of thirteen. My teacher at the time, John Fonville—a quietly brilliant man, a kind of poet-philosopher of the flute who was, and to this day remains, a hero of mythic proportions for me—plopped *Density 21.5* on the music stand in my parents' living room one afternoon. I thought it was the strangest and most beautiful drawing I had ever seen. A maze of straight lines, swells, jet streams, stars shooting in space. High notes, low notes, but no licks, nothing to "practice," I thought. My adolescent hubris took over: EASY, I estimated; this should take me a few days. John glanced at me wordlessly, as if to say, "Not so fast, Chase."

John gave *Density* no introduction. He simply stood up and played the piece from start to finish—an astonishing 4 minutes that could have been 4 seconds and that just as easily could have been four hours. I listened to him expertly finesse pianissimos the thinness of sand, make oceanic swells that turned the bottom notes of the flute into a trombone-like thunder, sustain piercing high notes that evoked sirens and, perhaps most strikingly, transform the instrument into a drum for a brief moment, slapping the keys down like mouse-traps and allowing the instrument to naturally amplify these outbursts in space. In the passage's silences he was a furnace of tension, as if something ferocious, horrific was about to happen. And yet there was beauty and lyricism everywhere in this piece, even in the most aggressive gestures. When he finished the last howling high B—a spectacular siren that must have roused every dog on the block—I was reeling. I didn't want it to be over. It wasn't a piece of classical music I had just heard—it was something else. What was it?

"Rad..." was the word that came out of the jungle of unfortunate orthodonture in my mouth. "Pretty rad, right?" he said, sounding suddenly comfortable in the North San Diego Country vernacular. "Work on it this week. The dynamic exercises I gave you will help." That was it. He let me loose with it.

My 7th grade existence at that time was a jumble of pimples, daydreams, a decaying baseball career—the boys had out-grown me, bogarting my place as the only-girl star of the Encinitas Little League, and I was too proud to join the softball team (they pitched underhand, for starters). Increasingly, my days were filled with countless hours of frenzied flute practice, terrorizing my neighbors with Anderson etudes and fourth-register exercises early in the morning and long into the night. After school, I would play along with old Jean-Pierre Rampal records, envisioning the living room as an enormous concert hall and imagining myself just like the joyous fat French man, with a big chest and an even bigger belly emanating an empire of sound. (I was scarcely four-and-a-half feet tall).

During my practice the day following the *Density* lesson, I stared at the score—at the bottom of the first page a little asterix took my eyes to a footnote: "Written for the inauguration of the first platinum flute in 1936, performed by Georges Barrère. *Density 21.5* is the density of platinum." I processed that like any 13-year-old would: 1936 seemed like a very long time ago, and platinum seemed like a far cry from the aluminum Armstrong that I used to hit tennis balls with. My mind wandered: what would a tennis ball sound like if struck by a platinum flute? Who was this Georges Barrère fellow, and did he too contemplate turning his flute into a baseball bat?

I decided to take the plunge. Playing it through for the first time in my parents' living room, a carpeted acoustic I resented when I wanted to sound "big," I realized that the instrument itself, not the room, could actually resonate on its own. In *Density*, the flute could just be the flute. Every note—the husky, hollow middle C-sharp, the naturally bright and ardent middle D, the crass C above the staff, the nasal and downright nasty E above that, the primal low C, and the wailing, penetrating highest D— these little jewels with their peculiar little imperfections, from the breathy bowels of the instrument to the screeching stratosphere, could be themselves, just as they were, like rugged islands dotting an ocean of air.

It was a before-and-after moment in my life. Little did I know at the time that this piece was also a before-and-after moment for the history of the flute literature, for the development of the instrument, a work of art not to be surpassed in impact—in a word, in density—in the remainder of the 20th century and well into the 21st.

In an instant, I was free from the tyranny of having to play every note the same, from the 19th century "model of good flute-playing" in which smoothness of sound is upheld as the sacred quest; in *Density*, I could feel sound for the first time not just as line, but as light, as heat. Air to metal. Metal to air. Some notes were irrepressibly bright, others were dark, some were fuzzy and others were as pure as sine waves. They connected like dots on a complex matrix of lines, but the parts were in effect the sum, and the sum was the parts. There was no need to make anything homogeneous, blend-y, pretty, one-sounding. Beauty here was about stripping off the mask and letting each sound make contact with the metal in its own raw, unaffected way.

As I struggled through the piece that night for the captive audience of our family dog Siegfried, I imagined my body as a vast, black chamber, with waves of light in fantastical fluorescent color schemes darting rapidly around it. I felt power for the first time in my playing, and a different kind of power than the satisfaction I had felt when I had executed a difficult technical passage or spun a sweet line of Debussy—this was new. This was deeper, darker. This was a new kind of music. What was it? Whatever it was, I was hooked. I wanted no more of the old stuff. *Density* was all there was.

*   *   *

I waited anxiously for my lesson next week, eager to share my findings with John. At first blow in front of more than a canine audience, I couldn't quite get through it all, but John responded warmly after my first stumble: "Toto, we're not in Kansas anymore," he said with a chuckle, and I knew I was on the right track. Over the next several months, we worked to unlock the piece together. We studied the key click passage, looking for ways to give those precious thirteen non-notes each a different timbre, like little points on a curve, each its own tiny universe of finger-to-metal, metal-to-air buoyancy. John taught me how to count the rests without rushing through them; and then how to venture beyond the "counting" and, with the help of my own heartbeat, simply know their value in my chest. We worked on controlling and varying vibrato, so that it could be by turns pure like a boy soprano and raucous like an electric guitar. He helped me discover the right balance of force and finesse for the extreme register shifts. I memorized it, working to get every passage into my body.

A lot of things happened outside the world of *Density* that year. I went to my first, and last, junior high school dance, where I was mercilessly ridiculed for wearing a bright yellow satin oversized men's shirt; I stood grumpily on the side of the dance floor all night wishing that I could diminuendo into nothing, like the recapitulation on the second page of *Density*. I got "trash-canned" by several 9th grade jocks one morning—I was the perfect size, just small enough to stuff all my limbs into the school recycling bins—and dug myself out from a polyphonic sea of pop cans and beer bottles. I hung my baseball glove up in the closet for good that year, unable to accept that I should pitch underhand and with a needlessly large ball. I discovered and became obsessed with the poetry of e.e. cummings. My brother gave me my first joint.

Later that year, I was asked by my junior high drama teacher—a wonderful, gentle man who was my saving grace at the proverbial prison of Dieguéño Junior High School—to "play something" for the 9th grade graduation ceremonies. Notably, there was no music program at this public school; the band program had been cut the year before, and the priorities at this institution were firmly aimed at the two crowns of Southern California existence: Surfing and Football. What would I say? What would I play?

At that point in my life, I had no problem playing for thousands of people, but the thought of getting up and playing for a group of older students at my own school, and on the football field no less, was beyond terrifying. I lay awake at night dreading it, imagining flocks of jocks jeering, screaming, throwing things, calling me queer, laughing me off the stage. For several days I pondered all the ways that I could get out of this snare—I invented bizarre illnesses; I concocted a plan of falling dramatically ill during Phys Ed on the track the afternoon of the event and being sent home to recover...

And then, one day on a walk home from school, it hit me—I would play *Density*! This was not classical music, and it was not Guns N' Roses. It was beyond all that, better than all of that. I would hit them over the heads with it as I was hit over the head with it, they would love it as I loved it, it would move them as it had moved me, and I would fill the Dieguéño Junior High School football field with ecstatic rays of light the way I had done so in my living room for the family dog. They would be rapt! The runt of the litter, Clarita, the tomboy, the walking fashion faux-pas, would suddenly be an exalted hero. They would clap and cheer so wildly that I would have to play it a second time, and they would listen even more intently on the second hearing. My fantasy whirled in my imagination and I saw local news stations covering the event, taking pictures of me posing with Siegfried...

Tragically, my brilliant idea was not met with enthusiasm that evening by Mama and Papa Chase. The Chases, both musicians themselves, had been exceptionally tolerant of my practicing, but they put their foot down about the *Density*-at-graduation proposition. No way. Not appropriate. Not over our dead bodies. No discussion. End of story. I pleaded, begged, gave righteous and hyperbolic sermons about the Liberation of Sound. There were tears. There were doors slammed. There was a stand-off.

A few days later, a family friend—Alice Parker, the choral director, composer-arranger and all-around luminous wonder of a woman—came to the Chase house for a visit. She was in town to lead one of her famous "Sings," marvelous gatherings in churches or gymnasiums or community centers in which she teaches a group of people to sing together in ways they never imagined they were capable. Alice was a kind of grandmother figure for me, one whose very presence inspired me; she had sung to me as a baby, she had taught me and my brother volumes of songs, and she had taught me how to bake bread as a little girl. Naturally, Alice was brought into the Chase State-of-the-Union family drama over lunch: Varèse at graduation. Whose side would she take? Certainly she wouldn't let me down...

As it turned out, Alice took no one's side. She listened patiently to my tirade, then she listened just as patiently to my parents'. She asked me calmly, "If you weren't going to play Varèse, Claire, what would you play?" I considered my options before responding, because I sensed that I was somehow already being painted into a corner: Vivaldi, Mozart, Debussy...no, these were all pieces for which I had to admit I had special places in my heart; I needed to mention something even more ridiculous: Gaubert, Ferroud, Chaminade...the epitome of flute "schlock"...no, but what if I got stuck with one of those? Heavens, what if I actually had to play the Chaminade for the 9th graders?! I would actually die. Okay, I've got it, I thought, the most typical, the reddest herring of all flute repertoire: "*Danny Boy!*" I would play *Danny Boy*, I replied, sloughing it off, assuming anyone in their right mind would share my adolescent disdain for such an obvious choice. But as soon as the words came out of my mouth, I knew I was stuck. Shit.

Alice smiled wisely and said, "Young lady, get me some manuscript paper, a sharp pencil, and get me my sun hat." I did as she said, for there was a sense of austerity in her voice I had not witnessed before. "And write down the lyrics of *Danny Boy* as you remember them, with your own spacing of the words, where you breathe, where you hear phrase-breaks. Don't look it up, just write what you remember, as you hear it in your head, and quickly."

If it had been anyone else, I would have fired up my protest and refused to get down from the liberation-of-sound soap-box. But Alice was a godlike figure for me, and I would do absolutely anything she told me to do. So I wrote down the words as I remembered them—spaced like an e.e. cummings poem, with one word per line at times, and long rows of silences where I imagined rests.

o   danny boy   the pipes
             thepipesarecalling
  from glen   toglen   and down
          the   mountain   siiiiiiide

I handed her the paper, and with a little glimmer in her eye she set out for the back yard, hat in hand, where over the next several hours that sun-drenched afternoon she proceeded to write a stunningly beautiful setting of *Danny Boy* for solo flute, deftly incorporating my strange interpretations of phrase-breaks. To Claire from Alice, 1993—Leucadia, CA was scribbled in pencil after the end of the last note.

The notion that a piece of music could be written for someone— with someone, because of someone, springing up from some happenstance event in a fleeting moment, be it a stand-off with one's parents or the inauguration of the world's first platinum flute—was another before-and-after-moment in my life. Little did I know, this discovery would become as important as the discovery of *Density* earlier that year. I knew somewhere deep in my being that this is what I would do with the rest of my life—I would commission music, I would turn everything I experienced into a reason to make something new, and I would start a lifelong project of trying to give birth to the new *Density*. It was an odd paradox that that journey began with an unlikely setting of an old-fashioned tune, one of such mystery and beauty that it has confounded scholars and musicians alike for centuries.

The graduation day came and went; I played Alice's heartfelt version of *Danny Boy*, and I felt a quiet pride about having given the world premiere of something that was written for me, something I participated, albeit reluctantly, in bringing into being. In the end, no one booed me off the stage; no one erupted in rapturous applause either. Needless to say, the news cameras never showed.

✶   ✶   ✶

A few years later, when I turned eighteen and made my Kennedy Center debut, I programmed *Density*, much to the horror of the concert presenters. I was an adult then, I told them—I could vote, after all—and I could now make my own repertoire choices, thank you very much. I felt vindicated, of course, and the experience of playing that piece in such a big hall was one I cherished. Still, though, I never felt like I mastered the piece. There were things I couldn't do yet the way I heard them in my mind's eye, the way John had played them. I wanted to simply let the instrument be the instrument, let the flute make contact with the body and let the breath make contact with the gut and let the heart do the rest. That's what *Density* required. Why was it so difficult?

I studied the piece again and again in conservatory with different teachers over the years, amassing more knowledge along with, inevitably, more hangups. At one point when I was visiting home on a school break I called John, whom I hadn't seen in years, and asked if I could play the beast for him, "for old time's sake." He accepted my offer enthusiastically, but when I played the piece through for him from beginning to end in a brightly lit UCSD classroom, he seemed unimpressed. "It sounds like French music, Claire. You sound like a great flute player. But you're not playing the piece." I went back to the practice room as a 20-year-old and tried unsuccessfully to recreate my initial adolescent encounter with the piece. In the months that followed I tortured myself practicing it in dead spaces, in live ones, standing up, lying down, kneeling, running, walking, hanging upside-down off the side of the bed. I sang it through, I played it on the piano, I analyzed it, I beat it to the ground. I tried everything but I could not find my stride with it. Finally, I admitted defeat and put it down.

Ten years passed without touching *Density*. During that time I devoted myself almost entirely to creating and commissioning new music, premiering dozens of new works for flute—pieces of complexity, pieces of performance art, pieces of minimalism, pieces for built instruments, deconstructed flutes, installations for flutes, operas for flute, concertos, sculptures, soundscapes. My life as a musician was lush with discoveries, some less successful than others but each one leading to an invigorating new search, a renewed hunger for new modes of expression and transmission, with and without the instrument.

Hundreds of concerts and what seemed like lifetimes later, I finally picked *Density* up and dusted it off in 2010 for a performance at the Lincoln Center Festival. Here we go, I said to myself, recalling my very first reading of the piece. No excuses this time. I fell madly, recklessly in love with it once more, as if I were thirteen all over again. *Density* immediately entered the rotation, and I have since then played it some fifty times in concert—sometimes I get a little closer to my ideal, sometimes I stray further away from it. But the search continues to intoxicate me.

Chou Wen-chung, Varèse's longtime assistant, pointed out to me wisely when we spoke of the piece recently in what was once Varèse's garden on Sullivan Street, that he was not "one among many;" he was the "one all alone." The willpower of the "one all alone" has resonated resoundingly for me in my journey with this, Varèse's only solo work, from my very first encounter with it as a lonely adolescent to my current plans to record it for release next year. Steven Schick, a beloved mentor of mine and an unparalleled Varèse interpreter, often mentions to me and my ICE colleagues in rehearsal what Kafka said of Borges—that he was so important he influenced even those who came before him. I imagine that this must also be true of Varèse, and emphatically so in the case of *Density*, which became the standard by which all the great 20th century flute landmarks hat followed it would be measured—Boulez's 1946 *Sonatine*, Berio's 1951 *Sequenza 1*... Surely it must also have influenced the great works for solo flute that came before it: Bach's solo *Partita* in a minor in 1718, Debussy's *Syrinx* in 1913...

In my current daydreams, I muse that I will be 58 years old in 2036, at the 100th anniversary of the piece. I dream that I will have commissioned and premiered the 21st century *Density* by then, a work that will singularly change the definition of the instrument. What will it look like? What will it sound like? Where will the newest innovations on the flute, humankind's oldest musical instrument, take us? A generation of flute-players will have devised new tuning systems, discovered volumes of new techniques, written encyclopedias of new performance practices, reached new extremities of virtuosity, discovered groundbreaking new ways of integrating technology with live performance.

There are some days that I am certain that solo flute playing will have pushed itself firmly into the realm of performance and conceptual art by the mid-21st century, that we will have exhausted the concert form as we know it. Then there are days when I am so moved by the promise of a few notes in the palm of a hand, uttered with the simplicity of an exhalation, that I have faith all over again in melody itself as an agent of change throughout the ages.

Oskar Fischinger once famously told a young John Cage: "Everything in the world has a spirit that can be released through its sound." Varèse unleashed this spirit for the flute, for the one all alone, in these staggering 4 minutes of music. Did he go as far as one could go, metaphorically and otherwise? Of what will the *Density* of our time be made? Of osmium? Of signal processing? Of wood? Of carbon? Of flesh? Of air?

BLANK SCREEN

ANNA CLYNE AND ELIZABETH TASKER

"Do you feel overwhelmed *when you begin a new project?*"

"Actually no. At the start there is just the idea I want to explore and no mistakes yet! It's exciting. Later, I might spend weeks trying to find a fault that is difficult to track down amidst what I have written."

"I feel the same. With the blank screen there are so many different directions the project can take, and the options are as vast as the imagination. Electronics have had a dramatic impact on my process, though sometimes it's hard to know how two different worlds will interact."

"Absolutely. I have tried to add multiple effects into the same project that ended up getting a completely wrong result. But once, I put something in that I wasn't expecting to be important and it ended up being the focus of the project!"

"Me too. It's funny that I can spend months on a piece that ultimately results in 10 minutes of music."

"For me it's the complete opposite. I spend months, and the project models the evolution of the Universe through 10,000,000,000 years."

As this conversation reveals, technology has revolutionized many fields from music to astronomy. I have known Elizabeth since we were 3 years old in our hometown in England, where we started our exploration of electronics by playing 1980s computer games. I am now based in Chicago as Mead Composer Residence at the Chicago Symphony Orchestra, and Elizabeth holds a faculty position in the Physics & Astronomy department at Hokkaido University in Japan. Despite the disparate nature of our fields, we both utilize electronics extensively in our work and we face many of the same challenges.

Advancements in technology have dramatically transformed the process of music composition and performance. From the days of the telharmonium, the first instrument to make music by electrical means in 1906, through the development of records, radio, and synthesizers, to chip music, experimental art music and popular forms of dance music, music technology has developed fast and in many directions. Composers today, of all genres, incorporate electronics into many aspects of their work, be it the use of notation software, the creation of pre-recorded tracks, live interactive electronics, sampling, amplification or the myriad of electronic instruments.

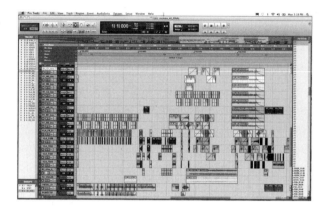

Technology is more accessible than ever before. What was once only available at high-end studios can now be achieved from a laptop in the comfort of your own home. The world of music and electronics is vast, and these new technologies allow for exciting experiments and completely new explorations of sound. Whether it be Redolfi's *Sonic Waters* which placed loudspeakers in public pools for the swimming audience, Pink Floyd's infamous sampling in *Money* or Bjork's vocal processing in *Medulla*, electronics provide a playground for music beyond traditional acoustic instruments and ensembles. To discuss all the uses of electronics in music would result in a long-winded ramble. So instead I'd like to focus on electroacoustic music, specifically music that combines acoustic ensembles with pre-recorded tracks ("tape"), compositional accidents and some day-to-day benefits of electronics in music.

Whatever the medium, we all start at the same point. The exciting, yet sometimes daunting, blank screen, canvas or paper. At the beginning of writing an electroacoustic work, the process can be aided by a structure to allow flexibility between the two elements. What comes first—the instrumental music or the tape? Or is it a back and forth between the two? The composer also has to consider how the live musicians will coordinate with the tape. Or perhaps (s)he prefers complete freedom between the two elements, or a combination of these. If synchronization is preferred, the composer can choose to notate the prominent pitches or gestures from the tape part, alongside the music for the live musician(s). This can allow for a greater freedom between the two elements. However, other options for a tighter synchronization could include the use of a click track or stop watch. Then comes the process of making the tape—splicing, manipulating and layering. These traditional, and previously laborious, techniques can be easily replicated with current editing software such as ProTools, Logic, or the wealth of free software available online. Speakers, microphones, mixers, headphone-splitters, a playback device and a sprinkling of extras such as effects pedals—the performance of this form of electroacoustic music is completely dependent on advancements in technology, and today's musicians and ensembles are pioneers in bringing this music to life.

One of the most exciting aspects of composing is not knowing the absolute outcome at the beginning, even if certain parameters, such as duration and instrumentation, are already set. Accidental mistakes, spurred by electronics, can add interesting surprises to a new piece. You can be certain that electronics will malfunction at some time. It's just a matter of when. One personal example involves an orchestral piece, "rewind". Originally I had intended the opening measure to start with a fast propelling rhythm in the strings. This now starts at measure 10, and is preceded by a rumbling D drone in the low strings and brass. When playing back the file, the playback function froze on the low D in the basses for a good 15 seconds before finding the power to keep scrolling forward. I liked the drone that resulted, and it stayed.

Sometimes the use of electronics can also solve some more day-to-day challenges, such as finances. Emerging choreographers, for example, generally have very limited funds to hire musicians. Create a piece for solo instrument with a belting, rich and carefully panned stereo tape part, and the choreographer gets a full sound for the cost of just one musician. Of course, electronics is not limited to chamber ensembles; it can breathe new life into the orchestra, and can reach millions across the world through the internet, as in the recent incarnations of the YouTube Symphony. Technology has allowed composers and musicians to create and develop some wonderfully original new paths in music making, and has facilitated a freedom in the process. In some ways it has also brought composers and musicians closer in collaboration to experiment with, explore, and further develop these technologies.

As the conversation with Elizabeth demonstrated, the impact of electronics is far from being limited to music. What was so entertaining about our conversation was the similarity of the problems we face; anyone overhearing us would have trouble deciding if we were two composers, two scientists or maybe even something else entirely. Elizabeth explains it from her perspective:

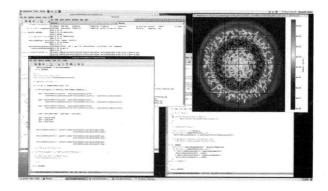

One of the main problems astronomers face is that they are confined to our planet with a single view of space. By using computer generated models, astronomers can visualize the Universe from different perspectives and test theories as to how the galaxies and stars are made. The final goal of any such project is to match the model to the real thing. Like with instrumental music and electronics, it is sometimes hard to decide what should come first; should astronomers take an observation of a star and try to match it or should they model how a star is formed and then compare to the finished product?

Research is also full of surprises. Like Anna, some of the most important results in my work are more due to serendipity than scientific planning! Once, I added a gentle heating source to a model of our galaxy. This heating genuinely exists, but it seemed very small compared to other forms of heat from exploding stars. To my surprise, there was a huge difference to the galaxy's structure because this steady heating produced a larger cumulative effect than the violent, but intermittent, explosions. The impact this had on a galaxy became a main focal topic in my paper.

Sharing computer code has also become a key part of astronomy research. Code development is very time consuming and by exchanging routines, research can progress much more quickly. The computer program I use for my work was jointly written by many scientists who work together to update and add to the package as well as help with problems. While Newton was not considering electronics at the time, his words "if I have seen further than others, it is by standing on the shoulders of giants" have never been more true.

The increase in computer power makes it possible to run complex models on desktop PCs. While the largest and most up-to-date results are still run on supercomputers, different ideas can be tested quickly and easily on cheaper machines. This frees scientists to explore new ideas that they previously might have been unable to try due to the amount of power needed. Ever wanted to see would happen if the Earth was twice as big? Me too, let's try it!

The rapid growth of technology has changed the way we work. It has birthed a whole new batch of musical techniques from electro-acoustic to purely electronic works. It has also allowed cheap exploration of new ideas and techniques that have never before been possible. What is perhaps most surprising is that it has done all this for many (if not all) other disciplines too. Perhaps the most exciting of all these developments is the ability to easily try out new sounds and combinations that have not been heard before. Whether you are a staring down a bow or a telescope, the possibilities are not only endless, but they are right at your fingertips.

BUILDING MUSIC
(An Architectural Method of Composing)

JOHN CORIGLIANO

It would be hard to imagine a sculptor chiseling a finger from a 10-ton block of marble, and then wondering what figure the finger would be attached to. Likewise, one would be puzzled by an architect who first designed the cornice of a window, and then built the building to fit it.

Yet this is the method of many composers who have discarded the forms (architectures) of the past, but have not found new ones for their works. Starting from a few notes or chords (a microcosm) and taking a musical journey of whim and fancy to a conclusion seems to be very popular way to write. Using forms of the past, or inventing new personal ones—that is, dealing with the entire work (the macrocosm) first, and dealing with the details (notes, rhythms, etc.) later is less popular.

I can understand the reluctance to use the traditional forms of the past. They seem to be a sort of pre-fabricated "Levittown", and using them gives up part of the creative process.

However, creating new architectures that create that necessary balance between the familiar (repetition of an idea) and the new (new material) is an option that any composer can take.

If we exclude the extremes of balance—serialism, with no repetition, and early minimalism (a rebellion against serialism) that repeated things endlessly and, like serialism, was anti-architectural—there is a whole middle ground of tonal and non-tonal music that can be constructed before it is actually written.

What do I mean by that? If one accepts the fact that the human condition needs the yin and yang of comfort and danger—home and the outside world, play and work, or, in other words, repetition (security) and variety (insecurity)—one can see how the traditional forms work.

Major ideas are given alphabetical symbols. Thus, ABA or AABA tells us that there is recognizable music (A) that alternates with different recognizable music (B). The basic ternary (3-part) form gives us material (A) that gives way to new material (B), and then returns to the original material (A). Often the original "A" is repeated, so that we feel (and remember) it. Simple—yes. Simple-minded—no.

All other forms grow from this idea of a major idea alternating with other ideas, and the result of this is that the listener is able to put together the pieces of a work as they fly by (no small feat.)

In my 20's, I used variants of traditional forms (Sonata-Allegro, Rondo, etc.) because I was learning my craft, and was dealing primarily with the rhythmic and melodic intricacies of the world around me, and therefore used the forms to organize my material.

Ten years later, however, I became fascinated with the idea of shaping each piece individually. For example, my oboe concerto of 1975 is in five movements that each display a technique that is unique to the oboe. The idea of building the piece this way came from my listening to many other oboe concerti. Since the oboe is basically a melodic instrument with a somewhat limited range, I felt that these concerti would sound fine if played on a violin, flute, or clarinet. My goal, therefore, was to write something truly "oboistic"—something that could not be played by any other instrument.

The first thing I did (in collaboration with my soloist, Humbert Lucarelli) was to make a list of all things that the oboe did that were either difficult or impossible for other instruments. Next, I chose the techniques that were most interesting to me (five ideas were chosen) and ordered them so that each movement set up a need for the next movement.

Thus the first movement was based upon the traditional use of the oboe as the instrument that sounds the "A" for the orchestra's tuning. The entire orchestra was tuned by the oboe and the attitude was mostly fast and boisterous.

The second movement was lyrical and long lined, (the trademark of the oboe) and featured the oboe in conversation with the other woodwinds.

The third movement was very fast and featured oboe and the percussion section. In this movement, the oboist played multiphonics (strange electronic sounding chords produced by special fingerings and blowing techniques.)

The fourth movement was arch shaped and dramatic pitting the solo oboe against the strings. The thing that made this movement especially "oboistic" was the fact that the oboe (unlike most other instruments and the human voice) is louder and coarser in its lowest register, and becomes thinner in its higher realms. Thus, the dynamics of the arch started softly, with a high oboe, and the arch took the oboe down to the bottom of its register, where the dynamic was loud.

The final fifth movement, the mood was that of a joyous Arabic dance, with the soloist playing his oboe in an Arabic manner. In order to produce the raucous and pungent Arabic sound (not unlike an early shawm), the soloist was instructed to put his lips (which ordinarily rest on the double reeds to produce a cultivated sound) on the *string* which binds the two reeds together.

Thus the five movements placed in order read: *Tuning Game* (fast, full orchestra); *Song* (slow, features oboe with solo winds); *Scherzo* (very fast, slow middle) oboe multiphonics with percussion group; *Aria* (slow and intense) oboe with string group; and finally *Rhieta Dance* (fast with slow sections) using solo oboe and full orchestra.

Architecting a work does not limit one to one way of building structure. My clarinet concerto was based on three things special to the piece: the legendary virtuosity of the soloist, Stanley Drucker; the fact that my father was concertmaster of the commissioning orchestra (the New York Philharmonic), and had died shortly before I was commissioned; and finally the charismatic and theatrical conductor of the work, Leonard Bernstein. Obviously, in building this concerto, I utilized personal experiences rather than qualities of an instrument as the inspirational germ.

Later works would develop this idea: The *Pied Piper Fantasy*, written for impish James Galway (who happened to also play a tin whistle); my first symphony, written for my friends who had died of AIDS— and one who was dying while I wrote the piece dedicated to him.

At first, I conceptualized these structures by writing them down in words. The result was that I could scan a page of typing and see what I was trying to do for a half-hour or more of music. Later, I have come to drawing the structures, much the way an architect draws a blueprint.

I take one or two sheets of 11x17 paper (a standard size) and lay them lengthwise. If I mark off one inch to signify 1 minute, that gives me up to 34 minutes for two pages (which can be placed side by side.) I can try to draw a line that indicates the intensity of the work at any moment (sometimes the softest passage is the most intense, although it is usually the loudest.) I can draw vertical lines on this map to indicate movements or sections, and create symbols for themes. I can make notes of tempi, dynamics, rhythmic figures, and the return of material as well as a new notation for new material. I use words to describe things (i.e. Fr. Horns in *Circus Maximus*: "wolf calls") so that I can both remember them and use them developmentally.

The result is a real outline of a piece before the piece has been written. This is immensely important, as one can trouble shoot things ("why do I approach every climax with a crescendo, and then get softer with a diminuendo?" "what about a sudden change from soft to loud? A jagged way of getting softer, so I don't do the same big gesture every time?")

I can ask questions of the shape and then re-draw it and fix things. Much better than writing eighty pages of music only to find these problems when one goes to the rehearsal.

The shape and structure of each of my pieces is different. The reasons for the differences are based upon the questions I ask myself before I start writing. "Why am I writing this piece?" "What am I trying to say?" To me, these are the basic questions a composer asks himself (herself) before beginning to work.

This is not for everyone. It is a personal way of dealing with the highly arbitrary act of composing. It makes it possible for me to find material, because I know what that material is needed for. It makes eclecticism more logical, because the choices made are less arbitrary. And most of all, it helps answer that question all composers have when faced with a blank page: "What do I do next?"

LIFE PRESERVER/IN THE WILDERNESS

JEREMIAH CYMERMAN

"It's a strange courage
you give me ancient star;
Shine alone in the sunrise
toward which you lend no part!"
—William Carlos Williams

Life Preserver

I've never felt as if I've belonged anywhere. My entire life, from childhood, has been marked by unhealthy and persistent feelings of loneliness, alienation and misunderstanding. As a boy in rural Upstate New York my family and I lived on an Ashram, a new age intentional community founded on Hindu principles, and rather than taking Hebrew lessons or playing sports I was learning Sanskrit and participating in summer performances of the Ramayana. Despite being only 45 miles north of New York City the predominant cultural attitude of Monroe, New York in the early 1980s was one of intolerance, bigotry and small town small mindedness. By any standard we were poor and I never had any new or brand name clothing. My mother drove an old beat up car and on the Ashram my mom, brother, sister and I lived in a 600 square foot, 2 bedroom shack. Everything about us, from head to toe, diet to clothing was different and through bullying & ostracisation my status as a less-than, something worse than a nobody, was brought to my attention on a regular basis. When I was 10 years old, around the first time that my father went to prison, my family and I moved to Atlanta, Georgia where the overwhelming attitude of mean-spirited intolerance was intensified and caused even further feelings of alienation. At various times in my childhood I was subjected to different types of abuse and very early on in my life I would look at myself in the mirror with repulsion at the pathetic and grotesque creature that looked back at me. I was skinny, had greasy hair, pale skin and a very distinct look of "victim" written in all capital letters across my over-sized forehead and in my poor posture.

Turmoil and chaos followed me throughout my teenage years. In the 9th grade, my family once again packed up and moved to an incredibly remote part of the North Georgia mountains. Blairsville, GA[1], a nightmarish town filled to the brim with despicable and vile rednecks, was like a prison sentence to a young, imaginative and sullen teenager. Like a caged animal I was constantly taunted, harassed, picked on and generally treated as if my very presence had violated some strange law known only to the native sons of this god forsaken town. Two days before my sixteenth birthday my step-father who was also my best friend suddenly died, completely devastating any emotional stability that existed in my home. Two months later, after his second prison sentence, my father was deported back to Eastern Europe. The following summer I came home one day and my mom was gone. She left a note saying that she was gone to Spain to figure some things out and didn't know when she would be back. I spent the next two months alone, drinking heavily, crying and entertaining very real thoughts of violence and suicide.

1. The 1972 film *Deliverance* was filmed primarily in Tallulah, Georgia which is located about 30 miles east of Blairsville, GA.

Growing up in an environment so full of misunderstanding and so short on nurturing I was constantly at a loss and struggling to find something good, something kind, something safe, something warm, something comforting ANYWHERE. It just seemed that at every turn I was met with a series of obstacles and systems of standards & values that shut me out of any place where I would have hoped to have found acceptance. I was bound for failure. I became enraged and deeply depressed. When you're a young person, living in chaos you NEED someone to throw you a life preserver. It's like being adrift at night, in a sea of black, drowning. You need a flotation device to save your life and the tragedy is that you may not even be aware that one exists. You need someone or something to guide you to it. Sadly, many people are never able to keep from sinking. For me the thing that pulled me back in and saved my life was music & creativity in general but more specifically, the comforting solitude that I found making music in my bedroom, alone, by way of multi-track recording. It was there, in the sound world that I began to inhabit at age thirteen that the seeds of the value system that guides my life and work were first planted.

*   *   *

I was 13 years old when my mom bought me my first four-track recorder, a Vestax MR200MKII. From the first moment that I turned it on and began to create layers of recorded music I was hooked. I felt a light inside of me turn on. All of a sudden, none of the pain that had been plaguing me for so long had any effect on me. I was bulletproof! Sitting in my room, alone, with the lights dimmed I began to take part in a ritual that delivered me to a place where I was in control. I was in a place where no one could tell me that I was wrong. No one could tell me that my ideas were stupid nor question my musicianship, intelligence or character. Once the headphones would go on they became my shield and the world became mine to explore. I would spend weekends, staying up to all hours of the night, surrounding myself with various instruments (usually electric bass, guitar, some Native American drums, a recorder and a Casio keyboard) and create bizarre miniature compositions that followed a logic that to this day I don't fully understand. I felt inspired. I felt as if I was soaring. Every piece that I made during that time was to be part of an album that I had entitled *Uncle Rabbit Presents*. The music was terrible and I can't help but feel embarrassed listening to those tapes today but this was my salvation. I think back on those late nights of staying up long past everyone had gone to sleep, headphones on, headphones always on, and my heart weakens remembering the purity and imagination with which I approached those recording sessions.

> "DESTINY is a feeling you have that you know something about yourself nobody else does. The picture you have in your own mind of what you're about WILL COME TRUE. It's a kind of a thing you kind of have to keep to your own self, because it's a fragile feeling, and you put it out there, then someone will kill it. It's best to keep that all inside."
>
> —Bob Dylan

It seems so simple, but in order to survive and thrive as a creative person I think you must have a strong and personal value system. It took me a long time to understand this. Defining a system of values by which you can live your life, make your art and to which you can hold yourself responsible is the ultimate life preserver. You have to have a personal sense of poetry and aesthetics, an inner compass that can guide you when you're lost and a personal vision that can protect you when you feel under attack. It's an underlying sense of what you know to be right and what you need to move forward in your own work and without it you're lost. I spent so long, as a teenager and into my adult life in New York City, beating the shit out of myself for feeling as if I wasn't as good or as worthy as those around me. I felt like everyone was doing things right and I was doing them wrong. The truth in the matter is that I was doing something wrong, I wasn't being true to my own values and standards. I was letting a set of standards that had absolutely nothing to do with me or with anything I ever wanted convince me that my work was somehow not as important as others. The world is full of judgment and the heretics will always be in the wings, waiting to ask questions like "Yeah, but can he *really* play?" The last thing, the very last thing a creative person needs is to let that line of questioning influence them. The world can be unstable and often feel that at any moment the ground beneath you is going to cave in but in moments of creation you are your best you. You are free and uninhibited and the work that results from it is your gift to the world.

> "My life is nothing but pressure. All pressure. This pressure is like a heaviness. It's always on top of me, this heaviness. It's always there since I'm a kid. Other people wake up in the morning, 'A new day! Ah, up and at 'em!' I wake up, the heaviness is waiting for me nice."
> —Rodney Dangerfield, *No Respect*

Music is many things to me but as a listener and as a composer it is most powerful when the focus is on intensity of experience. My fundamental aesthetic sense is dark. Maybe it's my X factor but I'm not interested in music being fun or entertaining. I'm not interested in things being precious or cute. I never wink at the audience nor is my tongue ever in my cheek. My work is informed by profound personal experiences, dark and light. While I certainly enjoy and value listening to a lot of "fun" music, at this stage in my life and "career" (what a nasty word), when I set out to work on new music my heart does not lead me in that direction. What I am most interested in an artist's vulnerability. It took me a long time to accept and embrace that in my own music. Through the anger, the dark aesthetics, the feedback and distortion I think it is ultimately my goal, consciously or subconsciously to expose that vulnerability and all else that lies beneath the surface, to convey the feelings of love and groundedness that I experience in the moment of creation.

In the Wilderness

The Album

The album is to me, above all else, the ultimate art form. I am a clarinetist, a composer, a recording engineer and an improviser but most of all I think of myself as a recording artist. The recording studio and the album are the canvas that inspire me most and the place where I truly feel that as, an artist, anything is possible. Every step of the way, from the very beginning when I start jotting ideas in my notebook to actually being in the studio, a ritual-like event in which every spirit involved is working in perfect sync to realize the same outcome, there is no greater pleasure that I know. Through liner notes and artwork I am able to offer clues and invite the listener into my sound world even further and in every CD that I've released I have made a concerted effort to share the love and enthusiasm that went into the production. My educational background is in music production and since I was very young my favorite way to pass the time has been to get lost in my albums, poring over every last detail of the music's origin. Whether it be *Pet Sounds* or *Check Your Head* I have learned more about music by obsessing over the most minute details of records in my collection than any music school could ever teach me. When I was young, confused and alone it was my record collection that helped me to make sense of the world. While I did very poorly in almost all of my classes I could tell you at the drop of a dime, to the very second, where the bad edit in Slayer's *Angel of Death* is (3:18).

All of my recorded output deals with, on some level, what I have come to refer to as *extended studio techniques*. These techniques, including creative mic placement, hyper & micro editing, tape manipulation, cut & paste strategies, extreme mixes that take full advantage of the stereo field and various other approaches, contribute to creating a recorded music that places as much emphasis on the sonic presentation of the ideas as the compositions themselves. On these CDs the mix is the composition. My work with extended studio techniques stems from the previously mentioned need to look within and create a world of my own rules, a world where nothing would feel impossible and where there could live a music that is its own strange bird. My first record to deal with these ideas extensively was *In Memory of the Labyrinth System* for solo clarinet and computer processing. Recorded over the course nine months at different locations all over the world, the album was heavily inspired by Pierre Fatosme's work with Andre Popp from the 1950s. Constructed entirely from meticulously edited fragments of clarinet improvisations and extended studio techniques *In Memory of the Labyrinth System* is a very unapologetic record. There are no chord changes, rhythms, harmonies or any other ideas typically associated with music. Upon reflection I see the importance of this record being my first official release. By establishing an identifiable sound world, a sonic environment in which the music takes place, I feel as if I was staking claim in a musical landscape that I could call my own.

Starting with my next album *Under a Blue Grey Sky* (2010 Porter Records) I began to place more emphasis on developing my harmonic voice as well as to rely heavily on a process that I have come to refer to as *Timeline Editing*. In all of my music improvisation is an essential and primary ingredient. There is nothing like bearing witness at the moment that music is being discovered and that feeling of discovery and excitement is something that I want audible in my music. Timeline editing refers to the way that I negotiate capturing moments of improvisation and dealing with them with extended studio techniques in post-production. Essentially the idea is that rather than editing a piece to fit an idea, the idea (duration, dynamics, density) is set by the improvisers with which I am working. However long the idea is (2 seconds to 5 minutes) all of the editing and processing happen around and in response to the music is created by the improvisers. I record a musical event of any length and process it according to the time line created by the musician. The result is a dense electronic music with an inherent breathability that feels organic.

> "I like the imperfection and it added to the color. It enriched the color, this out of tune quality. Just like I like my piano out of tune a little bit. It's warmer."
>
> —Morton Feldman

One of the main limitations that I place on myself in the studio is to never try to make my work sound expensive. I make most of my music in my apartment and to try to make my records sound like they were made at Sear Sound would seem foolish. There is great freedom in this approach. Attempting to express the infinite cry of longing with little more than an M Box and an $800 intermediate model clarinet presents a challenge that is both maddening and satisfying. When working in my home studio, in private, I experience something that feels like absolute freedom and joy. Responding to only my own rules and limitations and working for several hours straight I become completely abuzz with ideas and creativity I feel as if the entire world could implode in on itself and I wouldn't give a fuck. I become unshakable, a man possessed. It's a powerful feeling and not like when you've had too much to drink and start mouthing off to the wrong person. It's different. It's encouraging, it's life saving, it's vindicating. It's real. This is the feeling that I try to convey in my recorded music.

"What is written without effort is in general read without pleasure."
—Dr. Johnson

In some circles of musicians it's not at all uncommon to hear the following sentiment: *"Albums are just business cards for getting gigs."* While I can't even begin to fully comprehend how a musician could bring them self to utter something so profoundly ignorant and cynical towards music, the very thing that gives our lives meaning (!!!), I can testify that in almost every case the type of musician who would make such a statement makes albums that, just like most business cards, do not age well and end up in the garbage where they belong. And I don't even want to get started on the use of the word gig. I shudder every time I hear it used. The only time that I have ever played a "gig" is when I've reluctantly accepted a performance opportunity because I needed the money or because I felt like I needed to do someone a favor. I play concerts.

Amplified Clarinet/Solo Performance

"The Edge... there is no honest way to explain it because the only people who really know where it is are the ones who have gone over. The others— the living—are those who pushed their control as far as they felt they could handle it, and then pulled back, or slowed down, or did whatever they had to when it came time to choose between Now and Later. But the edge is still Out there. Or maybe it's In."
—Hunter S. Thompson, *Hell's Angels*

In the last seven years I have performed roughly 150–200 solo concerts. For about two years the bulk of my concerts were solo performances and while I believe that they have evolved into their own unique and identifiable musical entity, incorporating elements of extended clarinet techniques, amplifier feedback, mic placement and live looping, I would say that my interest in solo performance began with being completely taken by the solo saxophone music of Evan Parker. I think that this is a common story, particularly for woodwind players. Starting with clarinet and alto saxophone my initial experiments with solo performance were cheap imitations of Evan's laminal approach to creating "illusions of polyphony", combined with some of Zorn's animated extended techniques & sense of timing and interspersed with some piss poor approximations of "free jazz". Without the ability to circular breathe, and more importantly without a concept, these initial forays were pathetic. I spent hours and hours trying to create something that would at least resemble a cogent musical idea. My first solo concert lasted for 5 excruciating minutes and ended with me slinking out the back of the venue, my tail firmly between my legs and a heart full of defeat.

"Ever tried. Ever failed. No matter. Try again. Fail again. Fail better."
—Samuel Beckett

It is no dumb luck or stubbornness that has kept me pushing forward in the path to find a solo voice, nor do I think it is an innate sense of quality control, which is something that continues to be learned over time through experimentation, trial and mostly error. I think the main driving force that has kept me chasing the goal of creating a solo set was the same thing that has kept me locked in with my headphones since age thirteen: Being alone, in the wilderness, trying to find my way out. I thrive on the solitude that goes along with embarking on the path of composer and solo improviser. To shape an extensive language, or at least contribute to, for an instrument in the context of creating a body of solo work seems like what it must be like to be a travelling folk singer, developing his songs over the course of a lifetime. Like any long form composition, creating one's own language, particularly for solo improvising, is largely a matter of coming up with a concept and then whittling it down until you've discarded as much as possible, refining and refining it as you go until you've cast away as much as possible leaving yourself with just a tiny pebble or two with which you can begin to build from the ground up.

After about two years of on-again, off-again experimentation I think that my breakthrough came with the decision to incorporate live electronics into solo performance. Similar to my studio work I felt it best not to use computer programs that would require any complex programming or patch writing skills. I also didn't want any type of pedal that I felt would do any of the work for me. I wanted a raw and fucked up sound and to that end I use only a small consumer grade mixing board and guitar effects pedals. There is no piece of gear in my set-up that cannot be purchased at Guitar Center for more than $350 and none that requires any ability to program or write patches. This approach does not stem from an attitude or anti-intellectualism nor any sort of caveman aesthetic. My goal with creating music is to find myself lost in hypnotic states of bliss, agony, catharsis and release. With my hands and mouth already being occupied by the clarinet I need to be able to stomp on things and have the resulting sounds keep me moving forward in the composition.

The first roadblock that I encountered with incorporating electronics into my work was that I felt that I was somehow emasculating the form. Granted it's been a self-imposed roadblock, but I think as much as we might like to deny it, there is an element of macho boneheadedness that free improvised music has inherited from jazz. Could I create a solo music using electronics, that was still centered around the clarinet, that would be as powerful as say Parker, Braxton or Zorn? Am I somehow cheating by creating a loop when any of the aforementioned musicians would just circular breathe? By layering sounds via delay pedal or looper am I taking the easy way out instead of putting in the hours to create polyphony with the instrument alone? These are tough questions. They challenge the value system and musicianship of the performer and represent a crossroad, a place where one will choose to proceed or pull back. While I do feel confident in the work that I've done with clarinet, electronics and amplification over the past seven years I have also been sneered at and condescended to by more than one musician as soon as I pull out my bag of effects pedals. This attitude from my peers, and in some cases heroes, stings. It hurts like a motherfucker. After an entire childhood of rejection from the people around me I want so much for my peers and for those that I admire to respect me and my work and once again I find myself in a position where I must refer to an inner compass, one that I hope is steering me in the right direction.

Often after performances people who are interested in incorporating electronics into their own music will approach me with questions. I usually respond with a question of my own: "Well, what is it that you want to do?" It's depressing how rarely people have an answer. In conceptualizing my own approach to playing an acoustic instrument with live electronics my first concern and jumping off point was signal flow. I had a sound in mind, I had certain things that I wanted to be able to pull off and I realized that I needed to have as much control over the individual components of the performance as possible. The solution was to run everything through my own mixing board. A large percentage of the concepts that inform my solo performances deals with my relationship to the clarinet and to the mixing board. Taking the approach of a dub mixing engineer I treat the mixing board as an instrument in itself and with a lot of detail and attention paid to signal flow I usually use 4–8 inputs to offer me as much control and variation within the sound as possible. While I don't have an exact number I try to keep roughly 75% of my solo performances centered on the possibilities afforded to me by the clarinet, using the electronic components to provide an ambience in which the music is presented. Having a good handle on signal flow and having individual sends on my board gives me the opportunity to move between sound worlds in real time performance without abrupt changes.

My live performances with clarinet, amplifier and effects, particularly my solo sets, are largely about creating an immersive sound environment where the listener feels completely overwhelmed by a very menacing presence coming from the stage. I believe that music should be experienced in as three dimensional a setting as possible and I feel that my performances are most successful when there is a palpable sense of anxiety and tension. Just beyond the tension is love and until I can get there I like to hear sounds distort, to hear the PA crackle and sputter and to ultimately bring the music to a place where there is an intense shared feeling of fear between the performer and audience. I hate the fourth wall in any form and my best shows are the ones where I feel as if I have at least put a dent in it.

✻   ✻   ✻

Late one May afternoon in 2005, after a particularly good meal at the Second Avenue Deli, I was walking home and saw something strange and beautiful as I looked up at the sky just over the Williamsburg Bridge. Forming a giant half circle that seemed to stretch clear across the East River was a fresh vapor trail left by an airplane. At different points in the trail's body there seemed to be a number of different hues, shapes and ornamental details. The sky was a gorgeous clear blue and for the few minutes that the trail lived there, the stretch of sky over the East River was an unrivaled work of beauty.

To this day I have no idea if what I saw was some kind of art project or just a beautiful and happy moment that I happened to experience because I looked up rather than down. Who knows? Maybe what I saw was a figment of my imagination… What I do know is that looking at this short lived gathering of condensation I felt like I was receiving a message. When you create with honesty, love and integrity, the work, just like the vapor trail that was burned across the sky, will reach people in ways that you never imagined. The kingdom of god is within you and when you share yourself and your own experience with the world you make it a better place, if only for a moment.

Ad astra per aspera…

TO [RE]THINK OF MILTON BABBITT

DAVID FULMER

When Milton Babbitt passed away in early 2011, I was upset not only because of the loss of a very close and personal friend, mentor, and compositional figure, but also because the classical music world lost a distinctly unique composer. Milton was a bold composer, and he was never afraid to take risks. As I look back and think about our composition lessons, I am continuously struck by the originality of his observations and anecdotes. His perceptive capacity was staggering, and it was an extraordinary event to watch him look carefully and analytically through a musical composition. He was never preoccupied with the obvious, but rather intrigued by piquing his students' interests in the small intricacies and details of any compositional surface. He cared deeply about decision making and allowing a composition to withstand analytical scrutiny. I often feel that many lost sight of perhaps the most valuable tool that he had to offer; an open ear for any aesthetic of musical design. Unfortunately, because his aesthetic was so fortified, many of those who were less comfortable accepting that type of highly sophisticated compositional rigor tended to collapse into feeling obligated to write music in a certain idiom, leading to a dishonest attachment to a compositional technique. Could this be why the term "serialism" is plagued still today with a tarnished reputation? Perhaps it was the academic arena that created this atmosphere, but I am certain that it was not Milton Babbitt. Relentlessly, he strove for every student to create and cultivate an individual sonic universe. Equally at home discussing Beethoven's sketches, Brahms' *op. 118*, or any recent composition performed in New York City the week before, his ears were always open—and always in tune. In this way, he was ageless; he was extremely sensitive to compositional trends, new developments in sound research, and the advent of new performance possibilities and performers. His music is fresh—each piece behaves in a different manner, and provides an elegant solution to a fascinating musical pursuit.

I am always anxious to perform his works often and to repeat them every chance that I have. Years ago, I did not expect that sentiment from every new music performance group around town. It was a great relief, and gave me great deal of satisfaction when I came across another performer who felt as compelled about his music as I. It was understood that many were scared to attempt difficult music like Babbitt's. Every aspect of the composition is difficult—the notes, rhythms, timbres, dynamics, etc. I look at the current landscape of performers, particularly in New York City, and it is true that we are in the "golden age" of the new music ensemble "as specialists." Performers are surprisingly young, and surprisingly brilliant. Even more, they are eating up new music for breakfast, lunch, and dinner. The most exciting detail about this feature is that most all of the ensembles are interested in "difficult music." No longer does only a "token" 20th century composition find a way on a classical music program. The current horizons are expanding, and the music of Milton Babbitt is finding new homes. The phenomenon is quite simple really—his music was far ahead of its time, and with new blood pumping voraciously throughout the new music performance cults, Babbitt's music is highly treasured for the boldness and unapologetic approach of style. Like all great artists, Milton spoke loudly and without fear. When I began performing his music in my teenage years, surrounding musicians—certainly not the diehard fans—would quickly and haphazardly label it as "thorny" and "math music" because of a limited and warped introduction that was prescribed to them in some elective Musical Survey course at some point of their musical education. Today the concert scene has changed, and just recently I heard the words "gnarly", "vibrant", "ferocious", and "kaleidoscopic" being used in a pre-concert lecture describing Milton's music. Performances of all genres of contemporary music are reaching new peaks every day, but particularly those of very difficult musical scores.

Milton's music changes with time. Whether on stage performing, or in a study listening with a score, the musical surface illuminates different shapes and contours upon each hearing. I have listened now to the celebrated cellist Fred Sherry perform *More Melismata* a half-dozen times. Each performance has been different than the last—and the energy from witnessing the physical rigor of the performance never ceases to engage audiences to a new level of commitment. After the first performance of the solo cello work, I remember saying, "Every bow stroke was different, and each note had a different length, attack, release, and position of contact." Fred later said that it was the biggest compliment that he was paid. I meant every word of what I said; his execution of the mesmerizingly difficult score exhibited the greatest virtue of Milton's music—complete and utter diversification. It is true that no two notes in the entire work are congruent. One of Milton's greatest contributions was the way in which he manipulated our sense of hearing and the act of "listening." He changed our processes, and explored sonic landscapes that provided new methods of perception.

One of the greatest pleasures I had with his music involved the preparation of his complete string quartets with the Zukofsky Quartet. While all four members of the group admired the composer and had an affinity for his music, we all heard the musical designs differently. The transformative process that occurs over a short amount of time is hard to describe. After working out the complexity of rhythmic simultaneities, balancing the delicate arrays of dynamics, and figuring out the page turning dilemmas, a new surface emerged from the pages. Bar-lines no longer existed, and what first seemed like dense counterpoint turned into a lyrical tapestry of melismatic phrases. The typical rehearsal tactic of announcing a bar number in order to begin a passage was now replaced with, "let's start at the phrase with the D minor pillar—the sul ponticello passage with the condensed registration." That description was clear enough so that four people could navigate coherently through a 624-measure, 29-minute work. Of course, to execute his music on stage was the real adrenaline rush. I would liken it to something dangerously fun, perhaps skydiving, or some extreme sport that requires a signed waiver before participation. You are on the edge at all times, pushed to the limit, and there are no nets under you. Even small detours in the midst of his compositional webs can cause embarrassing breakdowns. BUT, when you do cross the finish line with your musical partners running perfectly adjacent to you, there is a glorious sensation—physically, mentally, and musically.

Milton's approach to composing should be a model for all young musicians. He believed strongly in musical integrity and finding an individual voice that resonates in meaningful ways. He was a true steward of the industry; his sense of compassion and understanding of the human condition was remarkable, and his respect for all composers, no matter the aesthetic intentions of their music, remained forever intact. He loved music.

Elliott Carter said it best, "Milton Babbitt is the most original composer I know."

BEHIND THE MASK
OR
I DIDN'T KNOW WHAT TIME IT WAS

JEFF GAUTHIER

I'm pretty sure it doesn't really exist (or at least not the way we experience it), yet we all seem bound by it. I believe our experience of time is a construct imposed upon us by our biologically limited perceptions. In other words, time only exists because our biology is finite.

By definition, music can only be experienced in time. Yet experience tells us that human awareness exists only in the moment, and therefore outside of time. How do we know this? Isn't the "I" of your awareness the same "I" that existed 20 minutes ago or twenty years ago? I'm not talking about your thoughts, knowledge or experience. I'm talking about the observer that is you, the "I" that is me. Therefore, to really experience music, one must continually re-focus one's awareness in the moment. If the awareness slips, the music passes us by. This reminds me of a line from the Bruce Lee movie, *Enter the Dragon* often quoted by Nels and Alex Cline (sometimes in unison): "It is like a finger pointing to the moon. Don't concentrate on the finger or you will miss all that heavenly glory."

The whole idea of composition actually demolishes the concept of time. It can sometimes take weeks or months to compose a piece of music that in performance lasts only 20 minutes, and performances can vary radically based upon the performer's concept of time. Perhaps this is why so many of us are addicted to the art of improvisation, which can only occur in the moment.

So by what process does the timeless observer/composer create music that can only exist in time? In my experience, the act of composition is the conscious unraveling of isolated moments of inspiration over the imaginary canvas of time. Coded within these moments are a composer's lifetime of knowledge, experience, emotion and technique. Composition is the process of decoding these moments of inspiration, then re-arranging and re-expressing them over time.

Some composers (like Mozart) hear finished pieces in their head and simply write them down. I've never had this experience. I improvise musical ideas in my head or on my instrument, but these ideas must be transcribed, unraveled and decoded to create a fully realized piece. In my idealized process, musical ideas present themselves as kernels of inspiration containing much of the material from which an actual composition can be unraveled. Since this is an idealized process, the reality is that most of my ideas are worked out through trial and error. But on the rare occasion when there is a direct connection between the moment of inspiration and the creation of a finished piece of music, the process can be a vibrant and magical experience.

Where do these inspired moments come from? I find they generally occur spontaneously during times of profound relaxation, usually when I least expect them. Sometimes they occur while walking, or in the moments before sleep. The implication is that the relaxation of everyday thought processes, (processes that may actually inhibit inspiration), is the key to allowing that inspiration to occur. The experience I'm about to relate occurred during an evening of fun and relaxation among friends, drinking, laughing, listening to music, and opening my awareness to the inspiration of the moment.

The piece *Mask* was written in late 2001 during a Christmas vacation in Guanajuato Mexico. Guanajuato is an old Spanish colonial town nestled in a valley surrounded by picturesque hills. All over the town are many old churches, each containing handmade iron bells in various states of disrepair. On Christmas Eve the church bells begin ringing around dusk, and continue sounding throughout the evening, building to a frenzied tintinnabulation at midnight. While all this is going on, the local residents walk from door to door carrying dolls wrapped in swaddling clothes while they ask for shelter. Usually they are satisfied by a Christmas cookie or a healthy shot of tequila or mescal.

I was staying with friends in a beautiful home in the hills of Guanajuato. The wall of one room was covered with many beautiful handmade Mexican masks, four of which are shown below[1].

1. This collection has now been donated to the Museo Del Pueblo De Guanajuato by Ann Troutner and Paul Marioni, in the name of Arq. Francisco Pichardo.

Example 1. Masks.

My friends and I had begun drinking the local tequila early in the evening, and by the time midnight rolled around we were feeling suitably festive. Just as the bells reached a frenzied crescendo at midnight, Billie Holiday came on the radio singing a soulful rendition of the Richard Rodgers song *I Didn't Know What Time it Was*. This tune can be found in almost any fake book.

The combination of tequila, church bells, and soulful singing awakened a profound experience of timelessness that I was inspired to recreate the next day by writing a new piece of music. I took a cue from all the handmade masks on the walls and had the idea to hide the melody of the song *I Didn't Know What Time it Was* behind masks of newly composed music, and to treat the song to various mask-like settings throughout four connected movements. This concept is not without precedent as it is a common jazz or bebop practice to write new melodies for chord changes of jazz standards, or to reharmonize melodies of well-known standards.

The next morning (after dealing with a bit of a hangover) I sat in the room with the masks and started sketching the music for an introduction, which contained the ideas for all the newly composed music that would follow. As I didn't have a violin or piano, I was forced to sketch all my ideas directly to manuscript paper. And, as I didn't have the sheet music for the Rodgers tune before me, (it wasn't a song that I knew) I was forced to dredge it up from memory, which explains why my version differs somewhat from the original. After sketching my ideas for the introduction, the task before me was to unravel the themes for the following movements from the kernels within the introduction, and find ways to embed or hide the Richard Rodgers song within the newly composed music. I decided to state the verse of the song twice (reharmonized differently each time), the first time during the first movement, and the second time in the second movement. Then I decided to disguise the bridge of the Rodgers tune as plainchant in the 3rd movement, and then reprise the first reharmonization of the verse at the end of the last movement. In this way the form of the original song (Introduction, AABA) remains intact throughout the four movements of the new piece.

As most of the music I write is written for my ensemble the Goatette[2] consisting of myself on violin, David Witham on piano and keyboards, Nels Cline on electric guitar, Joel Hamilton on bass and Alex Cline on drums/percussion, the instrumentation was already set. All these musicians are excellent improvisers, so as always the written material is just a jumping off point for improvisation. A recording of *Mask* can be streamed from this link: http://www.crypto.tv/mask

2. In a spectacular lapse of judgment, I call my group The Jeff Gauthier Goatette after my childhood nickname (the Goat).

Mask begins with an introduction of newly composed music, which contains most of the elements of the music that follows. Notice that the motif in measures 4 and 6 represents church bells.

Example 2. Introduction.

After more introductory material, a vamp (also foreshadowed in the introduction) signals the beginning of the first movement.

Example 3. Vamp.

As the first movement unfolds, there's a short melody in the violin, followed by a reharmonization of the verse of the Richard Rodgers song played over the vamp.

Example 4. Verse Reharmonization I.

An electric piano solo over the vamp is followed by a recapitulation of the melody. On cue a variant of the first theme of the introduction announces the end of the first movement.

Example 5. Variant.

Then, a new vamp in 6/4 time based on the bell motif of the introduction (measures 4–6) begins the 2nd movement. The theme of the 2nd movement (based on an inversion of the vamp) is introduced, and then the verse of the Richard Rodgers tune emerges over the 6/4 vamp with yet a different reharmonization.

Example 6. Verse Reharmonization II.

An improvised violin solo follows with a restatement of the first melody and verse. The music finally winds down over a two-chord vamp (measures 12 and 13) and devolves into a spacious group improvisation. Slowly Alex Cline the percussionist introduces various gongs and ringing percussion, which represent the church bells of Guanajuato. This part of the piece is embarrassingly literal, so much so that every time I hear it, I start to feel a little bit drunk and flash back to that moment on Christmas Eve. The church bells (gongs) grow in intensity over 2 or 3 minutes as the rest of the musicians improvise similar sounds. After a while the violin and bass come in with the bridge of the Richard Rodgers song played in unison as a kind of plainchant (yet more church references). This is done in four statements.

Example 7. Plainchant.

After the final statement, David Witham quotes the actual song *I Didn't Know What Time It Was* on the piano in the style of Jimmy Rowles, an old friend and the pianist on the original Billy Holiday recording[3]. This might be the only clue to the listener who wasn't in on the concept that Richard Rodgers' music was being referred to throughout the piece. After the piano quotes the tune, the bass starts what I call the "Timeless vamp" in 7/4, which also signals the beginning of the 4th movement. Slowly the guitar and violin come

3. In the 1980s I produced an album by Jimmy Rowles and his daughter Stacy Rowles called *Looking Back* for Delos Records. Toward the end of his life when he was being followed around by a tank of oxygen, if you asked Jimmy how he was doing, he'd say in that gruff, sardonic way of his, "Well, I ain't buying any more green bananas." Sadly both Jimmy and Stacy are gone now, and have no idea what time it is.

in, and the vamp builds to a raging guitar solo by Nels Cline. The effect of going from this spacious church bell movement to a raging guitar solo is stunning.

Example 8. Timeless Vamp.

After the guitar solo builds to a frenzied peak, the Timeless vamp is reintroduced, and then a melody based on the whole tone scale of measure 3 of the introduction is stated four times in contrary motion.

Example 9. Contrary Motion.

This section continues into a restatement of measures 11–14 of the introduction, and then a recapitulation of the melody of the first movement, which is finally followed by a drum solo over the Timeless vamp which is repeated ten times until the piece ends abruptly. Bam!

Look, it ain't Stravinsky, but *Mask* is one of my favorite pieces to listen to and to play, because it so directly reflects its moment of inspiration. For this reason, the musical and programmatic references seem to me to be deeply layered and full of meaning. The writing of *Mask* helped me to define a process of composition that I continue to follow to this day. I hope that it will be of interest to others.

I'd like to thank my dear friends and band mates, the Lads o' the Goatette for their collaboration and friendship. They are all geniuses in their own rights, and they all contributed mightily to this piece and its recording. This band has been playing together for almost twenty years (I've been playing with Nels and Alex for over thirty years), and my life will forever be richer for it.

The Jeff Gauthier Goatette:

Jeff Gauthier – electric violin
Nels Cline – electric guitar
David Witham – piano, Wurlitzer electric piano
Joel Hamilton – bass
Alex Cline – drums, percussion, gongs

Recorded by Rich Breen.
From the album *Mask* (CG112) on Cryptogramophone Records.

PERFORMANCE AND INTERPRETATION

ALAN GILBERT

The following is a slight adapation of remarks I made at the New York Philharmonic's Erich Leinsdorf Lecture on April 4, 2011. Because this is, essentially, a prose adaptation of spoken reflections which were given in a particular context—involving a live audience and musical demonstrations that included a spontaneous interaction with another participant— it cannot effectively capture many nuances that would have been palpable at the event. If you are curious about the recordings I played, or want to see my exchange with the Orchestra's Principal Oboe Liang Wang, for instance, or observe the vocal nuances in the concluding Question and Answer session, you can watch the video of the lecture, which is still available at http://nyphil.org/concertsTicks/leinsdorf_webcast.cfm.

When I spoke with my father recently he asked me what I was planning to speak about at this lecture. I told him "interpretation"; he chuckled and said, "Well ... at least it's not too ambitious a topic."

Yes, well, ambitious or not, that's the subject.

A quick definition: interpretation is that which leads to increased understanding of meaning. There are many objects or topics that are open to interpretation: the stock market, a person's tone of voice, a diplomat's speech at the UN, a poem, the Japanese government's reports on the current nuclear crisis, a painting, the Bible, a symphony. These things all have meaning; an interpretation can make that meaning clearer.

I've thought about this, specifically with regard to how it relates to what a musician does. Over the past few months, as I've been preparing for this talk, I've also read a lot, and I've had inspiring and wonderful chats with Randy Butler on the subject of interpretation. Randy is a bass player in the New York Philharmonic, but you may not know that he is also a certified philosopher—I should properly call him Dr. Butler, as he has received a doctorate in philosophy from Columbia University. I've enjoyed the conversations I've had with him over the last year or so, and I accept responsibility—all the help he's given me notwithstanding—for any philosophical deficiencies and errors. In no way are they his fault.

While I've had thoughts on the subject and, for a long time, have tried to deal with the topic in a way that would feed into my actual work as a musician and performer, one thing has become clear during this last period, especially from what I would call my crash course in rigorous philosophical thinking with Professor Butler: this is a daunting subject, and there are many who have gone much farther and deeper in their pursuit of answers than I possibly could. Furthermore, every time I've started to feel that I was close to an understanding, invariably a slew of new questions would suggest themselves, and the horizon of closure would move farther away.

And yet, I'm very happy to be able to grapple with the huge question of interpretation since it has, I think, helped to refine my own approach to music making and could possibly lead to a greater awareness for listeners, by developing a greater understanding of interpretive choices all performers must make.

When I defined "interpretation," I spoke of "meaning," which implies that music has meaning. This actually is an assumption that deserves a bit more discussion. Meaning in music is elusive—in fact, there are those who have said that music has no meaning. Nevertheless, for this discussion, I will be bold enough to posit that music does indeed have meaning, albeit not in the concrete or overt way that the word "apple," for example, has meaning. Still, a performer interprets a piece of music by playing it in a way that is designed to enable its audience to understand the piece's meaning, and I think we can all agree that it's not enough just to represent the notes in the score. There must also be emotional understanding that adds meat to the bones of the score.

But what is meaning in music? Is it necessary to defend the notion of music as having meaning? As I just said, there are those who have said that music has no meaning *per se*—that it is essentially an empty shell that can only provoke individual responses that are not intrinsically related to whatever quality the music holds. I could be tempted to counter this nihilistic attitude first by pointing to the many functions that music has served over the millennia. For one thing, music has crucially served as a call to religious life, by the shofar at Rosh Hashanah, masses for weekly or funeral rites, or other types of music used for rituals in other religions. Music has also inspired people in battle, in declarations of love, and in other communal, social, and personal forums. Today, many art forms—art song and opera, Broadway musicals and film—are human expressions in which music contributes to the text's meaning. How could music, especially in cases where it is an accompaniment to narrative, possibly lack meaning?

That having been said, I'm much more comfortable with a non-rigorous, intuitive response: music has meaning because it so palpably provokes deep emotional responses in people.

Partly I think I'm drawn to this approach to this profoundly important question because I'm far from being a true scholar—I lack the intellectual tools that academics use to effectively carry a convincing philosophical argument very far. Still, my belief that music does have meaning lies on an even more basic level: as a musician, believing in the primacy of meaning in music could not be more fundamental as a defining point in who we are and what we do. Furthermore, the idea that we must constantly search for meaning and truth in music is, I think, the guiding light for most musicians, and it provides a framework for stylistic choices: why would it even matter how we decide to play a given piece we were not pursuing a goal of meaning? It does matter, it must matter, because otherwise we would have no compass to guide us in our interpretative decisions.

Of course, music's meaning is ineffable, precisely *because* it picks up where words leave off. How often have music lovers felt something incredibly powerfully as the result of hearing a piece, a phrase, or even a note of music, without being able to express or understand why we had that particular feeling? Amazingly, these musical moments can seem unbelievably precise, although there may be no words to describe them.

For a long time I have considered a particular question: is meaning in music determinate, or absolute? Or, essentially, is there only one true meaning in a given work of music? And there is a corollary question: is there therefore only one right, or best, interpretation? I know that this is provocative, not to mention practically meaningless, since one of the things that makes music great is its ability to—and I use the word advisedly—*withstand* interpretation. I think we all love the fact that a piece such as Brahms's *First Symphony* can be played, and has been played, lit-

73

erally in thousands and thousands of different versions, many of which could reasonably be called definitive. But I'll throw out an image that has resonated with me over the years: that of a piece of music being represented by a mountain, with the interpreter's task being akin to a climber's attempt to scale that mountain. One mountaineer might be on the south side of the terrain, where it is sunny, and another might be on the north, where it is raining: same mountain, same piece, different outlooks. As they get closer and closer to the top (that elusive, perfect interpretation, perhaps?) the weather on both sides of the mountain is more and more the same ...

Is this nonsense? Perhaps. But this image does account for differences of approach, not only individually, but also historically. Performance practice has changed enormously through time as tastes have changed.

I am presenting some musical examples to try to frame this discussion, and also to show how it can be possible for really, really exciting and superlative interpretations to be widely divergent.

Take the beginning of the last movement of Tchaikovsky's *Sixth Symphony*, the *Pathetique*, by the Leningrad Philharmonic, conducted by Mravinsky, in 1960. [musical excerpt] This is really very poignant—it doesn't wallow in suffering, but clearly expresses deeply felt pain.

Here's another version of this is played by the New York Philharmonic, conducted by Leonard Bernstein, in 1986. [musical excerpt] The exact same passage of music, literally twice as long. I was at these performances; what Bernstein did with the symphony was really unique, and I think that the final movement literally lasted twice as long as it has when led by anyone else. It's a different kind of suffering, and it was Lenny's way to draw it out. It was almost as if he enjoyed it and he really didn't want to let go of the pleasure of the pain.

Illustrations of different approaches, each of which is arguably equally convincing.

Back to my reflections: tastes and historical contexts do change, as do the expectations of audiences. This leads to an important and perhaps evident point: music is one of the arts that essentially requires the added dimension of the audience. Musicians, as interpreters, bring the music to life for the listener. Thus, the interpretative goal is to share and explain the meaning of the work to others.

Parenthetically, I must add that I don't discount those musicians for whom reading a score is like reading a book; it's just that the common aspect of music as a social contact between performer and audience is basic, and is the subject I'm addressing today. This is in contrast to, say, a painting, which is primarily about the direct relationship between the work and the viewer, or receiver. No interpreter is part of the equation. Even an explanation from an expert, which might well add to the viewer's understanding of the painting, is not intrinsically part of the artistic process: the explainer is also a viewer.

So here is the crux of the matter: what is it that happens when a performer interprets a piece of music for an audience? There are three elements involved:

- The work itself, that is, a piece of music; the musician/interpreter; and the receiver.

- There is also the two-sided aspect of the conception of the work— that is, the interpretation—and the performer's capacity to communicate that conception. A musician might have conceived a brilliant idea of how a piece should go, but if the performance is under-rehearsed, or there is a technical deficiency, for whatever reason, the audience might not understand or even have the chance to receive that conception.

- Another variable involves the audience and the expectations it has brought to a performance. As an example, I point a performance I led in Hamburg as a benefit for Japan. It was clear from the beginning of the concert that the audience had come with the expectation that the music would be meaningful. There was a palpable sense of "Event." And so, while the orchestra and I could probably have stood more rehearsal to refine the performances further, there was a deep connection felt in the hall between the musicians of the NDR Orchestra and the public, and I think that everyone agreed that the music came strongly to life and was profoundly meaningful. This illustrates the role, in fact, the *need*, for chemistry between the musician and audience members. If people come to a concert with a degree of apathy, for whatever reason, it can be difficult for a performer to overcome.

That is, of course, not to abdicate in any way the responsibility of the musician. A musician must know the music so deeply that all interpretative choices add to the listener's understanding of the music. How is this done? There are infinite levels to interpretation, but I would point to two as being primary: formal and emotional. A successful interpretation both reveals the structure of the music, and plumbs the depths of the emotional journey it follows. Obviously, this is only possible if the performer truly understands the music on both of these levels.

Formally speaking, this understanding leads to an interpretation that allows the listener, consciously or intuitively, to "know where he is" in the piece. In music composed with formal clarity (for example, Sonata-Allegro form, or Rondo form), this means that the music must be presented in such a way that one feels whether one is, to put it simply, heading away from home, or heading back. Some music is not so clearly structured, and here the listener must be helped to know that very quality of the music—that he or she is on a freer, less rooted journey.

Emotionally, the richer a performer's sense of the range and relative saturation of character and feeling of music, the more compelling and colorful the interpretation will be.

I'm fascinated by, and am a believer in, the hermeneutic approach to interpretation. That is to say, I think that the whole of a work can only be illuminated with reference to its component details, and the details only meaningfully exist with reference to the whole. This is the idea of the hermeneutic circle. One can picture a ring (that is the whole work), with smaller rings around its circumference. These smaller rings are details or localized events that are parts of the whole. The whole thing is reductive, in that each smaller ring can be considered a "main ring," if you will, and have its own set of smaller rings that constitute its many components. You can picture the elements of a piece of music—the overall shape, the movements, the sections, the themes, the melodic fragments, the accompanimental figurations, etc., getting smaller and smaller in detail.

An important responsibility for an interpreter is to address as many of these elements as possible, and to balance them so that there is an organic equilibrium, so that all the details fit into the whole and the whole is naturally built up from the details. This natural approach allows the music to speak for itself, and maintains the primacy of the music over the interpreter, who is, after all, only the vessel through which the music flows, ideally without impediment, to the listener. This equation is highly sophisticated and complex, however, because the personality of the performer is not unimportant—on the contrary, it is essential to successful musical communication.

The performer/interpreter must put his or her imprint on every musical moment and idea: music cannot come alive if the performer approaches it with a passive attitude about letting the music speak for itself. If, for example, a passage of music is characterized by swashbuckling, daring flair, the performer must embody these exciting qualities as fully as possible. Likewise, on the other end of the emotional spectrum, quiet, introspective music needs to be imbued with the necessary stillness and calm—actively realized, even if the passage is, in its effect, neutral. Music making like this is necessarily informed by thousands, if not hundreds of thousands, of interpretative decisions, made both during the preparation for the performance and also spontaneously as it happens.

But here's the conundrum: ideally, decisions should never be perceived as such. That is, an interpretative choice that calls attention to itself, or a performer who makes decisions that jump outside the organic hermeneutic circle, automatically fails what I might call "the naturalness test."

As a performer, it is tempting to make such choices. We seem to be in an age in which interpretative agendas are often celebrated, in which some listeners are apparently thrilled when they can identify "interpretivisms." I would never presume to deny an audience anything it might take from a performance on any level, but I do feel that vividness of personality should not come at the expense of integrity of musical line. I think that is what Leonard Bernstein and Isaac Stern—two great interpreters, neither of whom at all suffered a lack of personality—were referring to when they singled out *La Grande ligne*, or "The Big Line," as the most important quality of a great performance. I am quite sure that what they meant was that a performance, or interpretation, of a work must aspire to have a natural flow from beginning to end, in which all the details and landmarks along the way assume their proper place and proportion within the context of the whole.

Erich Leinsdorf, in his landmark book, *The Composer's Advocate*—a book I read long ago and reread recently, and that has always been an inspiration to me—points to tempo, or, more precisely, the right tempo as the essential element in interpretation. He even goes so far as to note that Wagner felt that interpretation is entirely about finding the right tempo. I think that line and tempo are inextricably related, and they help define each other. Finding "the right tempo" allows for the possibility of the existence of a *Grande ligne,* and a true line throughout a piece, or even in a particular section of music, practically speaking, determines the tempo.

I find these concepts fascinating in the context of the orchestra/ conductor paradigm. It is not an exaggeration to say that I expend most of my interpretative energy in my work with orchestras in striving to address these two musical qualities, line and tempo. I will try to give some depth and breadth to defining these ideas, but at the same time I also hope to show that their successful realization is the basis for a healthy relationship between an orchestra and a conductor.

Line in music is storytelling, and cannot be separated from musical character. It is all about ebb and flow, about the pace and energy behind the unfolding of the music. One of the elements that must—and can—be controlled is how the music moves forward. Sometimes music must be allowed to meander without input of energy—to coast. Sometimes it needs a huge amount of push. Some music must go forward as if reluctantly. Other moments need to be kept from skittering away. An image that I have used when working with student conductors illustrates these various modes of forward progress: I tell them to imagine that their conducting arm is constantly swimming through different media, perhaps air, helium, mud, honey, or almost, dry concrete. It all depends on the desired expression of the music and on how the flow needs to be managed. I might add that creating a natural flow does not necessarily preclude discontinuities and surprise: these are important narrative tools that must have their rightful places and rightful emphasis in the music's course.

Clearly, this point is very close to that of tempo, and may even come close to helping one understand what we mean by the "right tempo." Let's accept that there will be a certain tolerance around the notion of tempo: from day to day and from moment to moment, according to circumstances, there will be a certain variance in tempo. Acoustics play a role; one's heart rate, the particular constellation of musicians involved in a performance, as well as any number of factors, come into play. And yet, I fundamentally believe that there exists a "right tempo" for every moment of a given piece, one that allows the music to exist with maximum expression and emotional resonance. This tempo brings out the fullness of character and lets the musicians tap into their range of feelings about what the music suggests.

There is an interesting interplay between sound quality and tempo as well. A certain richness and intensity of sound makes slower tempos possible without feeling slow—I will often ask orchestras to out fill the time with sound. Conversely, an overly heavy sound quality makes a fleeting tempo impossible. The appropriate character and sound quality provoke tempo, and the other way around.

In the past, I've often spoken about the relationship between orchestras and conductors: I truly believe that the ideal balance has each and every musician fully engaged and committed so that each individual's energy and enthusiasm can be fully utilized in a way that is consistent with a common flow set up by the conductor. Interpretation needs to make this possible.

I like the chapter headings in Leinsdorf's book because they list the areas of interpretation that have to be considered, by conductors:

"Knowing the Score"
"Knowing the Composer"
"Knowing What Composers Wanted"
"Knowing Musical Tradition"
"Knowing the Right Tempo" (there are actually two chapters on knowing the right tempo)
"Knowing the Conductor's Role"

Leinsdorf's premise is similarly compelling: musicians should be faithful to the composer's intentions. I would perhaps state his point in another way, carrying it a step further: musicians should be true to the essence of the music, and they must do so in a way that fully engages their personal point of view.

I've been speaking about line and tempo—these things have to be fully digested and convincing in a conductor for an orchestra to be inspired. Simply put, musicians have to be confident about when and how to play their notes; they will never produce inspired sounds if they don't understand or trust the rhythmic tempo flow and the conception of the music presented by the conductor.

I have often been asked what I do when a musician plays a passage differently from the way I imagined it. My answer: "it depends." What it depends on is in what way, and to what degree, it differs. If it alters the basic line and tempo disturbingly, then I ask for adjustment—or, I should say, if I'm completely convinced in my concept, then I have to ask for adjustment. However, it does happen that somebody plays something with such fantasy and such convincing quality that I think, "Wow, okay, I'm all for it, let's do it," but even in these cases I try to stay true to the conception I have already developed. More often than not the differences are subtle, and it is often thrilling and wonderful to be surprised and challenged in the musical moment.

I might class musical choices into macro and micro subcategories. On the micro level, it is not only possible but also desirable to have individual initiative at play. Furtwängler described a performance as being like a river: always the same, and always changing. If at the bend in the river the water takes more time to cross a certain rock, it's still the same river.

I asked our wonderful Principal Oboe Liang Wang some questions about what he looks for in a conductor and how he comes up with his own "personal musical integrity" in the face of being conducted, and to what extent he feels that he has to leave his own musical personality at the door when he comes onto the stage to play in the Orchestra.

Liang Wang: Before I go into the first rehearsal, I put tremendous amount of thought into a piece of music, but I try not to let my musical personality get in the way of the composer's intentions, as I interpret it myself as a musician. So, as much as possible, I try to give up my personality as a musician before I come to the rehearsal. Still, it comes through anyway, I think; that's the beauty of individual musicians gathering around playing. When I play, or interpret, a passage in front of a conductor, I also look at him—it's actually a very complex moment. When you look at somebody and their gesture is supposed to tell you about the musical line and also the preparation of the whole solo, I think it's really key to not disturb the flow of the music, but here and there not to lose your personality as a musician, which give a little bit of spice to the music. That way it makes it interesting, I think.

That's why sometimes the best conducting is not conducting. It's just letting the musicians play. Seriously, that is actually an important, let's call it, skill. It's certainly an area that I think is important to be aware of as a conductor: to know when you can bank on the inspired contribu-tion of the musicians and to know when it actually will resonate most powerfully by not being too determined about how it should go.

I guess the point is that there are moments in which different micro choices, as I am now calling them, can work equally well in the big context; that's why, if anything, I think I've learned more and more to let the orchestra make decisions. But it has to be in a context that is very clearly set up from the beginning.

Interestingly, a quality in a conductor that I think virtually every orchestra member I've ever spoken to appreciates is the idea of their being allowed them play. They say, "Oh, we love this conductor, he just lets us play." I find that interesting—clearly there's a consensus among orchestra members that that's a good quality. And to reveal a little bit of my sort of secret response to that, I think it's important for a conductor to make sure that the orchestra does feel as if you're just letting them play while, at the same, you set up such an inevitable compelling flow that you are creating a direction that has to be followed, even without everyone noticing.

I confess to a certain sense of futility in talking about something that, at the end of the day, really defies verbal articulation—how can I describe the sense of rightness and inevitability, of magic and inspiration that a great performance has? Words can only begin to describe what we feel in our hearts when music making reaches the depths of humanity. I had the pleasure of performing Mozart's *E-flat Piano Concerto, K.482*, with Emanuel Ax, and after the concert some orchestra players and I were trying to articulate why it felt like one of the greatest Mozart performances we had ever been part of. Manny made some obvious interpretative choices—he wrote his own cadenzas and changed some notes that are disputed in the original manuscript—but, for the most part, the music flowed effortlessly and sincerely, without interpretative agen-da. No obvious points were being made, but the music felt freshly inspired and deeply considered at the same time. I had never heard the last movement capture the fleeting mix of gentle nostalgia and charm as beautifully, but I am unable to say how Manny achieved that. The musi-cians and I finally admitted that there may well be no easy explanation: Manny simply feels the music naturally and is able, pianistically, to bring the music to life so that it sounds inevitable. I have a feeling that the best music making similarly eludes easy description and explanation.

Earlier I spoke about the elusive quest for the perfect interpretation. Even if there are determinate meanings and values in music—and I think there may be—music making and interpretation result from the combination of human beings and the music that they are playing. With the human element there is changeability, uncertainty, and fallibility. Perhaps this is why an interpretation that feels inevitable is so powerful: we hear people making human choices that seem aligned with perfection, and truth.

*   *   *

Editor's note: Alan Gilbert's discussion was followed by a Q&A, an adaptation of which follows.

Question: *What are your thoughts about the "original performance-practice" movement? The question, as I think I heard it, essentially concerned the "original performance practice" movement?*

Alan Gilbert: *I think that there's been something of a pendulum swing, as far as that area of music goes. I'm glad you brought this up, because it's a pretty interesting area.*

Times have changed and approach to performance has … I wouldn't even say it's developed, because that might imply a kind of progress, but it has certainly transformed and evolved over time. And there are examples—fascinating examples of performances from fifty, sixty, seventy years ago—that actually make you laugh now, and seem quaint and bizarre. I can't imagine that that was the response at that time because they're often by really famous artists who were then quite important; in fact, imagine that they were held up as paragons of interpretation. But tastes change, and it's not in fashion right now.

There was a very strong—I would even say dogmatic and exaggerated—movement that was really hard line, about performing Baroque music, in particular, but also about a lot of music written especially before the 19th century. There were a number of people who said that this is the way it had been done when the pieces were composed, so this is how it should be done now, and there's no other way. A lot of musicians who grew up with the "freer," "more romantic" approach to playing Baroque music, let's call it, were often ridiculed and told that they were just wrong, that their approach was old-fashioned, and now we have to do it this new way.

I think we're kind of coming back to a more reasonable place. I believe that music has benefited from the scholarship and the research of that period of hard line "original performance-practice movement." I think we've learned a lot: I think that tempos have probably come a lot closer to what the composers intended.

It's an interesting area, the question of tempo as it relates to pulse, because if you get used to playing a piece and feeling it, say, with four beats in a measure, then if it's marked "andante" you have to make each of those four beats feel like walking, whatever that is—it's not an absolute tempo marking, but it means "walking." One of the most important things that I think people learned, or were reminded of, was that you don't have to feel these measures in four; you can feel them in two. In order to make the andante feeling, you end up with a completely different result if you're trying to make each of those two beats in the measure feel like walking, as opposed to four, a much more flowing tempo, which could be even as much as twice as fast as what people had gotten used to.

One of the wonderful attributes of the New York Philharmonic, and many other orchestras, is the capacity to play a huge range of music and a huge range of styles. I don't think it's necessary to attempt to play it in a way that some scholar has called "correct." I don't think it really matters. As I said earlier, I think music can withstand interpretation. I'll never forget a performance of a Bach chorale, "Jesu, Joy of Man's Desiring"—very poignant, wonderful music—that provoked giggles from certain people. It was played by four student saxophone players, and it probably sounded kind of funny, but I remember feeling that the music was absolutely stunning. And that's what I mean by music's being able to withstand interpretation.

So what I do with the New York Philharmonic is to try to use what we've learned in a way that's consistent with the training and the experience and the point of view that the musicians themselves bring. The New York

Philharmonic, I think it's fair to say, is more flexible than it was, say, forty years ago.

As far as that goes, if you hear older recordings of Baroque music performed by the New York Philharmonic, it sounds very different from what you'll hear today from the New York Philharmonic playing "Messiah", which we do every year. And we've had period specialists conduct, and they've led wonderful, wonderful, very convincing performances. I think that has changed even in the last ten years. I remember that when the Orchestra started doing that, it was new, but now all the musicians not only know it, but they come into these weeks of Baroque music expecting to be asked to play without vibrato, and to approach early music in what we call a "historically informed" way. But they use modern instruments and play at modern pitch, and I think it works very well.

The point is that stylistic questions actually are, finally, pretty small when compared with the bigger issues that musicians deal with all the time. I'm not saying that style is not important, because it's really important, and one of the things that I try to do—not just with Baroque music or Classical music—is to make sure that the New York Philharmonic has a stylistically distinct approach to every piece it plays, and to every composer it plays. Tchaikovsky should be played with a different stylistic approach from the one we use when we play Mozart.

I know that I have kind of talked around the subject, but I hope that gives you a little bit of a sense of where I stand on that one.

Question: *Do external factors, like the reason you were giving the benefit concert for Japan, united the audience and the soloists and the whole orchestra so they gave an even more emotional, perhaps, or a better performance than they might otherwise have.*

Alan Gilbert: *I'm sure that's absolutely true. I think it's very hard to say how much of the feeling in the concert hall was from a sense that the music itself was meaningful and how much was because of the circumstances surrounding the event.*

I think many of us will never forget the performance that the New York Philharmonic gave of Brahms's "German Requiem", the first concert it played after 9/11, with Kurt Masur and Tom Hampson and Heidi Grant Murphy. It is a piece that, first of all, the New York Philharmonic and Masur had played many times brilliantly, but it did come to life, and I'm sure that the musicians were inspired in a special way.

What we try to do on what we could call a "normal" concert—although I hope there is no such thing as a normal concert at the New York Philharmonic—is to play with that sense of emotional urgency, although I think we would all perhaps agree that it's okay not to have every concert inspired by horrible tragedies.

Question: *I'm interested in the relationship between programming and interpretation. Do your guest conductors choose their soloists because of their interpretation, or are they chosen separately and the conductor understands what the soloist is about?*

Alan Gilbert: *The question about how soloists are chosen—whether because of an interpretative point of view that we're looking for—is interesting. But it's a little broader than that, I would say. I'll answer a different question that you didn't ask, first. When I work with a soloist, and I think when most conductors work with soloists, the understanding is that the approach and the interpretation of the soloist is the one that is going to carry the day. There was a famous performance of Brahms's First Piano Concerto played by Glenn Gould, conducted by Leonard Bernstein, in which Bernstein issued a disclaimer at the beginning of the performance, saying that he didn't agree with the interpretation that the audience was about to hear. Yes, that was uncool, I would say, but that's what happened. We certainly wouldn't do that: that soloist might not come back if we had that much of a disagreement.*

But, essentially, when soloists come, it's to present their version of the piece. We often know more or less what we're going to get, and we're looking for someone who will present something that is personal and compelling, as well as virtuosically dynamic. That's an area that I thought of addressing in the talk but I didn't really get to—the idea that there is a technical com-

ponent to performance that is absolutely crucial.

I don't think there is any such thing as a performance that has no interpretative point of view, because no point of view is in itself a point of view, but there is such a thing as a performance that is gratifying and thrilling simply because of the physical execution, if you will, of the playing. And that is undeniable. I mean, it's thrilling to hear a pianist play all the right notes in the first Chopin Étude, whether or not they interpret the piece, if you know what I mean. That is an important thing that we look for in soloists also, but certainly not the most important.

We want someone who will bring a personal take on whatever piece they're playing. If you bring a cellist to play, there are not that many different pieces that cellists are going to offer, so there's a good chance that in the span of, say, ten years you might hear four or five different versions of the Dvořák Cello Concerto, so I think it's important for the audience and the people who stay with the orchestra over a period of time to be able to hear different points of view. And that's what we hope soloists bring.

Question: *Maestro, I can understand how you can sometimes develop a rapport with a solo instrument, allowing one instrument to offer a different interpretation of a passage in a piece of music. How do you develop that same sense of trust with 100 musicians in allowing them to interpret a piece of music without the benefit of the beat of the conductor?*

Alan Gilbert: *Yes, well, that's pretty much* **the** *question, isn't it?*

The idea of conducting, as I briefly touched on, is to come with a developed and hopefully inspiring point of view about the music—I guess that's what we're calling an interpretation—and present it to the orchestra in a way that is understandable, so that the orchestra can play along, if you will, and that your point of view is inspiring and convincing so that they buy into it and use their capacity, goodwill, enthusiasm, and energy to play their appropriate part in the interpretative process.

That is far from a given. I really can't overstate the importance of having natural, convincing rhythm as a conductor, so that the orchestra can trust their own rhythm. It doesn't sound good if people are not able to use their own sense of musical flow in a way that they can trust, if they're not sure when the next note is going to happen. I am not only talking about playing steadily in tempo; I am talking about bending the time in a way that people understand it, so that they can go take the curve in exactly the same way, with the same banking and the same speed as everybody else. That's what conducting is, and that's what we strive for.

But again, at the end of the day, it's an indescribable alchemy that happens. And I guess all I can say is that when it happens—and it does happen quite a lot at the New York Philharmonic, more at the New York Philharmonic than almost any other orchestra—that you know it when it happens, and it is not something that you can explain or that you even necessarily want to explain. Suddenly everybody is totally on the same wavelength, and the most important thing is that the music feels as great as it should, and there's an enjoyment both on the playing side and on the listening side.

Question: *When you are starting a piece with the Philharmonic, in Baroque and Classical music, if you listen to four or five great recordings, vastly different versions by great orchestras and conductors, how do you decide which you think is the most definitive or the most accurate? And in more modern music, how does hearing the composer conduct or hearing the composer play an original piece weigh into your decision more heavily?*

Alan Gilbert: That is actually two questions. How do I decide which version to take as my own, if I listen to different records? And, with a modern piece of music, is it helpful to hear the composer perform the piece?

The answer to the first question is that I almost never listen to recordings when I'm preparing for a performance. I try to have a one-to-one relationship with the score. Frankly, I actually find it difficult to listen to recordings of a piece that I'm performing, even if it's great, because it is different from what I'm trying to do. So I try as much as possible not to listen to recordings.

If a modern piece has been composed and performed by the composer him or herself, then it can be interesting. But using a recording is a shortcut to learning, and I don't think it leads to a personal point of view about the music; it's taking on somebody else's approach to the music.

WE ARE ALL BEETHOVEN

JUDD GREENSTEIN

In a 2010 article in *New York* magazine, Justin Davidson asked about a series of then-upcoming Beethoven performances at Lincoln Center, "Can Ivan Fischer put the shock back into *Eroica*?" ("Beethoven's Kapow", *New York*, March 21, 2010) Davidson astutely turns on its head the notion that musical literacy or foreknowledge of repertoire is a necessity for listening to classical music, suggesting that those acquired skills or prior encounters may actually inhibit the radical experience that an uninitiated listener can have with a masterwork like Beethoven's *Eroica* Symphony; familiarity and "understanding" can limit one's openness and the capacity to be truly moved or even disturbed by the psychological and emotional messages or implications of such a work.

Davidson writes:

"For much of today's public, even the most thoroughly tilled symphonic turf has become unexplored terrain. The orchestral Establishment treats that widespread musical illiteracy as a disaster, but it's also a chance to give works of *Eroica*-like stature an infinite number of premieres. The fact that many audience members have never heard the piece should be a bracing thought for the players on the stage: To dispense revelation is a daunting responsibility.

"Classical-music neophytes often worry that they don't have enough background to appreciate a performance, but the opposite is often true: They're the ones who listen without preconceptions and who are primed for danger and unpredictability."

This is an insightful message that sheds an encouraging light on our role as contemporary composers. As the creators of new work, we accept the responsibility of presenting that work to the uninitiated: that is the definition of a "premiere". But even non-premieres are *functionally* premieres for nearly everyone in attendance at a contemporary music concert; rare, indeed, is the performance of a recent work where a majority of attendees have heard that work before. The music we write is music for which most hearings, now and into whatever future we may imagine, will be first hearings. Our work will receive, in Davidson's words, "an infinite number of premieres". "Danger and unpredictability" are our daily bread and, given the explosion in both the number of composers and the amount of new music being written, as well as the increased availability of that music via the internet, it's hard to imagine that the trend will ever tilt back toward the creation of a stable audience of listeners who are regularly familiar with our work before they hear it performed.

This trend doesn't just apply to the music we write, but also to the music we consider fundamental to our compositional voices, the bedrock of our personal musical histories. Just as Davidson's Beethoven interpreters can't assume an audience with prior knowledge of Beethoven, neither can we. The Canon is gone, if it ever really existed at all. Furthermore, with the increasingly dissolving barriers between traditional musical genres, the likelihood that a listener will share a composer's given musical history, the personal "Canon" that informs him or her, is vanishingly low. There are too many threads of music on which to draw, for listener and artist alike. The very idea of being part of a musical "tradition" is called into question by the many traditions and histories that inform the musical voices of today's composers—and songwriters, and producers. History isn't over, but the myth of a universal History has been shattered, replaced by the small, personal histories of given communities and individuals.

The absence of a Canon and a Tradition doesn't leave us completely untethered or disconnected from one another. A Canon is not only about the works it contains, but is also about the cultural conditions that it reflects. Even in the absence of a core set of works, we can discern a common approach to cultural consumption, a way of looking at the world that underlies our contemporary thought and behavior. It seems that we've made a necessary adaptation, as people living in a culture with altogether too many choices at all times: we've become experts at scanning the surface features of a huge quantity of information, choosing which from among the many options are worth more of our time. We're not passive recipients of a received culture or tradition but instead are active participants in picking and choosing the specific combinations of interests that make up our own, individualized micro-cultures. Because we're not seeking to recreate existing cultural norms, we're not merely "tolerant" of the New but are in fact demanding of newness and strangeness. Finding something truly New in the haystack of cultural offerings is an elevated prize, its strangeness feeling all the fresher for the difficulty in discovering it. The crotchety among us might argue that this scanning-the-surface renders our culture more superficial than in previous eras, but that misses the point. The depth is still there for those who seek it, lying beneath the various surfaces, ready to be explored once the choice has been made. We're just insistent that there be a compelling indication that the investment will be worthwhile. More than ever before, we're aware of the "opportunity costs" of the choices we make because we're continually bombarded with tantalizing-seeming cultural options.

I am certainly describing an idealized form of today's cultural consumer, one who is actively forging his or her own cultural pathway and is not merely following the tides and trends that surround us at any given time. But traditions are tides, too, and carry their own dangers. It's not at all clear that a tightly-guarded, monolithic Canon is a better foundation for a healthy relationship between art and society than is a radically open playing field, even one where internationally-owned corporate cultural products are constantly threatening to drown out smaller entities. But in any case, again, the genie is out of the bottle, and while the past can offer us important models for consideration, it can just as easily misguide us if we try to replicate those models from earlier eras that had their own cultural norms and conditions. If our task as an arts community is to find ways of introducing cultural products of depth and substance to as wide a public as possible, we have to respond to this world, not try to force the solutions of prior generations onto a contemporary cultural consumer who will reject them out of hand.

This is a relatively easy case to make so long as we are speaking theoretically about the method of presenting new art to new audiences. Some people might put more stock in Traditions or History than I am suggesting we should, but it is generally uncontroversial to say that arts presenters should be attentive to the cultural context in which they are presenting new work. But what of artists ourselves? This kind of self-reflection is usually the domain of arts administrators and educators and academics, not artists, who are "supposed" to be shielded from these questions, left to our own devices without concern for the context in which our work is made. In fact, nothing is guarded more carefully by composers than the "right" to not consider the audience for our work. This mentality is a reflection of a pernicious myth that has arisen since the Romantic era: the ideal composer as isolated genius, divorced from any forces that would alter his or her art from the perfect form that it takes in his or her uncorrupted mind. Here you can think of Conlon Nancarrow in the Mexican desert or Charles Ives in the insurance industry; each of these two great composers have mythologies surrounding them that are, in their own way, versions of this perfectly walled-off composer ideal, making work that the world was not yet "ready" to hear. Even late Beethoven falls into this category: protected by his fame and clear status as the most important composer of his time, as well as the popularity of his more "accessible" works, he was free to write what were then inscrutable quartets and other radical works. What is fetishized in these stories is the composers' independence from popular appeal; they were writing "for themselves" alone and therefore able to take chances that the marketplace would have otherwise rendered impossible.

In dialogue with other considerations, this story, about the need for composers to be allowed to act autonomously, is extremely valuable. Particularly in a cultural context where traditions have eroded and market forces threaten to drown out any other considerations, it is absolutely imperative that artists be given safe spaces in which to take chances and try out new ideas. It's also critical that those artists whose work is excellent but doesn't happen to conform to the present whims of the cultural marketplace not be left out in the cold. Just as importantly, the purely "free" market is itself a deeply destructive myth—much, much more dangerous than anything that composers might invent about ourselves—so even providing a counter-narrative to that mythology is a critical element in improving our culture. Championing values other than those that are purely commercial is a powerful function and an end unto itself, one that art and artists are extremely well-positioned to deliver. And, like most publicly-supported creative research endeavors that fill in gaps in the commercial marketplace, the return on the "investment" will at times take forms that have a broad impact, with some seemingly insular music having great appeal or influence among audiences or composers, immediately or down the road.

Those are the good things about the story of the composer-as-island. The problem is that the same story can easily be used as the principle or sole lens through which to view our work as composers, defining the relationship between that work and the broader world of music. Today, composers have an entire infrastructure at our disposal that allows us to behave as Nancarrow or Ives might have, without needing to move to Mexico or to take a job outside of the field of music. We are shielded by walls of our own devising, with our music heard mostly by other music professionals or a small number of devotees of contemporary art music, and rarely by the public at large. This condition is highly lamented by most composers, who seem to ignore the fact that this condition has been created by composers ourselves. In demanding safe spaces for our music, reflecting our mythology of isolation as a condition to be cherished, we built walls that keep others out but also keep our music in. We have our own venues, labels, and media outlets, attended and followed by the same small community, one that is (thankfully) very supportive but also very insular. The story that we have told ourselves about ourselves has led us down roads that reflect that story, but in so doing also feeds our collective isolation as a community, limiting the possibilities for broader audiences to engage with the work we create.

My life as a composer is intertwined with an effort to collectively emerge out of this isolation, entering into a dialogue with the wider world of music. My colleagues and I who share this effort are constantly asking questions about our own experiences as composers and musicians, assessing what is successful and unsuccessful about our lives in music both in terms of our own happiness and also in our impact on society, at large. Are we fulfilled by the performances of our music, for composers, or by the new music that we play, as performers? Are we playing for the audiences we desire, in quantity or quality or diversity of every kind? Are we collaborating with the kinds of artists with whom we'd like to be working? Are we happy? Are we improving our culture or our society? These and many other questions of similar stripes are not necessary to ask if one is content to put one's head down and write, regardless of the circumstances, but for those of us who are not so content, we thankfully have the ability to make changes to suit our interests and needs.

One of the most difficult areas of speculation about contemporary art music and its relationship to the broader world of contemporary culture is the question of what music is "accessible" to a wider audience. My music is often branded with that word, thoughtlessly thrown out as praise by classical musicians who rarely engage with new music at all, or bitterly used as a term of dismissal by composers who work in a different style. I wouldn't even bring the term up at all except for its ubiquity, as well as what that ubiquity can tell us about the lack of sophistication that we bring to our strategies for cultural engagement. "Accessible", used as a blunt instrument, is obviously deeply reductive and therefore meaningless for reasons that circle back to my original point: what does it mean to be "accessible" in a cultural landscape where listeners are coming from every possible direction, and therefore require many different access points? The notion of a work's accessibility, as commonly used, implies a connection to a set of expectations—a link between the musical expectations of the expected audience and those also "expected" by the piece. In other words, it implies a tie to a tradition, with a set of musical parameters tied to that tradition. If our contemporary culture even vaguely resembles that which I described above, with its micro-cultures and personal histories, this strategy, of accessibility by way of adherence to a tradition, is fundamentally flawed.

My question, for myself and to our community, is what it would mean to reconsider the notion of "accessibility" for the cultural landscape in which we actually live. If we start from the description of our current cultural consumer as someone who scans broadly, looking for engaging points-of-entry that imply Newness and depth underneath, can we as composers craft music that offers these points of engagements and welcomes new listeners, unfamiliar with any specific tradition, into our world(s)? Can we write for the cultural community in which we are situated, or only for our own, insulated communities? This task isn't for everyone; some composers want to choose the latter path and write for limited audiences who share their values. But those composers need to stop pretending that the world "should" be a certain way that it isn't, that there's an injustice in the world not conforming to the artistic sensibilities that they prefer, and that we should mangle our strategies as a contemporary music community by being overattentive to the needs of composers who are not interested in creating a dialogue around their work and its engagement with broader audiences.

We can't pretend that we can have this conversation, a real dialogue around the work that composers do, without including the dirtiest of all topics: the music itself. It is delusional to think that we can find new strategies of engagement while speaking only of where our music is played, or how, but not what the music does in terms of sound and energy and form and everything else. This isn't a call to stop anyone from writing whatever they want to write, and it's certainly not a facile, juvenile call for "more tonality" or "rock influence" or anything so reductive or simplistic. It's a call to openly consider the question of how our music communicates meaning, across all parameters, and to consider what strategies we might employ to better engage with the cultural community in which we find ourselves today.

For me as a composer, this doesn't mean self-consciously examining each note for how it would play in Peoria, or in Pitchfork, or in *People*. That is a dystopian vision of an artist's life. Rather, I have made a deeply-embedded decision to write each piece as if it were my first, to try to keep the elements that I am using as clear and transparent as possible, to teach the language of the piece at the same time as I "tell the story", to never fall back on historical references that aren't themselves engaging without a knowledge of the history to which they refer. It's an approach that melds the didactic and the narrative, assuming nothing of a first-time listener but also engaging myself as someone intimately familiar with the material. I believe you can have it both ways, and feel very comfortable writing music this way (I know no other)—so perhaps that's why I am advocating for such an approach (this wouldn't be the first occasion in the history of music writing that a composer had made such a move). But in thinking theoretically, this feels like the type of approach—one version of this type— that would allow us, as composers, to speak across the boundaries of divergent infrastructures that have emerged to support different areas of music. In fact, it feels like a response to my own experience as a member of the broader cultural community, as someone performing the same activities of scanning and picking and choosing that I have ascribed to the population at large. To the extent that I am writing for myself, I'm writing for myself, on the Internet, looking for some compelling music to hear. I'm challenging myself to make the case, to myself: why would I download my own mp3, of all the mp3s in the world to be downloaded?

In the end, I come full circle on this question, returning to Davidson's account of Beethoven the revolutionary, introducing new forms of art into the world. It cannot be a coincidence that he, the most revolutionary of all composers, perhaps the only one who changed not just music but all of art, was also the composer who most thoroughly blended the didactic and the narrative in his compositions. There's a force and clarity to each idea, an announcement of each motif as a motif, and a repetition of those motifs in multiple forms to make sure that the listener certainly gets the point. New ideas are usually presented with new textures supporting them, helping the ear notice the change. There's often a dramatic stripping-down of motifs to their most essential elements, one or two notes rendered naked and bare for all to see, arriving as the centerpiece of development sections across Beethoven's compositional lifetime. There are the mighty codas, which read as "triumphant" to the Beethoven scholar who knows each measure by heart, but also announce the arrival at the conclusion of the movement, in no uncertain terms, to the novice listener. These features, and countless more, are as exciting on the hundredth listen as on the first, in different ways.

Should we—could we—write like Beethoven? Not exactly, but here's yet another thing to learn from him: how to write for an audience that could not possibly be prepared for what you have to say, either because nothing like it has ever been said before (Beethoven) or because there are too many things being said at once in the world (us, today). As composers today, we are all Beethoven, and at the same time we're also all Beethoven's ignorant audience sitting expectantly at the premiere of the *Eroica*, not knowing what will come next but open to the possibilities.

TROUBADOURS' DILEMMAS

HILARY HAHN

At the security check at Heathrow Airport this morning, a security woman took away my cough syrup. It was very nice cough syrup, available neither as a prescription nor in a tiny size, allergen free, alcohol and drug free, impossible to find outside North America. I was getting over a sore throat, trying to not cough on everyone during the desiccating flight, so naturally I was annoyed. But there was nothing I could do about it.

This got me to thinking, in a roundabout way, that it is remarkable to what lengths people go to bring music on the road, when in fact, it already exists in many forms in nearly every city there is to visit. Hundreds of instrumentalists can play the same pieces. Even if concertgoers want to hear a specific performer, the Internet and recording technology make it possible for that person to be heard without being physically present. Looking at the situation dryly, it could seem that the only practical reason for musicians to travel the world is to enable audience members to walk out of their houses, stroll down the street, watch an out-of-towner concertize in the local hall, go to a favorite restaurant for supper and then sleep in their own beds, get up, and go to work or meet their friends for brunch at the corner cafe the next day. Which is a wonderful scenario to take part in. But is it outdated? Somehow, we take it for granted that the performer or entertainer comes to town. Other entities that people want to see stay put and do alright: architecture, amusement parks, restaurants, cities, shops, and so on. Tourists seem happy to travel to those. So why is it the musicians who are hitting the road and not the audiences? It could have gone either way, but this is where we wound up. There must be good reasons.

I am not complaining. This lifestyle is intriguing. The reality is not as glamorous as it might appear from the outside—but it is still pretty amazing and I am grateful for these life experiences. I am a little ashamed that I was annoyed when my cough syrup was taken away. After all, I spent an evening at the Prado museum in Madrid last week and I'm looking forward to shopping for yarn in Glasgow on the other end of this flight. I go from Rio to Berlin to Seoul, for work. For work! I get turned around sometimes. It's nice to get lost by stepping out your front door, for the simple reason that your front door has changed since yesterday. Yet through technology, I'm never far from the people and hobbies I rely on to keep my balance. It is a really nice setup in many ways.

The traveling, however, is awkward. First, there's the instrument. Will a gate agent try to stop me from taking it on board? Will somebody try to jam a suitcase on top of it once it's in the overhead compartment? What if I need a bow rehair for a recording but I don't know any luthiers or bowmakers in town? Then, planning logistics: days spent in embassies waiting for work visas, flight and hotel decisions to address, what to play in two years, when to take a break, which priorities might still be important down the line and how to fit them into the demands of the music, what the program order will be in a particular recital program a year away, and finding a convenient time to add in concerts for an unexpected project. Those are good problems to have, but they eat up mental space. The logical part of my brain tells me that yes, I need to think about these things now. But most days, the instinctive part of my brain doesn't feel capable of making those kinds of decisions.

There's the preparation process to keep in mind, too. Traveling throws a wrench in practicing and routine. Changing repertoire is stimulating but unpredictable: pieces take their own sweet time, and practice conditions aren't reliable in the midst of travel. When I'm not at ease, I don't progress. Sometimes I wish I could go to the same work space every day: an office, a studio, or a dressing room in which I feel particularly comfortable. When it isn't there to return to, I conjure it in my imagination, but this wastes creative energy I could be putting into the music. Hauling luggage spends physical energy. Jetlag leaves me bleary, stumbling through the day at what feels like 60% functionality. Every type of lifestyle has its downsides; these are the peculiar challenges of traveling to make live art. The irony is that this sort of touring threatens the fragile continuity of artistic development at the same time that it both demands and rewards it. In short, there are a lot of reasons why travel is not a helpful aspect of performing. Solutions do exist to all of these individual challenges—but they treat the symptoms, not the cause.

Ideally, a musician would choose freely between time spent visiting these wonderful places, seeing the world, and being pushed out of one's element; and creating in a consistent environment. In a spontaneous world, recordings would be made on three days' notice, when a piece is ready in the right way or a collaboration is poignant, and repertoire could be decided at the beginning of each week. Fewer strategic decisions would need to be made. Willpower could be freed up for what appear to be more important artistic pursuits. In reality, the ideal probably isn't ideal. The trick is to find a good middle ground. Every person should be free to work in the way that is easiest for them. I think that that in itself is a solid goal.

One thing to consider is how the negative effects of travel on our work affect the people we are traveling to. How can we honor those who value us, if we aren't thinking clearly or our fingers barely want to move? How can we deliver when our ideas are weak? This would apply, in reverse, to concertgoers, who add artistic input of their own. Listeners have ideals too. They strive for a certain experience. They communicate their involvement often silently but strongly. They too may struggle with the same issues as musicians, but in ways that get much less attention. For those facing the stage, the question might be, How can we bring our best to the table even when we aren't feeling connected to the performance? I don't have answers, but it is worth thinking about. We should not be reckless with audiences. They are smart; they can tell when things are falling apart.

"Accessibility" is a big word in classical music these days. The term is typically applied to compositions and concert settings. What about logistical accessibility: where can the artist travel to easily; what improves everyone's shared efforts; and what allows us to consistently attain a high level of performance? Which elements are important when creating opportunities for artistic growth?

I would like to see more openmindedness within the presenting structure, so that musicians can follow their instincts and work in ways that speak to them. If someone needs to spend half their day in a sunny art studio or rowing on a river or practicing on the porch of a farmhouse, he or she should not be exempted from a fulfilling performing life because of these factors. It is crucial to specifically invite artists to follow their instincts. It should be acceptable to give a recital from one's living room, streamed to wherever people are interested in seeing it. It would be a relief to be encouraged to decide some repertoire on the concert day. If a musician wants to spontaneously bring an additional performer to collaborate with, well, why not? Like in any career, there are many days when it would be helpful to be able to turn around and take a rest if the work isn't going well; the best way to avoid such a situation is, of course, to rework how things are scheduled in the first place. The next time a traveler wants to take off for somewhere other than where the plane is heading, it could be constructive for him or her to start a discussion with others about creating a more favorable structure. We could all learn from each other's ideas. Imagine the fantastic contributions that could be made if everyone was in a position to reach their full potential.

These suggestions may be impractical right now, but somebody has to be the first to see where they lead. We have to be ready to support those pioneers. Experiments can only truly be tried and understood if all of us in the field are open to new possibilities. A tendency—and an understandable one—is to keep things as they are because that is what we know. With administrators, presenters, and managers run ragged by expectations, it's no wonder flexibility is a strain. It's impressive how many performers are currently experimenting by redefining boundaries. A lot of other people across the genre are also trying very hard, pushing their capabilities to the max. Regardless of the results, that is phenomenal to witness. That shows that the will is there. The environment hasn't quite caught up, but if we keep inventing, it will.

Wherever our efforts may take us, I hope that musicians never lose the benefits of traveling for their craft. At an embassy reception on a recent trip to Iceland, diplomats from three countries separately mentioned music as a form of cultural ambassadorship. Their point was that this art form transcends language barriers. It had been a long time since I gave that some good thought; it is easy to get caught up in pondering what the score wants to say and forget what we convey by playing in a country we weren't born in. Even going to school with fellow students of over a dozen nationalities is nothing to sneeze at. Though politics within the field can be fierce, when it comes to issues outside of rehearsal, classical musicians tend to be careful with each other. With a few important exceptions, there is an unspoken agreement to look past those differences to focus on what brings us together, so that we can create a musical statement as one composite voice.

Musicians fill a unique niche in the broader community of roving citizens of the world. We work in areas filled with people from all kinds of places, and we do so within a communicative art while changing location nearly constantly, from concert halls to capitol cities to the hotels we stay in. That is part of the tradition of music, and classical music is more tradition based than any other discipline I know of. We revere what has come before, even if we rebel against it. A fat passport and a working knowledge of airports and cities one passes through every year represent rites of passage, part of the romance of being a musician. So we have to stop every now and then and think about how neat it is that we get to do so many terrific things, all because of a set of notes that is arranged and rearranged in endless combinations.

Through travel, we work with colleagues with whom we would never cross paths otherwise, and that can be so musically enriching. Someone has to move around in order for two disparate people to meet! It is good to be forced to stay on our toes and to adapt to things we don't agree with. Having it our way doesn't necessarily push us to be better than we can imagine for ourselves.

And then there's the beauty of live performance with all of its difficulties, warts, and brilliance. One of my favorite things about classical music arises from the fact that we work with pre-determined materials. Each player's individual reaction to the confines of rhythm, notes, tempo, and dynamic markings is what makes each interpretation—and each evening onstage—different. Every venue offers new insights. It is near impossible to mimic a live concert, without certain elements present. Audiences feel this. They want to be there, in the room, when ideas are born. I think that that, in essence, is why musicians travel to audiences and not the other way around: the disconnect we struggle against as performers helps spur on our concert experiences. We can't go on autopilot all that easily when we are feeling disjointed. This imposed resourcefulness keeps the music vital.

So we keep traveling, tossing and turning like we are caught on a line, sometimes drifting, sometimes racing, sometimes fighting, sometimes freeing ourselves. But in the end, we are reeled in again, and we give in, wishing that we will be transported, through this next trip, to a better place.

THE INVENTED HORIZON IS FREE

MARY HALVORSON

From an early age, my primary focus as a guitar player has always been on composing, performing, and listening to instrumental music. However, sometime around 2003 I went through a phase where my listening habits changed. I had worn the bulk of my instrumental records into the ground and needed a break; I found myself listening to all sorts of music with vocals and lyrics. Inspired by the change, I began to wonder what would happen if I incorporated lyrics into my own music, and as an experiment, I decided to find out. Because lyric writing was an unfamiliar universe for me, I wasn't sure where to begin. So I decided to take some of the techniques I use for instrumental composing and translate them into similar exercises using text. This way the lyrics I wrote would have a kinship with my music, by virtue of sharing a common process.

For example, below is an exercise I use to explore new chords on the guitar. The concept is simple: fiddle with something until your intuition tells you to stop. Starting with a basic A♭ Major 7 chord, I gradually add, subtract, or change one or two notes at a time, keeping track of each step along the way. The idea is that the chord gradually morphs until a "blurred" effect is created. In some cases the final chord ends up being a slight modification of the original; in other cases it becomes something entirely new. Once I'm finished, the first four chords are discarded and I'm left with the final (new) chord to use as a starting point:

The text equivalent of this exercise would be to take a simple sentence and gradually morph it to obscure meaning and/or to create new meaning. Words can be deleted, added, or replaced with similar words a few at a time, in a train-of-thought manner. In the following example, I started with a saying from a fortune cookie that read, "You are free to invent your life." I then tinkered with the fortune cookie text a couple words at a time until finally settling upon a modified proverb, "The invented horizon is free":

You are free to invent your life. His life is free of an inventor. His life is escaping the invention person. Free escaping for the invention person. Free refers to the invention person. Referring to the free invention of person. The invention of free is referred to. The invention of reference. The help for invention. The horizon for invention assistance. The horizon for invention help. **The invented horizon is free.**

Another lyric-writing exercise I'll use as an example is a rhythmic game. Let's say I want to create three verses of lyrics consisting of 7 + 5 + 3 syllables, to fit with a melody. First, I'll find some text to use as a starting point. For the purpose of this exercise, I'm using the following excerpt from an article in *The New York Times* about electric cars. The next step is to highlight my favorite words, shown here in bold:

"A CENTURY ago, when **electric** cars were **popular—especially in cities** and among **women** drivers—they looked **discernibly** different from gasoline-**powered** automobiles. In the **age** of the **horseless** carriage, the transportation historian James Flink wrote, electric cars **looked even more like** carriages.

Those **early** electric cars were **upright** and **boxy,** just the look that today's designers are **trying** to **avoid.**

The electric cars on display this week at the North American International Auto Show in **Detroit** are **adopting** one of **two overriding** design philosophies: **make** it exciting, **or** make it **familiar.**"[1]

1. *It's Electric. Should It Look Electrifying?* By Phil Patton, *The New York Times,* January 6, 2012.

By discarding the un-bolded words, I have condensed the text into the following:

century electric popular especially in cities women discernibly powered age horseless looked even more like early upright boxy trying avoid Detroit adopting two overriding make or familiar.

I then choose from the above list to string together three verses of words, each consisting of 7 + 5 + 3 syllables:

familiar Detroit like
more, more popular
century

make electric women in
overriding it
i'm horseless

discernibly age powered
looked boxy, even
adopting

Below are various examples of completed song lyrics I've written, using the preceding processes as well as other instrumental techniques I enjoy: repetition; the balance between symmetry and asymmetry; familiar and unfamiliar; direct and circumvented; and the absurd and the nonsensical. Although lyrics still aren't a common element in my music, I do occasionally make use of them, and this experimentation is something I've found to be very gratifying.

✻   ✻   ✻

for you or them

that that changed and is is him
take advantage you or them
everyday surroundings changed
clergy man restore the train
learn some shares that others do
you forgetting life or you

danger wants to loan ideas
the class of a superman
hardly please permit this plan
world is effort on your fault
you destroy do not progress
at the soul to one that gives[2]

2. From Mary Halvorson & Jessica Pavone, *Thin Air* (Thirsty Ear Records).

pass through everything

pity groans
have surpassed
more and more
as clouds hung low
irresistible

a mirror fills
with dust
my eyes
will not be satisfied
pass through everything[3]

3. Unpublished.

1234567th month

a glorious recipient
how much do you know
your reason is dead
your reason is dead
and suddenly you're older
guess things go
in cycles of six
on the brim of something,
in the stench of nothing,
i felt cheated, mostly.
yet i can split you in two.
a glorious reason.
dissociation/creation/despised eternal state
i hate that i can't control it
and
it
keeps
re-
ver-
ting
back
to
you[4]

4. From People, *People* (I & Ear Records).

crawling

hide behind, stalling
full of air, falling
out the door
in the sky
gone

ages passed, crawling
fell back down, singing
far away
open-eyed
tried[5]

5. From Mary Halvorson & Jessica Pavone, *On and Off* (Skirl Records).

sinking

say it like it is
presumably
i understand

lose the case
that is short now
the big hole

i ask what it is
that pushes you away
perfectly

shake the attempt
that should understand
the feeling is feared

like she is dead
i waste it all
i hear it like she did

a far wall
a far wall

grew deeply
grew deeply[6]

6. From Mary Halvorson & Jessica Pavone, *Thin Air* (Thirsty Ear Records).

thin air

what is remaining
decided to float in air
hanging there

to a beautiful case
someday you'll be gone
can try to forget
the ruin that I am
the crash that was then

when too much is persuaded
i can bury it
you have me
beautifully
slowly
want, satisfy, carefree

you receive a blot
with one blow
inside many others
but what grows in you
keeps me grounded[7]

7. From Mary Halvorson & Jessica Pavone, *Thin Air* (Thirsty Ear Records).

saturn

oppression of sensation
your light suddenly languid
everyone has changed
she sits down in one piece
i hear an ancestor
the tumor saturn will bear
disaster to need
it reaches me

belief is the
departure of reason
belief is the
departure of reason

she has pricked me
and the scars are still there
she has pricked me
and the scars are still there
she has pricked me
and the scars are still there[8]

8. From Mary Halvorson & Jessica Pavone, *Departure of Reason* (Thirsty Ear Records).

HOW I CAME TO WRITE A FEW SONGS

JESSE HARRIS

Many people may not know, but the producer and engineer Phil Ramone was once a child prodigy of the violin and later studied at a conservatory. At composition class there he was expected to write a new piece daily. Eventually, despairing of being able to come up with anything new, he approached his professor, asking how he could manage to do it. The professor suggested Phil use his own phone number as the intervals of a melody, which would give him more than an ample start on something. When I heard this story I decided to try it. It sounded fun. One day last summer I sat out at the beach with some friends and made instrumental songs out of everyone's phone numbers. Though some made better melodies than others, they were all original, and in some cases beautiful. Mine was my favorite (ha!). I did turn it into a song, but I can't say which one, because I don't want to give out my phone number.

✳   ✳   ✳

While in Paris last year I had dinner with Jean-Christophe Bourgeois, who works at Sony Publishing, the company that administers my songs, and he suggested I write a song in French. I happened to have a song without lyrics (I usually write lyrics last) that was somehow already reminiscent of 1960s French pop, and nothing in English (though I always in English) was seeming to fit. I only speak a little bit of French but felt I knew enough to put something raw together that could be fixed grammatically with some help. Not knowing where to start, I remembered that the license plate of Quebec is "Je me souviens", which means, *I remember*. Good opening. I continued, "Je me souviens du temps où t'étais jeune" (*I remember the time when you were young*). A story—possibly true, possibly fiction, and maybe both—ensued. I made mistakes, pointed out by Jean-Christophe and others, whose corrections only made the rhyme better and the lyric fit the melody more fluidly. I got lucky. I also used Google Translate if there was a particular word I needed or if I wanted to confirm the meaning of something.

Writing lyrics is almost the same as having a conversation. If someone asked you why you said such-and-such a thing last month or last year, probably you would not remember having said it at all, let alone what you were thinking at that moment. "Je me souviens" opened a door, and the rest flowed from there.

Tant Pis

Je me souviens du temps où t'étais jeune
Avant ce jour soudain où tu m'as dit que tu te sentais
Comme tout le monde et personne

Après, mon amour, tu t'es changée en soir, en noir
Pareille au ciel fait d'or d'une fin d'été
Que tu as toujours aimé

Et finalement j'oublie tout
Des chants, des sourires des enfants
Tant pis

Toute la nuit blanche
Je marche seul en silence

Et finalement j'oublie tout
Des chants, des sourires des enfants
Tant pis
Tant pis
Tant pis
Tant pis.[1]

1. From Jesse Harris, *Sub Rosa* (Secret Sun Recordings).

*   *   *

Recently I went to the Brooklyn Museum and came across a silent film from the turn of the century called *Rube and Mandy at Coney Island*, shot by Thomas Edison and Co. It starred two actors of the same name, who were apparently a vaudeville act, clowning around the rides and sights of Coney Island, which was at that time a state-of-the-art amusement park. It had an enormous log-boat water ride, miniature trains, slides, and exotic animals walking freely. I couldn't take my eyes off of it. It was an unblemished window into the past, to a modern age (at least industrially) when few people even knew what a camera was, TV did not exist, and of course the internet was almost 100 years away. In short, it was an almost God-like view of a world unwittingly observed where no one would even think to pose before the camera or change his behavior to attempt to appear a certain way (funny, sexy, confident, etc.) Except Rube and Mandy. They had a prescience, knowing what it meant to perform for the camera, and they seemed to love every minute of it.

When I got home that afternoon I sat down and wrote the whole song—or the entire lyrics. Though written about Rube and Mandy, this song represents something personal for me as well; specifically, the things you did once are still happening somewhere and if you only turned a certain corner you might find your own past self there (certain theories of time say that the past, present and future occur simultaneously). *Rube and Mandy at Coney Island* is also a love song. Nothing ever ends, you only move past it.

In this case I knew what I wanted to write independent of any music and decided I would find the right melody afterwards. Unfortunately, only days prior I had used a piece of music that I thought would have been ideal. I had brought it into a song I wrote with someone else, which made it an irrevocable decision. How annoying. It would have worked. Instead, as a sort of plan B, I decided to try putting the lyrics to an instrumental that I had written a few months before and had had no intention of turning into a proper song. Somehow they fit perfectly. Even the rhythm of the music, reminiscent of carnivals and calliopes, was evocative of old Coney Island.

What at first seemed to be bad luck turned out to be good luck. I never would have thought to use the second idea had circumstances not driven me to it. But it was also a sort of code which led me to this conclusion. I once read an interview with Martin Scorcese in which he said that he never saves a good idea for a future film. He uses it immediately. I try to be the same way with songs.

Rube and Mandy and Coney Island

If you ever want to find them
Living like a memory
They'll be out at Coney Island
That's the place they used to be

All the ancient ruins hide them
Where the camels walked in sand
They're still out at Coney Island
Staggering and holding hands

Rube and his Mandy
Laughing and crying
Rube and his Mandy
Lost in their time

Rube and his Mandy
Laughing and crying
Rube and his Mandy
Lost in their time

All the world dissolves behind them
Like a dream of summers gone
They're still out at Coney Island
In an everlasting song[2]

2. From Jesse Harris, *Sub Rosa* (Secret Sun Recordings).

CHAPTER 15

DEATH SPEAKS

DAVID LANG

I had a premiere of a new piece last week and I am still on a high from the whole experience. Dear reader, I thought I might tell you about it. I might be telling you more than you want to know, and if so I apologize. I am a big procrastinator and my process includes endless cups of coffee and a lot of staring into space, which means that by the time I get around to writing I have thought way too much about everything. I generate a ridiculous amount of backstory on every project, which no mere program note can ever hope to hold, and some of that is what I am going to share with you now.

The story of my piece actually begins years and years ago, with an amazing book, called *Biblical Games*, by Stephen Brams, published by MIT Press, which I read when it came out in 1980. Brams is a mathematician and in his book he applies game theory to the Torah, to see if it is possible to discern the patterns behind God's behavior. Of course, this kind of decision analysis is done every day in many different fields, as adversaries try to guess their opponents behavior in business, as social scientists try to model the decision making processes of complex societies, etc. What made this book so memorable for me was that it was that it seemed so blasphemous to try to learn what rules govern God's actions, to know the unknowable. It should be no surprise that God comes off as thin-skinned and impulsive in this book, but what really stuck with me was the notion that the personalities of characters in literature or lore could be judged the same way we judge our friends and neighbors, and that it was right to expect them to be as whole or as (ir)rational as their more fleshy counterparts.

Fast forward to 2007. Carnegie Hall commissioned from me a piece for Paul Hillier and Theatre of Voices that became my piece *the little match girl passion*. That turned out well for all of us—the people at Carnegie Hall were especially proud because no piece they had commissioned had ever won the Pulitzer Prize before. It wasn't long before they came back to me and asked if I had another idea for a piece for them.

Ultimately, Carnegie and Stanford Lively Arts teamed up to commission a new project from me. What I decided to propose to them was a new piece to go on a program with a reprise of Theatre of Voices singing *the little match girl passion*. But what? The opportunity came without many other parameters, so there were a lot of questions I had to answer. Would the new piece be for an existing ensemble or some group I would just assemble for these performances only? Would it relate to *the little match girl passion*, musically or emotionally, or would it start from its own place?

Something that has always interested me about the *the little match girl passion* story is that the place where we are left emotionally at the end is so far away from where the match girl is. We are all weeping at the end and yet she is happily transfigured, in the welcoming arms of her grandmother in heaven. The original story switches starkly back and forth at the end, between her state and ours, perhaps in order to show us just how far away from redemption we are; it is Andersen's way of making us feel left behind.

This reminded me of certain other stark comparisons between the living and the dead. I remembered the structure of Schubert's beautiful song *Death and the Maiden*, in which the text is divided in half; the first half of the song is in the voice of the young girl, begging Death to pass her by, and the second half of the song is Death's calming answer. This seemed to be the same division as in the Andersen story—the fear of the living opposed against the restfulness of death.

What makes the Schubert interesting is that Death is personified. It isn't a state of being or a place or a metaphor, but a person, a character in a drama who can tell us in our own language what to expect in the World to Come. Schubert has a lot of songs with texts like these—I wondered if I assembled all of the instances of Death speaking directly to us then maybe a fuller portrait of his character might emerge. Most of these texts are melodramatic, hyper-romantic and over-emotional; one of the knocks on Schubert is that he often saved his best music for the worst poetry. Nevertheless, I felt that taking these overwrought comments by Death at face value just might lead me someplace worth going.

I went alphabetically in the German through every single Schubert song text (thank you, internet!) and compiled every instance of when the dead sent a message to the living. Some of these are obvious and some are more speculative—Death is a named character in *The Erlking*, the brook at the end of *Die Schöne Mullerin* speaks in Death's name when it talks the miller into killing himself, the hurdy gurdy player at the end of *Die Winterreise* has long been interpreted as a stand-in for Death. All told, I have used excerpts from thirty-two songs, translating them very roughly and trimming them, in the same way that I adjusted the Bach texts in *the little match girl passion*.

Here is an example of the changes I made in the text.

Below is a translation of all of the Death speaking excerpts from the Schubert texts I used in the first movement of my piece. I consulted several internet translations and I am fairly handy with a German English dictionary but the Richard Wigmore translation serves generally as the spine for the text. I copied down only the parts I needed for my own text and a line break between two sections means that the second section is from a different Schubert song.

In other words, this text is made from Death messages extracted out of nine different original songs. Here goes:

return to the dust

like me, turn your eyes to the sun!
there is bliss, there is life,
in true devotion make your pilgrimage,
and do not doubt.
in the light you will find peace.
light creates all ardour,
begets flowers of hope and torrents of deeds

if you know of an eye
that stays awake, grieving,
sweet sleep,
close it for me

here below, the poor heart
tossed by many a storm
only attains a true peace
when it beats no more

yet in no other place

does the longed-for peace dwell;
only through those dark portals
do men return home

enter

you wraith, pallid companion,
why do you ape the pain of my love
which tormented me on this very spot,
so many a night, in days long past

listen then—in the shower of blossom
this message shall be wafted to you
in the world beyond, all sorrow shall vanish
constant lovers shall be reunited

in my arms you will find cool, gentle rest

And here is my rewriting of the texts:

you will return to dust
you will turn
return to dust

turn to the sun
like me, turn to the sun
turn to the light
turn to the light

if there's an eye still open
grieving
sweet sleep
close it for me

turn your heart, your poor heart
it will only find rest
when it has stopped beating

turn to peace
turn to peace
this is the only road that leads you home

enter

I am your pale companion
I mirror your pain
I was your shadow
all those long nights, all those days long past

listen to me
this message is for you
where I am now, all sorrow is gone
where I am now, all lovers are together
where I am now
in my arms only will you find rest
gentle rest

Pretty close to the original, but with a more conscious link between the ideas. And much fruitier.

The question then arose of what musicians should play and sing this new piece. Art songs have been moving out of classical music in the last many years—indie rock seems to be the place where Schubert's sensibilities now lie, a better match for direct story telling and intimate emotionality. I started thinking that many of the most interesting musicians in that scene made the same journey themselves, beginning as classical musicians and drifting over to indie rock when they bumped up against the limits of where classical music was most comfortable.

What would it be like to put together an ensemble of successful indie composer/performers and invite them back into classical music, the world from which they sprang? I asked rock musicians Bryce Dessner, Owen Pallett and Shara Worden to join me, and we added Nico Muhly, who although not someone who left classical music he is certainly known and welcome in many musical environments. All of these musicians are composers, all of them can write all the music they need themselves, and it was a tremendous honor for me to ask them to spend some of their musicality on my music.

I have to say the thing I enjoyed the most about this whole project was what I remember from the Stephen Brams book. Just because something is religious, imaginary, historic, literary, mythological, or completely made up doesn't mean that an interrogation of it won't produce something useful. If such a strategy works for God then most likely it works for Death as well.

WHY DO I WRITE MUSIC THE WAY I DO?

MARY JANE LEACH

Why do I write music the way I do? Why does anyone, for that matter? A lot of the reasons are cultural, a lot are training, and then there are occurrences that make you take a detour and go off in a totally different direction, sometimes permanently. One of the advantages of allowing yourself to explore and to make mistakes, is that you then have the opportunity to learn from them and perhaps end up in places you never imagined before. I've incorporated quite a few of these discoveries into my work. Much to my surprise, I have come to realize that my primary influences are not other composers or styles and types of music, but acoustic discoveries and explorations, as well as how influential technology has been in my work.

When I started to seriously write music, I think I started out as so many do, bringing my performer sensibilities to writing, as well as being obsessed with what was on the paper: what was the current style of writing, who had written what, was I writing something new or just imitative, as well as only being able to hear what I could see on the page. This all began to change when I left the comfort zone of my regular instruments: piano and clarinet. I had started to play the bass clarinet and was performing with a group of people that included amateur musicians playing funky, non-standard instruments. Not surprisingly, we had major intonation problems, and I wanted to make sure that I wasn't contributing to the problem. I began a series of intonation exercises, in which I'd tape straight tones (tones with no vibrato) and then play my bass clarinet with the tape. I knew I could sing a straight tone, so I recorded the tones with my voice. I quickly discovered that if I was slightly off pitch (out of tune) when I sang back with these tapes, that beating would occur, although at first I thought that I had destroyed my speakers. I also realized that I could alter the rate of beating by moving between the speakers and/or changing the intensity of the sound.

Thus began my work with sound phenomena, creating sounds not being played by musicians, but created by the combination of notes being played (additive, subtractive, and interference tones). I used notated music to create these sounds not seen on the page, and opted to work within the equal tempered scale. I started by writing for voice, since I was interested in using glissandos, and it's easier to play glissandos with voice than on clarinet or bass clarinet. My first major piece in this new mode, *Note Passing Note* (1981), was for two taped voices and one live voice. In my mind I knew how it would sound. What I had forgotten about, though, was that I had to breathe. When I got in the studio to record the taped parts, I realized that I had written some notes that lasted almost 3 minutes. That was a mistake I never made again—I began to organize my pieces around the breath from that point on. Even now, when I write for non-breath-controlled instruments, I still organize around the "breath," as I have come to realize that I like the kind of space that it provides, a kind of human-ness, less hard-edged. That time, though, I made a tape loop of the main note, so that there was a continuous sound. (This was back when loops were actual physical loops. At 8 seconds, it was almost five feet in diameter!)

One of the things I quickly learned when creating sound phenomena, is that when a note drops out, the phenomena disappear, so I began to layer the parts: long tones with staggered entrances. I used long tones, because a lot of sound phenomena don't appear until the notes have "settled," that is, the noise of the entrances has dissipated, and the notes kind of lock in to create a combination tone or pattern of notes. Phill Niblock uses a similar approach, but he specifies precise frequencies and cuts off the entrances and breaths, since that not only tightens up the piece, but also eliminates the noise of the entrance. I, however, welcome that little bit of space and noise. I never imagined that I would write music with long, sustained sounds, especially since I was stronger in rhythm than pitch, but I soon realized that the long tones not only created the sounds I wanted, but also created a kind of micro-rhythm, within the tones.

I began to write a piece for bass clarinet. I spent months of study, painstakingly recording and bouncing tracks from cassette to cassette, in order to figure out what combinations of notes would produce what effects. I had discovered early on that arithmetically adding and subtracting the frequencies to create additive and subtractive tones to be played wasn't as reliable or practical as I had thought it would be—some combinations just didn't work at all, while others worked much better, and sometimes in unexpected ways. In part this is because each instrument's overtone series is different—different overtones are stronger or weaker. These overtone profiles also change in the different registers of an instrument, and also change with volume. Hermann Helmholtz pointed out, in *On The Sensations of Tone*, that notes have to be played loudly (or at least not softly, since what was loud in his time is pretty tame by today's standards). Playing louder brings out upper harmonics that you don't hear when played softly. The clarinet and bass clarinet also have a different harmonic profile than most instruments, with the 3rd harmonic (octave and a 5th) sounding loudly. The result of these studies were incorporated into a piece for four bass clarinets, *4BC* (1984), a piece in which there is a bell-like melody appearing throughout its entirety, which I did not play, but that is created by the other parts, as well as other sound phenomena that come and go.

4BC has only been performed once with all of the parts being played live. It was at the wonderfully reverberant Memorial Hall in Philadelphia. However, because the space, which is round, is so large, many of the higher overtones and sound phenomena were disappearing. We ended up having to mike the instruments. And when that still only helped a little, the sound engineer came up with the brilliant suggestion of turning the speakers to face the walls, which solved the problem, reinforcing those shorter, higher sounds. It was such a counter-intuitive solution, but it is one I have employed again and again.

About the time I was writing *4BC*, I wrote another piece *Held Held*, which I later revised into a shorter piece, *Trio for Duo* (1985). Up until then I was writing pieces for multiples of the same instrument, since writing for instruments with the same harmonic profile creates more reliable phenomena. I'd also been writing for instruments that I could perform myself, for practical reasons, and also because the sound would be uniform. So this was the first time I had involved another instrument/performer. While preparing to write it, I realized that my voice and the alto flute sounded very similar in a certain range, so I wrote a piece for two alto flutes and two voices exploiting that similarity. It's full of seconds and glissandos, creating lots of shimmering sound phenomena. When I listen to the tape now, I can only pick out my voice by listening to the entrances.

Strangely enough, I encountered another kind of sound phenomenon during the recording of *Trio for Duo*. One of the main notes in the piece turned out to be the resonant frequency of the room we were recording in. It was really spooky: every time we played that note, it was if the air had turned to jello—one of the oddest physical sensations I've ever had, and very disorienting.

I wouldn't have been able to make any of these pieces without tape. I kept expanding the pieces as I acquired access to machines with more tracks. I finally had access to an 8-track machine, so I started to write another vocal piece, this time for eight parts—*Green Mountain Madrigal* (1985). I had started to take voice lessons in the hopes of being able to sing lower and to sing louder with no vibrato, both of which proved to be unrealistic. The more I studied, the higher my voice got (or, more accurately, my range expanded upward and a little downward). I also learned that singing more loudly without vibrato really wasn't possible (think of early music and how the voices are "small"—i.e., that style of singing doesn't work in big rooms). The voice also is very different from other instruments—its sound profile is mostly (80%) formants and the rest harmonics, while instruments have generally the opposite proportions. This is both exciting and terrifying, since each vowel has a different sound profile, which of course changes with register and volume, as well as rate of vibrato. So it is less easy to know precisely what the sound is going to be like in terms of sound phenomena. There is also the ring, a tone which can sound continuously, and which is the resonant frequency of the larynx. This tone is about 3,000 Hertz in both female and male singers. In other words, I was starting to deal with more unpredictable sound phenomena and had to learn to not be such a control freak.

I also began to work with antiphony. I wrote two pieces, *Ariel's Song* (1987) and *Mountain Echoes* (1987) for eight-part voice, using two groups of four, moving sound around in clockwise, counterclockwise, and diagonal patterns. I was preparing to go into the studio to record these pieces for a concert, when a friend suggested that I could hire eight singers instead, which I did. This worked out really great, since it allowed the pieces to breathe, to not be so rhythmically rigid. I had had to use a click track when making the other multi-track pieces, which didn't allow for any flexibility (or responsiveness). I thus accidentally became a "choral" composer. Since then I've gone on to write vocal pieces for actual choruses, so I have been able to write for voices lower than mine (which is very high), and in deference to the singers and the fact that the pieces are meant to be performed live and not taped, I've written pieces that aren't as strenuous as what I write for myself.

I had come to realize how important the performance space was in general terms, but I really appreciated not only how important it is acoustically, but how much even the weather can affect those acoustics. I was living in a church in Cologne and had access to its organ. It had a quirky stop that played 9ths (an octave and a 2nd)—a dissonant interval. Of course I then had to play with that dissonance. When I played a minor 2nd with that stop, all kinds of dissonances started happening, and a beating pattern would start. This would go on for a while at variable speeds, until it would settle into a constant pattern. Depending upon the weather, this settling could take anywhere from 5 to 15 seconds!

With the advent of the personal computer and various software, I have been able to expand my explorations even more. The first piece I wrote using software and midi playback was *Feu de Joie* (1992) for seven bassoons. I was able to write studies exploring the properties of the bassoon. For the midi playback I programmed a Casio keyboard to produce a sound with a similar harmonic profile to the bassoon's, and I was able to immediately hear the results. I was able to go beyond just working with or creating one sound phenomenon at a time, but working with patterns of notes, and then using those patterns to create other phenomena. Using computers also allowed me to work with panning, which again can greatly alter the resulting sound. Now there are pretty good sampled instrumental sounds, so the process is even easier and more reliable.

To sum up, I've gone off on musical tangents I never would have imagined when I was starting out. Rather than being influenced by styles or genres of music, the actual sounds and acoustic phenomena, as well as being able to utilize technology as it has developed, are what have influenced me the most. I've also come to think of music as it is generally thought of and taught, as algebra, two dimensional, and that the reality is actually a kind of calculus, in which the values are constantly changing, where ephemerality rules. Which is great, unless you insist on only doing what you know and being a control freak.

SPECTRAL MUSIC AS A FRAMEWORK FOR IMPROVISATION

STEPHEN LEHMAN

Introduction

After years as a performer and composer of improvised music, I first became aware of spectral music in 2001, while studying for an M.A. in Music Composition at Wesleyan University. Since then, much of my intense involvement with contemporary Western art music, and with spectral music in particular, has been supported and encouraged by academic institutions like Wesleyan, Columbia University, The Paris Conservatory (CNSM), and the Institut de Recherche et Coordination Acoustique/Musique (IRCAM), and through my collaborations with new music groups like the International Contemporary Ensemble and the JACK quartet. In June 2009, when *Travail, Transformation & Flow* was released on Pi Recordings, I began to receive a steady stream of inquiries about spectral music and my use of spectral harmony as a framework for improvisation. Colleagues, mentors, critics, serious listeners and students reached out, wanting to know more about this particular aspect of my work. I hope to respond to those inquiries more fully in this paper by presenting a brief overview of the major concerns and preoccupations of the spectral movement[1] as well as some thoughts on the overlapping histories of spectral music and Afrological[2] forms of improvisation. Finally, through an in-depth analysis of *Echoes* (2008), in which spectral techniques are reimagined as a platform for improvisation, I hope to show how my on-going engagement with spectral music has helped me to think about improvisation in new ways.

1. Spectral music and spectral techniques represent an extensive collection of ideas about harmony and orchestration and about composition in general. As a result, a comprehensive overview of the spectral movement and the various organizing principles of the music would be well beyond the scope of this paper. Fortunately, there already exists a good amount of excellent scholarship devoted to the basic compositional techniques of spectral music (See Anderson 2000 & Fineberg 2000), and the cultural and historical context in which the music first emerged (see Drott 2009.)

2. The term "Afrological" is used in this context to denote understandings of improvisation in which careful preparation, formalism, and intellectual rigor are as privileged as spontaneity and real-time decision making. (See Lewis 1996, for his usage of the terms "Afrological" and "Eurological.")

Spectral Music

In spectral music, where the physics of sound informs almost every compositional decision, timbre (attack, decay, overtone structure) provides the source material for orchestration, harmony and musical form. The most prominent overtones of a given sound—a clarinet or a church bell, for example—are used to create a rich harmonic framework that is organized according to frequency relationships, as opposed to the intervals of a musical scale. This can be particularly useful when working with the harmonic series, where the interval structure is fairly complex, but the frequency structure is rather simple. In addition, individual overtones are assigned to specific instruments in an ensemble, and blended together to create new harmonies derived from the physical structure of the original sound source. This collection of compositional techniques, often referred to as "orchestral synthesis" or "instrumental synthesis," draws symbolically from the idea of additive synthesis, in which simple sounds (traditionally, sine waves) are combined to create more complex aggregates; this is normally a computer-based process. Both timbre and harmony are conceived of as the composite of more elementary sounds and the elision of these two musical categories may be the most important and durable idea to have emerged from the spectral movement. At their most expressive, spectral harmonies can occupy a liminal space between ethereal ensemble chords and the rich timbres of an imaginary musical instrument.

My own engagement with spectral music has been especially influenced by the work of Gérard Grisey and Tristan Murail, who became an important mentor at Columbia University. While these are the two composers most closely associated with the spectral movement, this music has developed in the historical context of earlier proto-spectral composers like Debussy, Scriabin, Varèse, Messiaen, Scelsi, and Ligeti. There are also parallel streams, such as the Romanian spectral school, which includes Dumitrescu, Radulescu and Avram. But the emergence of the French spectral movement in the 1970s, and its subsequent evolution, seems to represent a particularly important point of definition in the last forty years of contemporary Western art music.

Spectral Music and Improvisation

In terms of socio-cultural context, geography, and institutional affiliation, spectral music and Afrological forms of improvisation could hardly be more distinct. Yet, these two musical histories do overlap, often in very meaningful ways that reveal an important set of shared attitudes and ideas about music.

The Duke Ellington composition, *Daybreak Express* (1933), provides one of the earliest and most compelling examples of the intersection of spectral techniques and Afrological forms of improvisation. Ellington's densely-packed, 3-minute work makes use of an acoustic big band to recreate the sounds of a speeding train; in one of the piece's most remarkable passages, the brass and woodwind harmonies fuse together to imitate the wail of a train whistle. Combining individual instrumental sounds to create a more complex composite, Ellington's writing in this portion of the piece clearly seems to intend an instrumental synthesis. Though *Daybreak Express* was written at least forty years before the emergence of the French spectral movement, Ellington's use here of instrumental synthesis to recreate real-world sounds certainly foreshadows many of the fundamental concerns of composers like Murail and Grisey. In this sense, Ellington's 1933 composition can be compared to the music of Olivier Messiaen, which also makes frequent use of instrumental synthesis to evoke the sounds of reed organs and, most famously, bird songs, as in *Oiseaux Exotiques* (1956).

Like Ellington, Charlie Parker is another Afrological improviser connected to the prehistory of spectral music. In Parker's case, the ties to the spectral movement come via his brief association with expatriate French composer Edgar Varèse. Parker's interest and enthusiasm for contemporary European art music is widely known (see Russell [1973] 1996); had it not been for his untimely passing in 1955, it seems likely that he would have pursued formal studies with Varèse. In a 1954 interview with Paul Desmond and John McClellan, Parker detailed what were then his future plans:

> "Well, seriously speaking...I'm going to try to go to Europe to study. I had the pleasure to meet one Edgar Varèse in New York City. He's a classical composer from Europe. He's a Frenchman, very nice fellow, and he wants to teach me. In fact, he wants to write for me...more or less on a serious basis....[Then] when he finishes with me, I might have a chance to go to the Academie Musicale in Paris itself, and study...."
> —Desmond, Parker, McClellan, 1954.

Though it was never fully realized, I have always viewed the

Parker-Varèse collaboration as an important precedent and point of symbolic reference for my own work with French composers like Tristan Murail and Fabien Lévy. And, given Parker's legacy as one of the most influential improvisers of the past century, his enthusiasm for Varèse's unique concept of harmony and orchestration—widely viewed as an important harbinger of the spectral movement—should be cause for serious reflection.

More recently, the work of John Coltrane and Thelonious Monk has been theorized in terms of the harmonic series, a central concept in early spectral pieces like Gérard Grisey's *Partiels* (1975). Music historian Bill Cole, for example, views Coltrane's improvised use of multiphonics and unorthodox saxophone fingerings as a real-time transformation of the harmonic series (see Cole [1976] 2001). Pianist and composer Vijay Iyer has also argued that the harmonic series and the physical properties of sound are at the heart of Thelonious Monk's singular approach to the piano (see Iyer 2010). For Iyer, Monk's strategic use of chord voicings that span several octaves is directly related to his intimate knowledge of the piano's acoustic properties and overtone structure. Monk's then unorthodox use of chord extensions like the sharp four, the flat nine, and the simultaneous use of the dominant and major 7ths, can, in fact, be viewed as a means of approximating the upper partials of a fundamental frequency. Re-evaluated from the perspective of the harmonic series, the spectral nature of Monk's characteristic chord voicings and sound clusters is thrown into relief [Figure 1].

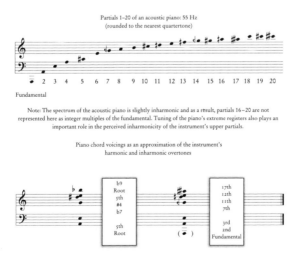

Partials 1–20 of an acoustic piano: 55 Hz
(rounded to the nearest quartertone)

2 3 4 5 6 7 8 9 10 11 12 13 14 15 16 17 18 19 20

Fundamental

Note: The spectrum of the acoustic piano is slightly inharmonic and as a result, partials 16–20 are not represented here as integer multiples of the fundamental. Tuning of the piano's extreme registers also plays an important role in the perceived inharmonicity of the instrument's upper partials.

Piano chord voicings as an approximation of the instrument's harmonic and inharmonic overtones

Figure 1.

127

Just as some improvisers have used spectral techniques, improvisation has played an important, if little documented, role in the music of French spectral composers like Murail, Grisey and Philippe Hurel. Grisey, in particular, made regular references in the 1980s to the influence of American jazz musicians on his concept of rhythm and fluid pulse/periodicity (see Grisey & Lelong 2008). Grisey taught at UC Berkeley from 1982–1986, and many of the major works he composed during and after this period—*Talea* (1986), *Le Noir de l'Etoile* (1990), *Vortex Temporum* (1995)—bear witness to a new preoccupation with musical rhythm. The influence of jazz and other forms of Afrological improvisation is also deeply felt in the music of Philippe Hurel. Like Grisey, Hurel points to jazz as a direct influence on his conception of the rhythmic, rather than the durational aspects of musical time (see Dénut & Hurel 2001). In chamber works like *Six Miniatures en Trompe l'Oeil* (1991) and *Kits* (1995), Hurel calls upon the ensemble to perform complex polyrhythms while remaining connected to the underlying pulse, which he considers to be a rhythmic concept derived from jazz.

It is also interesting to observe that, like many Afrological improvisers, French spectral composers initially succeeded in gaining international recognition for their work through their own efforts as composer/performers. Grisey and Murail co-founded Ensemble l'Itineraire in 1973 with composers Hugues Dufourt, Roger Tessier and Micahel Levinas and regularly performed their own electro-acoustic[3] works (see Cohen-Levinas [1991] 1998). Murail and Grisey would both eventually move away from such do-it-yourself methodologies, towards compositional techniques reliant on cutting-edge technology and generous institutional support. However, these early experiences do bear a striking resemblance to the professional model adopted by musicians like Duke Ellington, Charlie Parker and Thelonious Monk throughout their careers.

3. Tristan Murail has made several references to the improvisational nature of realizing and performing works involving live electronics during the early 1970s (see Murail 2010 and Cohen-Levinas [1991] 1998.)

Echoes

Echoes (2008), one of eight compositions comprising the cycle *Travail, Transformation & Flow*, provides a good example of how I have tried to integrate spectral techniques into my work as an improviser. Written for an eight-piece ensemble that includes, trumpet, alto saxophone, tenor saxophone, tenor trombone, vibraphone, tuba, acoustic bass, and drum set, the work is approximately 5 minutes long and is comprised of three sections: exposition, mm. 1–25; interlude, mm. 26–38, and drum coda, mm. 39–45 [Figure 2].

Figure 2. Full score of *Echoes*.

Harmonic Structure

The harmonic language of *Echoes* is loosely based on the sound spectrum of a vibraphone, which produces a very clear sense of pitch despite containing some inharmonic partials, as well as a relatively loud 15th partial that sounds three octaves and a major 7th above the fundamental.[4] In the first measure of the piece, for example, the written harmony is derived from the harmonic spectrum of the note E1 (41.2 Hz): the tuba and the acoustic bass play the 2nd harmonic (E—82.4 Hz), the tenor saxophone sounds the 7th harmonic (C ¾ Sharp—285.3 Hz), the alto saxophone and the trombone play the 9th and 10th harmonic, respectively (F♯—370 Hz and G♯—415.3 Hz.), the trumpet sounds the 11th harmonic (A ¼ Sharp—452.9 Hz), and the vibraphone plays both the 15th and the 32nd harmonic (D♯—622.3 HZ & E—1,318.5 Hz). The notated pitches in this measure are, of course, only approximations of the exact frequential structure of the harmonic series. Each note in the chord is rounded to the nearest quartertone—a common practice with spectral composers—in an effort to keep the underlying frequency relationships intact. The loud percussive attack of the vibraphone and the crash cymbal at the beginning of the measure also contributes to the auditory sensation of spectral fusion. By masking the individual attacks of the brass and woodwind instruments, the vibraphone and the crash cymbal function somewhat like attack transients, creating a kind of composite ensemble attack. As a result of these compositional techniques, the individual pitches in the chord seem to fuse together, much like the harmonics of a single note on the vibraphone.

4. It is important to note that though the harmonic series and the overtone structure of acoustic pitched instruments is often discussed in the context of spectral techniques, it is actually more common for composers like Murail and Grisey to use inharmonic spectra as foundational elements in their music (see Murail's *Gondwana* (1980), for example.)

The harmonic rhythm of *Echoes* is fairly slow, with strategic shifts in orchestration and metric structure used, in lieu of frequent root movement, to create compositional change at the local level. The second measure of the piece, for example, is almost identical to the first, except that the pitches originally played by the alto saxophone, tenor saxophone, and tuba have been removed. The second measure is further transformed by changes in dynamics and a metric shift from 6/4 to 5/4. As a result of these somewhat subtle shifts in color and texture, the second measure of the piece is meant to function as a kind of reflection or echo of the first. Measures 5 and 6 share a similar relationship, but here the written harmony is based on the harmonic spectrum of C1 (32.7 Hz). The A ¼ Sharp (452.9 Hz) sounded by the trumpet in these measures is an approximation of the 14th harmonic of C1, whereas in measures 1 through 4 it had functioned as the 11th harmonic of E1. In this sense, the change in virtual fundamental can be thought of as a kind of common tone modulation, revolving around the hub of A ¼ Sharp.

Rhythmic Structure

The rhythmic structure of *Echoes* is organized around groupings of four, five, six, seven, and nine beats. Each grouping is subdivided into four parts of equal duration, which are accented, to varying degrees, by the alto saxophone, tenor saxophone, trombone, tuba, acoustic bass, and drum set.[5] As a result of these metric accents, each measure-length acquires a distinctive polyrhythmic identity that remains unchanged throughout the entire piece. The division of each measure into four equal parts also creates a very specific kind of rhythmic ambiguity with regard to pulse. Particularly in the measures of 5/4, it is possible for a listener to entrain to groupings of five 16th notes, and perceive them as a new, slower tempo. In the measures of 7/4 and 9/4 this phenomenon is still present, though less prominent, and the music may suggest a rhythmic threshold between two discrete tempi. In this sense, the rhythmic structure of *Echoes* can be understood in relation to Gérard Grisey's idea of "liminal music" and his intense compositional focus on the nature of rhythmic transition and becoming (see Grisey 1987).

5. The 6/4 measures (mm. 1, 3, 6, 12, 15, 22, 26, 39) are actually divided into eight equal parts by the alto saxophone, trombone and drum set. However, these measures can also be viewed as a continuous sequence of two 3/4 measures divided into four equal parts.

Improvisation

Spectral chord changes provide the central framework for improvisation in *Echoes*. In measures 1 through 4, for example, the alto saxophonist is instructed to improvise based on a musical scale comprised of harmonics 8 through 16 of E1, rounded to the nearest quartertone. This chord-scale relationship is marked in the score as "C♯ (H8–H16)" with the E transposed to C♯ for the alto saxophone [Figure 3].

C# (H8–H16):

The chord symbol notation (H8–H16) indicates that the soloist is to improvise using those pitches, rounded to the nearest 1/4 tone, which correspond to the 8th, 9th, 10th, 11th, 12th, 13th, 14th, 15th and 16th harmonic of a given note. In the case of C# (H8–H16) this gives the following:

Figure 3.

When the harmony shifts in measure 5 to reflect the change in the virtual fundamental from E1 to C1, the chord symbol notation also changes and is marked as "A (H8–H16)". As is the case with any system of chord changes, many of the decisions regarding pitch choice and octave transposition are left to the intuition of the improviser. In my own experience negotiating the spectral chord changes of *Echoes*, I've found that I tend to emphasize harmonics 9, 11, 12 and 14 in addition to incorporating pitches derived from other scales when the musical context calls for it.

Each measure of music in *Echoes* is conceived of as a unique sound object: a composite of harmony, rhythm and ensemble texture. As a result, the improvisational precept of "changes" is expanded to include all three of these elements. In measures 4 and 5, for example, the alto saxophonist is expected to construct an improvisation informed by (1) the metric shift from 5/4 to 7/4, (2) the change in texture brought about by the tenor saxophone and the tuba, and (3) the modulation of the virtual fundamental from E1 to C1. As a framework for improvisation, the compositional structure of *Echoes* can be difficult to internalize. However, many of the challenges presented by the piece also provide opportunities for creative approaches to improvisation. An improvised solo on *Echoes* can be built around the microtonal pitch content of the spectral chord changes, but it is also possible to imagine an improvisation that uses the piece's rhythmic, textural, and dynamic changes as its foundation. For example, the drum coda at the end of the piece (mm. 39–45) can be seen as a platform for improvisation that privileges both rhythmic and textural variation. In lieu of chord changes, the percussionist is asked to negotiate a set of "dynamic changes," which are the result of rapid shifts in the number of accompanying players from seven (m. 39) to three (m. 40) to two (mm. 41–42) to five (mm. 43–44) to one (m. 45).

Conclusion

In a letter written to composer Hugues Dufourt in 1980, Gérard Grisey expressed his frustration with the term "spectral music," finding it too vague and inclusive. Instead, he proposed the term "liminal music" as a more apt description of the foundational concepts in his work (see Grisey and Lelong 2008). I would argue that this clarification may, in fact, point to the most significant link between French spectral music and Afrological forms of improvisation. Both of these musical traditions are built around thresholds of transition and becoming, where the exploration of a liminal terrain between two fixed identities can lead to a transcendent musical experience. Musical boundaries are central to spectral music: the lines between harmony and timbre, pitch and noise, electronic and acoustic, and rhythm and duration. In Afrological forms of improvisation, inquiry into such musical boundaries is further reinforced by the traditional and fundamental nature of improvisation as a creative practice situated at the thresholds of structure and disorder, understanding and mystification, and the known and the unknown.[6]

6. See Ruud (1995), for example, for a discussion of jazz improvisation as a liminal experience, and its application in a variety of music therapy techniques.

Ten years after my first encounter with Tristan Murail and Gérard Grisey's music, I am still exploring the relationship between spectral music and improvisation and continuing to make new connections and new musical discoveries. My hope is that this paper will illuminate some of the key ideas that inform my recent work and encourage similar research and experimentation in these musical areas.

Works Cited

Anderson, Julian. "A Provisional History of Spectral Music." (*Contemporary Music Review*, vol. 19, no. 2, 2000)

Cole, Bill. *John Coltrane.* (New York: Da Capo, [1976], 2001)

Cohen-Lévinas, Danielle. *Vingt-Cinq Ans de Création Musicale Contemporaine.* (Paris: L'Harmattan, [1991], 1998)

Dénut, Eric and Philippe Hurel. "Une Musique Résistante." In Eric Dénut, ed. *Musiques Actuelles, Musiques Savantes: Quelles Interactions?.* (Paris: L'Harmattan, 2001)

Desmond, Paul and John McLellan. *Interview with Charlie Parker.* (Boston: WHDH Radio, January 1954)

Drott, Eric. "Spectralism, Politics and the Post-Industrial Imagination." (Bjorn

Helle, ed. *The Modernist Legacy: Essays on New Music.*) (Farnham, England & Burlington, Vermont: Ashgate, 2009)

Grisey, Gérard. "Tempus ex Machina: A Composer's Reflections on Musical Time." (*Contemporary Music Review*, vol. 2, 1987)

Grisey, Gérard, and Guy Lelong. *Écrits: Ou L'Invention de la Musique Spectrale.* (Paris: Éditions MF, 2008)

Fineberg, Joshua. "Guide to the Basic Concepts and Techniques of Spectral Music." (*Contemporary Music Review*, vol. 19, no. 2, 2000)

Iyer, Vijay. "Thelonious Monk: Ode to a Sphere." (*JazzTimes*, January/February 2010)

Lewis, George. "Improvised Music Since 1950: Afrological and Eurological Perspectives." (*Black Music Research Journal*, vol. 16, no. 1, Spring 1996)

Murail, Tristan. Personal communication. (April 30, 2010)

Ruud, Evan. 1995. "Improvisation as a Liminal Experience: Jazz and Music Therapy as Modern Rites of Passage." (Carolyn Bereznak Kenny, ed. *Listening, Playing, Creating: Essays on the Power of Sound*) (Albany: State University of New York Press, 1995)

Russel, Ross. *Bird Lives!: The High Life and Hard Times of Charlie (Yardbird) Parker.* (New York: Da Capo, [1973], 1996)

RIGHTING WRONG NOTES

STEVEN MACKEY

Blues

When I was about 15 years old I read a quote from B.B. King in *Guitar Player* magazine. He said something to the effect of "The blues isn't a scale, it's a feeling." I had heard that chestnut in many forms and regarded it, at the time, as poetic and metaphorical. As a teenager I was preoccupied with scales, patterns, and fingerboard geography. Over the years I've come to understand it as more accurate and syntactically insightful than I originally thought.

Jimi Hendrix, in an extended solo (*Red House from Live at Winterland*, for example), might put all the notes in a chromatic scale in play and a lot of the microtonal territory in the cracks as well. A great blues solo is not constructed from discrete steps of a scale but from modes of behavior—bending, sliding, digging, insisting, stuttering, and moaning. Pitch, pitch inflection, rhythm and tone color are inseparable aspects of a projected emotional gesture. The *right* rhythm can make the *wrong* note (from the strict blues-scale perspective) *hurt* so good. There are no wrong notes only inauthentic or unearned affects. The scale does indeed dissolve behind pure expression. It's a feeling.

In Mozart *the harmony,* is expressed by the combination of melody and accompaniment working together, *harmony* is not just the chords or the alberti bass, ignoring the tune. Dissonance resolves to consonance allowing vertical cross-sections to be reconciled into harmonic units that concatenate into harmonic progressions. Fancy jazz is similar but the harmonic units have more elaborate taxonomies and you hear people refer to 7$\sharp$9 chords. Some blues and rock music is better conceived as contrapuntal not harmonic. It is stratified where the dimensions of melody and accompaniment or solo and rhythm section have somewhat independent modes of behavior. This independence is at the heart of the notion of blue notes: The minor 3rd and 7th preferred by the melody *hurt* so much better because they clash with the major chord routines in the rhythm section. These clashes could be called 7$^{\sharp}$9 chords, but doggedly pursuing an all-encompassing harmony seems to miss the point. It is a blue note because it sticks out like a sore thumb. Its distinctive color causes it to stand in relief, not be subsumed into the harmony.

The "emancipation of dissonance" in a rock/blues context is quite different than in the case of Schoenberg who coined the phrase. For Schoenberg, emancipation of the dissonance meant that any two notes could sound together. I suppose one could say, especially about his pre twelve-tone *expressionistic* works, that it was about the *feeling* (the *expression*) not the scale. However, there is a consistency of harmonic color and texture that subsumes everything into a single sense of *harmony* and as a result there aren't really any strikingly *wrong* notes. There are more and less gnarly chords but there aren't audible clinkers—*a chord* plus a note that is no-way-no-how part of the chord. Context alone articulates what the function of an interval is. There is no apriori functional difference between a 5th and a ½ step. Dissonance was emancipated; wrong notes were legalized, which kind of takes the pizzazz out of them.

In rock/blues the relative independence of solo and rhythm, a context for defining relative consonance and dissonance, and high tolerance for the latter, gives this music a palpable *inside* and an *outside* with respect to harmony. Inside the harmony would mean emphasizing notes that are quite resonant with and congeal with the prevailing bass and *outside* refers to notes that are less reinforced and do not blend in. An extended *Outside* would be forbidden in classical tonality and notions of *inside*, *outside*; consonance and dissonance are irrelevant to a rigorously atonal context.

The European avant-garde proposed a continuum connecting syntactical pitch relations and noise. To my peers in music history class who were raised with piano lessons and Clementi, the porous membrane between pitch and noise seemed challenging and un-musical but such a continuum is familiar in rock music. The expressive motivations that take Hendrix from inside to outside continue on to just as smoothly deliver him to squealing feedback, and the crushing hush of an abandoned Wa-wa pedal. Noise is just a particular color of being outside the harmony.

Beethoven

It wouldn't be much of an exaggeration to say that my life was changed by one note—the E♭ in bar 16 of the scherzo in Beethoven's last *String Quartet*, which I first heard when I was 19 years old. This is an exalted clinker, at once comical and terrifying. It is preceded by a repeated 8-bar theme and it takes longer than that, 9–10 bars, for the music to get back on its feet.

The impact is in part due to the vividness of the contrast that the E♭ delineates. The first 16 bars have a naïve, nursery rhyme quality. The four instruments interlock cooperatively and then … *bang!* The E♭ changes everything. Gone is the singsong. The triadic harmony collapses into eerie octaves and unisons. The wheels fall off the happily ticking triple meter and the music stutters in a disoriented rhythm and claws its way through E natural to get back to something like the beginning … although you can never trust the beginning again because the E♭ casts a shadow over everything. The bright A natural, major 3rd of the nursery rhyme is colored by a sinister tritone.

Sure you could give the E♭ a name and call it a flattened 7th of the scale and be done with it, but that explains nothing. It doesn't go down like a flattened 7th should, it goes up to a *normal* 7th. It is as if the music was aiming to just take a step down but slipped past the mark and now has to struggle to climb back aboard. It's a *wrong* note made *right* by the gesture. The gestalt of that note delineates an extraordinary character. In short, I am more satisfied with a description of how the note *feels* than I am with assigning it a functional label in the scale.

Do the Math …

My composition teachers were for the most part, twelve-tone composers. I was a student at the University of California at Davis studying physics and playing in a rock band when I first heard classical music and turned my attention toward composition. It just so happened that the senior composer there at the time, Richard Swift, was committed to twelve-tone technique. My scientist's head devoured the Babbitt articles on set theory and techniques of permutation that he assigned and twelve-tone music seemed to blend my interests—science and music—perfectly. I continued to grad schools that he recommended—SUNY Stony Brook and Brandeis—and furthered my education as a composer/theorist writing a PhD dissertation about twelve-tone music under the influence of Donald Martino. As important as the specific techniques that I learned in those years was the idea that a technique, algorithm, system, filter, etc., could be invented to get something interesting on the page. (More on that later).

After grad school when there was no longer anyone paid to be interested in my work and I was left to my own instincts the guitarist in me started to re-emerge with some tough questions. I remember believing that I had created the hippest, funkiest, rhythm ever with the new complicated rhythms I had learned to write, but when performed the music sounded dislocated, twitchy and without any physical impact. I realized that there was a little drummer in my head when I was composing, laying down a sweet groove and helping me place each note in the right spot. Against that grid my rhythm was interesting but there was nothing explicit in the music projecting that grid. Lesson learned: Meter needs to contextualize rhythm so that syncopation and offbeat-ness are palpable realities.

Then came the geeky algebraic equation: Rhythm is to meter as pitch is to tonality. Pitch and interval are contextualized by tonality as rhythm is by meter. I had rhythm, meter and pitch but I was missing the fourth variable—tonality—or at least some stable matrix with which to endow pitches with vivid and differentiated color. My blues guitarist instincts began to re-engage and I had to admit to myself that a ½ step was just not the same as a perfect 5th. That equation was the first step for me toward embracing the overtone series and harmonic spectra as an a priori context for re-empowering consonance and dissonance and enabling me to create a context for blue, outside and just plain *wrong* notes.

One work in particular—*Physical Property* (1992), for electric guitar and string quartet—is a constant reminder of this period since I continue to perform it regularly. I had very little time to write the piece, let alone practice it so it made sense to compose at the guitar to make sure everything fit nicely in my hand. Reduced to its essence, the guitar establishes an animated A/E drone—an A *power* chord—which unambiguously establishes a metric for understanding levels of dissonance. The 15-minute piece doesn't modulate from key to key to refresh itself. Instead, like an extended blues solo, it makes forays along a continuum delineated by A major chord tones, A mixolydian *insiders, outside* notes (E♭, F, A♭, B♭, microtones) and noise (scratch tones, slides, distortion).

That Reminds of the One About Two Musicians in a Bar …

There is a joke running around the music world, probably apocryphal but apt nonetheless: Thelonius Monk is sitting at the bar, following a set, looking despondent. His friend walks in and asks, "What's wrong Thelonius?" Monk answers, "Oh man, I played all the wrong, wrong notes."

In that spirit, guitarist Bill Frisell tells a story of his first day at the Berklee College of Music. After they passed out a chart of all the right notes you could play Bill immediately went home and experimented with what the wrong notes sounded like. I imagine him developing his personal sound, vibrato, sense of time and phrasing in order to make those wrong notes do the right thing in the tradition of the other great wrong-note musicians before him.

Deal

In the early-mid-'90s I had the opportunity to compose a concerto called *Deal* for Bill Frisell, drummer Joey Baron and the LA Phil new music group. I began writing music and then had the ironic vision of Bill squinting through his thick glasses trying to decode a notation intended to capture his personal style. So, I decided to allow him to do what he does best—improvise, survive, *Deal.* The same for Joey.

Suggested by a philosophical pre-occupation I had at the time that the universe doesn't make intrinsic sense, rather we as individuals must make sense of it, I invented a little system which begins with a randomly selected group of pitch-class sets and connects them into something logical using common tones. (J.K. Randall inspired this by handing me a stack of pages of randomly generated pitch class sets. I've written about this in *Current Musicology* number 67/68 Fall/Winter 1999.)

Since I was writing for an improvising electric guitarist with a background and sensibility not that different from my own I wanted to create a context which had a palpable, inside and outside. With any of these random pitch class sets I could organize and orchestrate to suggest an *inside* element with some kind of tonal pull and titrate out *outside* element(s) that seemed to occupy a different space in order to create a heterogeneous, poly-valent if not polytonal texture rather than a single, dense, freely atonal chromatic texture. While any one moment might radiate some kind of tonal identity (along with some wrong notes) the concept is fundamentally atonal since the succession of random pitch-class sets makes it impossible to string together a cogent progression. It is the job of the soloists to somehow make sense of, or give purpose *(feeling)* to the disjunctions.

Bill could then play inside the harmony, play with the twiddling outside and by virtue of his attention, make that a secondary inside. Or he could play a completely different outside element twiddling along on its own. What makes his performance work is his relentless commitment to the character of every note he plays. (Feeling not scale.)

Below is an example from *Deal*. This is similar to what the guitarist and drummer are given to work from. It is a reduction of the chamber orchestra part with some guidelines for the improvising soloists.

Each rehearsal letter (DD, EE, FF) represents a pitch-class set on my chart. DD is a realization of C♯, E, F♯, G, G♯, A, B. If presented with this set in my grad school days I would have probably focused on the chromatic tetrachord between F♯ and A as a way of disguising that this is one wrong note away from an A major or F♯ minor scale. Instead, in *Deal*, the big bass notes alternating F♯ and C♯, broadcast an F♯ minor gravitational field. The *wrongest* note is the G since it disagrees with the bass and the more resonant G♯ 9th in F♯ minor. The G happens in two strata. It thumbs its nose at the F♯ minor by being part of a dissonant ½ step moan (G/A♭) in the viola but it is also echoed in the background. There it is softened a bit by being part of a chromatic, linear step, G♯-G, instead of a cluster, which in turn is made more *consonant* by coupling in 6ths and 3rds with E and B.

In EE (C, C♯, F, F♯, G, G♯, A, B♭) the set is partitioned into the bass motion B♭-C and displaced 6ths in the tenor, G-A, which suggest an F major core. The F in the oboe enters as a sweet consonance but is immediately followed by the staccato chattering of the flute and trombone on C♯, F♯ and G♯ which represent clinkers in the works. The soloist can ignore or join those clinkers, or respond to the rhythm and articulation of the clinkers using different pitches and thereby suggest yet another element dangling outside of the F major.

There are some voice leading and motivic connections smoothing the succession of DD and EE but the move from an F♯ minor-ish world to an F major-ish world, each with some quirky notes attached, is not a conventional, strong progression and the soloist's are asked to do what they can to make give the little bumps some purpose. One advice I found myself giving Bill before the premiere was that he could move to the next harmonic unit well ahead of the orchestra to create the illusion that the orchestra was responding to him instead of him always responding to them.

It was quite late in the process that I added drums as a further extension of the idea of inside and outside. If the guitar is oblique or contrary to the orchestra but strongly reinforced by the drums there can be a sense of counterpoint between two *orchestras*. Or the drums can support the orchestra and leave the guitar hanging outside alone. Or the drums can nibble at the edges of the music with fewer harmonic consequences. There is actually a pre-recorded tape part with sounds of real world sounds which draw and even wider perimeter such that even the *outermost* notes, merely by being pitches, are on the inside compared to a duck quacking, dog barking or a phone ringing.

Groucho Marx

My little random pitch-class system was intended to be for *Deal* only but I was intrigued by the sound of the music and the process challenged my imagination in positive ways. For the next ten years I worked in this way; digging through random sets looking for ways to make both right and wrong notes speak. This led me to some glorious cacophonies that I would not have thought of otherwise and the process of finding the music in a group of notes, felt as much like discovery as invention. During this period I thought often of the Groucho Marx line "I refuse to join any club that would have me as a member." My version was, "I refuse to accept any idea that I can think of" and I enjoyed feeling *lucky* when I stumbled into something fascinating. (As someone said—"It's better to be lucky than good.")

Deal (1995) and *Dreamhouse* (2003), the first and last pieces written with random sets linked by common tones, were the only pieces that carry the method through rigorously from beginning to end. In the intervening works I would often develop material from a particularly interesting segment of the common-tone chain and develop that material on its own terms, using my intuitions about its potential, as if it was a *theme* in my notebook that I had invented from scratch. The point is that my interest in this system was not to guarantee coherence or logic or to insure the *supremacy of American music for the next 100 years.* It was intended to suggest surprising notes and challenge me to imagine vivid characters that would trump notions *right* and *wrong.*

"Where we're going we don't need roads."

The process of constructing my common-tone chains from a page of random pitch-class sets was time consuming and tedious. I would often spend a couple of weeks before beginning to invent music. I'm sure I could have had a computer program developed that would make the task quicker and easier but I firmly believe that the calculations, educated guesses, wild goose chases, and stabs in the dark, that led to the finished charts imprinted my brain with vivid impressions about the roles the notes might play. For each piece I essentially turned myself into a crackpot who anthropomorphized the notes I was wrestling with.

After a decade of work in this meticulous mode I just started to hear that way—quirky heterogeneous note combinations that often have a stable, gravitational nucleus and one or more peculiar satellites. My process is now entirely intuitive with no elaborate chart preparations yet I don't think the sound of the music has changed significantly across that shift in working method. This evolution reminds me of Doc Brown's DeLorean time machine in *Back To The Future* which initially required a rare grade of plutonium to operate but after exploring the time-space continuum a bit he discovers that banana peels will also work.

In a nutshell, I started life as a guitarist in search of blue notes, discovered classical music and *serious* composition in college at age nineteen, then embarked on a journey that took me through serialism and hare-brained schemes of my own design to a place where I feel I am writing intuitive music that I am uniquely suited to write, where blue notes again have their place.

"HE SAID WHAT?"

Questioning the Questions, Questioning the Answers

RUDRESH MAHANTHAPPA

When asked to contribute a piece to this volume of *Arcana*, I considered many topics of discussion such as my personal approaches to creating fresh vocabulary for improvisation and composition, musical synthesis with regard to my Indian-American identity, my experiences with racism and stereotyping with specific regard to my music career, multiculturalism and its (good and bad) impact on improvised music, an analysis of one of compositions and one of my solos, an unconventional analysis of a Charlie Parker solo, and the list goes on. The reality is that while my perspective on all these topics continues to grow, I do discuss them quite a lot in many other forums. I am beginning to feel like a broken record. For that reason I chose a more personal direction that still touches on similar subject matter but through a wholly different mode of engagement.

The past three to four years have been the busiest of my life and career thus far especially with regard to performing, recording, and teaching. Obviously these activities lead to a greater interaction with the public be they audiences, students, journalists, or the guy sitting next you on the train between Köln and Berlin. My sense is that most creative musicians have a manner in which they would like to be understood and perceived both on and off the bandstand. Not only do we want a performance to be well received but we also desire the "right" sort of commentary when speaking to audience members after a concert. We want the journalist to ask questions that are "important," "relevant," and "meaningful." It is an often occurrence that we harp on the comments made by someone who "didn't get it" or asked a "dumb" question or the enthusiastic listener who gravitated towards the "wrong" aspect of a performance or recording. We want our mission to be understood in full, a worthy objective without a doubt.

As I get older, I seem to vacillate between impatience and compassion. That is to say that I either have little tolerance for the interactions described above or I welcome most comments as mostly valid interpretations of my presence and work. The latter behavior is new to me. Fascinated by this, I am interested in revisiting a few of the irritating, thoughtful, and even moving questions and comments of the past and perhaps gain some perspective on the nature of the exchange that ensued. This is a sort of self-analysis. While I dissect the impetus of the instigator, I am more concerned with re-examining, questioning, or validating my responses and reactions.

Q: Where are you from?
A: Boulder, Colorado.
Q: Where are you really from?
A: Boulder, Colorado.
Q: No, I mean where were you born?
A: Trieste, Italy.

Now obviously this person is inquiring about my heritage/ancestry. I'm not sure why they could not just ask me that directly as I am now offended. I'm really from Boulder, Colorado and was really born in Trieste. Those are facts that could not be more real.

Friendly Answer: My parents came to the US in the '50s. My family had already settled in Boulder but I happened do be born when my Dad was on sabbatical in Italy.

Should have I understood the intended inquiry and initially answered accordingly? I don't think so as the hybrid nature of being Indian-American is a primary aspect of my existence.

Q: How often do you go back?
A: Go back where? Boulder?
Q: India.
A: India is not going back …

This is evidently part of the same family of questions. One that is exacerbated by often being listed in programs (especially in Europe) as being from India in order to ostensibly add an exotic flavor to the audience's expectations.

Q: How Indian are you?

Ditto and I'm definitely offended.

C: I can really hear the Indian influence in your music.
R: Really?

A loaded comment but one made with genuine positive intent and observation. Some of my work is very blatantly rooted in Indian music while in other cases that presence is quite subtle and personal. Did they really hear it or has the color of my skin and my long South Indian surname altered the way they heard the music?

Do I say thank you?

Once a (rather famous) fellow musician heard me playing a bunch of multiphonics and cited that as an obvious manifestation of my ancestry!!!

Another funny one is when people talk about hearing the Indian harmonies. Classical Indian music has no harmony; it's melody and rhythm. Maybe they mean sonority and it's a question of mistaken terminology.

The word "fusion" inevitably comes up if this conversation continues, a word that I have avoided and discussed in many interviews if one is interested to learn more.

C: I don't hear the Indian influence in your music at all except for maybe in the first piece.
R: Really? Too bad.

A similar thread but irksome to say the least. The commenter has implied that he knows something about Indian music or at least enough to make the comment. I come back to what I stated above regarding my ancestry vis-à-vis my work but posit that the influence would have been more apparent to this person if I had been wearing a turban. Was I supposed to wear my culture on my sleeve in order to entertain this person?

By the way, the first piece is usually a drone.

Q: If you were to try to describe in words the geographical space that your music explores, that space that is both India and the US, and yet neither, what would it be?
A: Well not to sound redundant, but I think "[hyphen]American" sums it up specifically. I am Indian-American and my music inhab-

its both of those spaces. More importantly, my work speaks to multiculturalism in the contemporary society while avoiding exoticism and stereotypes. All over the world, there are immigrant populations blossoming and their children are trying to define, redefine, invent, and reinvent who they are. Hybridity and bicultural identities are probably more prevalent than ever and some of the most interesting and engaging art is coming from these communities. These are my people. This is where my music lives.

This is from the tail end of an interview I did with Naresh Fernandes for "Time Out Mumbai." Naresh is a very astute journalist who is currently conducting a major research project concerning the early days of jazz in Mumbai. I thought the question was beautifully posed and consequently elicited a thoughtful yet concise answer that essentially sums up my mission. If I could review the journalist, he would get 5 stars.

C: I really hear a lot of Ornette and Dolphy in your playing.
R: Really? I never think of them as major influences. [Dismissively] Is it just because I'm playing an alto saxophone?

Friendly response: Beyond Bird, I've actually been more influenced by tenor players such as Johnny Griffin, Coltrane, etc.

Wouldn't it be great if a player of a different instrument or even a non-performing composer were referenced as an audible influence?? I'd love it if someone came up and said "I hear a lot of McCoy Tyner, Bismillah Khan, and Bartók in your playing." I'd probably kiss that person!

C: In a recent listening test/interview, you said that Paul Desmond was cheesy. I was shocked.
R: I didn't say that Paul Desmond was cheesy. I said that the recording was cheesy as in '70s CTI sounding cheesy. Paul had his own sound and I respect anyone who has an individual and unique voice, without question. However, I never gravitated towards his music. I never really liked his stuff. It never spoke to me. Is that so bad?

Is it so bad? Upon publication of this listening test, there were sev-

eral people who took issue with me not liking Paul Desmond. *Why is it so important to approve of my personal taste? Why do I have a feeling that no one would have batted an eye if I said that I didn't like Ornette or Albert Ayler or Rothko or Brancusi or Shakira or George Michael? I do like all of them by the way.*

In regard to the same article:

C: I was surprised that you didn't recognize Phil Woods.
R: [No response]

Why surprised? Are we responsible for being walking encyclopedias of jazz? I'm sure I can recognize a multitude of players and composers within a few seconds that many others cannot, but who cares?
Does this even dignify a response?
It all makes me evaluate the importance of knowing what an artist thinks about other artists. One on hand, such insight can be illuminating for a listener/reader/colleague and on another hand, it can serve to paint a target on one's back.

C (from a musician): I really like Indian music. I wrote a piece in 5/4.
R: [Somewhat dumbfounded silence]

C: It sounds like you're just playing free.
R: Nope.

Firstly, what is free? Do they mean spontaneously improvised music with no preconceived structure? I hardly ever do that and when I do, I'm usually blessed to be in the company of the greatest spontaneous composers I know such as Mark Dresser and Gerry Hemingway. Why the use of the word "just?" Is playing "free" easy?
If I was "just" playing "free," what was the music stand for?
Obviously there is an even larger issue at play here as I wonder how and why complex music and spontaneously improvised music are often lumped together by audiences and journalists alike. Do the extremes converge somehow? Are they really perceived as similar to the "average" listener?

149

Q: How much of that was improvised and how much was composed?
A: About as much as is when you hear a band playing a jazz standard. They play the head, folks take solos, and they play the head again. We did the same thing but it just so happens that the head was little more complicated with many sections, tempo changes, etc. and the solos occurred over that same form. We're not doing anything too different than Bird.

That last bit always get a chuckle even though I'm dead serious. I usually answer this question with compassion and understanding. It's a reasonable question ... I guess.

My good friend and amazing percussionist Dan Weiss just tells people "70/30" which always cracks me up and also seems to satisfy the person who has asked!

Q: Do you play music for a living?
A: [Somewhat defiantly] YES.

This question usually comes from a South Asian. Indian-American jazz musicians are still a rare thing so fellow South Asians are surprised to see me and/or surprised that my parents let me pursue this as a career choice as it is not a traditional path for my people. I try not to be acerbic when asked this because it is not a farfetched question. However, it is not something that you want to be asked after playing your heart out for two hours. It's a timing issue.

Why is it important to know if music is how I make my livelihood in that moment?

I have to say that I have been asked this question quite seldom in recent years which is welcome and significant to me but makes it sting even more when it does arise.

For a general public, it's probably easy to feel incredulous regarding the ability to make a decent living playing music unless one is a Top 40 star.

In some cases, audiences like the idea of (or even fetishize) the broke and struggling musician. I have twice experienced interviews where that was the all-pervading emphasis of the article far beyond my work. Eeesh. Glorified destitution.

C: I really liked the last piece.
R: Thanks.

The last piece is usually a ballad reminiscent of Trane, if I had to describe it.

But what about the rest of the concert?

The person clearly enjoyed himself or herself but am I annoyed because it wasn't the "correct" compliment? The one I wanted or needed to hear?

Clearly, this is my problem and not theirs. I should in fact be grateful methinks.

Q: Do you ever play ballads?

This person must have left before the last piece.

C: You play really fast.
R: Thanks?

Yes. I can and do play fast. The musicians that made me want to play music could play fast too. Maybe I do it too much?

Still working on this one.

Q: Why did you choose the saxophone?
A: My older brother played the clarinet and always thought the students in the high school jazz band were having more fun than he was having in the orchestra. He also told me that the baritone saxophone could rattle an entire room. This was certainly intriguing to a 4th grader. I had already been playing baroque recorder for two years and saxophone was an easy transition because of the fingerings.

This question always throws me off. I sometimes wish I had a more interesting answer. "I heard the saxophone and my life was changed forever" and the like.

More than that, I wonder why I play music. Do I derive joy from actually playing this instrument or is it the pleasure of playing and interacting with other musicians? Or is it the act of performance or even the satisfying sense of accomplishment?

151

I'm quite sure that I would not be satisfied playing the saxophone if no one ever heard me. Is that selfish? Am I needy? Who knew such an innocent question would call all my motivations into uncertainty?

I'd like to think that it could have been any instrument and the choice of the saxophone just happened to be the one that presented itself most readily. I'm certainly open to being wrong about that though.

C: You're so talented!
R: Thanks!

I actually hate the word talent. With the exception of physical/ athletic talent resulting from genetic coincidences, I'd like to think that environment is the prevailing factor in shaping one's life. Most anyone is capable of anything given nurturing and encouraging circumstances. If talent exists, maybe it manifests as hard work, dedication, and an open perspective.

Why do I believe this? For the simple reason that I have never thought of myself as being talented.

Q: How did you get into jazz?
A: I was playing the saxophone. There were not many other obvious genres suited to this instrument. I first heard Grover Washington Jr. and then Bird. I was hooked.

I like this one mainly because I'd like to meet someone who pursued the saxophone with the initial aspirations of being a rock or classical superstar.

Surely, there must have been someone who was inspired by Clarence Clemons or the '80s rock saxophone solos in songs by Supertramp, Men at Work, and Huey Lewis.

Any takers on that?

C: Your music requires a lot of knowledge even for an educated listener. It's difficult to understand.
R: Why? What did you need to understand?

Another loaded remark. I've always believed that my music can be enjoyed by anyone. There's a lot of passionate and energized storytelling at play. There are many levels of engagement for the listener and by no means is my target audience fellow musicians or a self-anointed intelligentsia.

This comment usually comes from someone who considers himself or herself an expert on jazz and clearly demonstrates that they possess that "little bit of knowledge" that has become a "dangerous thing."

C: Your latest album *Samdhi* reminds me of Mahavishnu.
R: Oh.

I don't really get this one. This album is definitely "fusiony" (as in jazz-rock fusion) but I didn't really check out much Mahavishnu though I know they were great! I did listen to Weather Report and the Yellowjackets when I was younger but they never seem to be referenced.

Does it really sound like Mahavishnu or does Mahavishnu sound like Mahanthappa?

Q: If You had to describe the meaning of the word music, what would You say? What is music for You?
A: Music is many things to me. It's the resonance of humanity and the human condition; it's the beauty of number (the building blocks of creation) in an audible form; it's the great communicator of culture and society both past and present; it's the only life force besides my wife that makes me want to wake up every morning and live like it's my last day on Earth.

From a wonderful interview with Tilman Urbauch for "Du Magazine."
This one made me smile for weeks.
I pondered the question for several days.
I continue to ponder the answer.

Thanks for indulging me in this inquiry of inquiries and analysis of answers.

CHINA DIARY

DENMAN MARONEY

From June 17 to July 11, 2007 I toured China with drummer Rich O'Donnell on a grant from St. Louis based New Music Circle, of which he was music director. Joining us were his wife Anna, born in China, her daughter Debbie, living in Shanghai, and her granddaughter Aida.

Rich and I met in 2000. I sent him a disk, and he gave me a gig. A year later he formed a trio with violinist Leroy Jenkins and me called "Unknown Unknowns" after a speech by Donald Rumsfeld, "things we don't know we don't know." Later Leroy made us a quartet with pipa player Min Xiao-Fen. That group gave one concert, at the Community Church of New York, produced by the Association for the Advancement of Creative Musicians. The concert was recorded and released as *Leroy Jenkins' Driftwood: The Art of Improvisation* (Mutable Music 17523-2).

Leroy died in February 2007. Rich wanted the rest of us to tour China in his memory, but Min couldn't go, so he and I went as a duo. It wasn't much of a tour: four concerts in three weeks. But it was a trip! For the first time in my life, I kept a diary. An edited and expurgated version follows, to which I've added explications of our music.

6-19-07 @14:45

Arriving in Shanghai, population 17 million, my worst fear is realized: no one is there to meet me! I phone Debbie. Her line is busy. At last she appears. She's a documentary filmmaker. Her husband Jonathan works for a company that does voice over IP.

This morning she takes Rich and me to East China Normal University, where we'll give our first concert tomorrow. We want to be sure they know our needs. I play "hyperpiano," meaning the keys with one hand and the strings with the other using prayer bowls, copper bars, steel cylinders, rubber blocks, and plastic audio media cases. I want to show this to our host and assure him it's benign. "I don't care what you do to the piano," he says. "I'm busy!"

Our translator, Elaine, asks us to explain our music, so she can explain it to our audience.

Rich makes his own drums. On the heads he sometimes deploys an assortment of wind-up toys. To the undersides he attaches springs, which resonate like flanges. His kick drum pedal, which he patented, has two mallets. One strikes when he pedals down, the other when he pedals up.

Rich and I have similar approaches to rhythm. We both play what I call temporal harmony, meaning layers of tempo related like the undertone series, the reciprocal of the overtone series, i.e. 1/1, 1/2, 1/3, 1/4, etc. If the time unit is an 8th note, then the first harmonic is an 8th, the second a quarter, the third a dotted quarter, etc. The first eight tones and durations of the undertone series of C7 are:

I can play multiple layers in each hand. For musical interest I vary their pitch, register, duration, dynamic, articulation, and rhythm. I may or may not use the pitch relations. Note e.g. that 3:4:5 is a first inversion minor triad, 4:5:6 a root position minor triad, and 5:6:7 a diminished triad.

Rich calls his playing technique "seesaw" drumming. He makes his own sticks and mallets as well as drums and pedals. Like a vibraphonist, he holds two sticks in each hand. Rhythmically, he can work each stick independently, so he, too, can play multiple layers of time in each hand. He plays what he calls conversational phrases, Moiré patterns, and swarming images.

We also discuss with Elaine our musical backgrounds and influences. How much she understands is hard to know.

We go to a dim sum house for lunch. Fabulous! My first meal in China!

6-21-07 @22:50

Yesterday morning we visit the Shanghai Urban Planning Museum. The centerpiece is a giant scale model of the city, which in reality is so huge that everywhere you go seems like the center. One diorama shows photos of the same locations taken by the same photographer in 1990 and 2006. Total transformation! The land across the water from the Bund (the strip of buildings along the waterfront built by Europeans in the 19th century) was vacant then and is filled with skyscrapers now. The newest, which will be the world's tallest, was supposed to have a rising sun on top, for the architect and anchor tenant are both Japanese. The government nixed this idea.

We lunch at a restaurant in the old city where both the Clintons and Castro had dined.

That afternoon we visit People's Park. Skyscrapers with odd crowns are visible through the trees. It's lovely. It's nothing like its namesake in Berkeley, CA, where I was gassed in the Sixties, not for protesting, but for cowering in a record store as protestors marching past were gassed.

We go to East China Normal University to set up for our first concert. A student recital is in progress. Two pianists are playing a Rachmaninoff concerto reduction. We finally get in the hall an hour before our show. In the interim I find a toilet with nothing but a hole in the floor and no paper. Somehow I avoid soiling myself.

The hall has microphones and a P.A. but no engineer. It's filling already, and I'm running back and forth between the stage and the booth a long way off. By the time the concert starts, I'm exhausted. I haven't touched a piano since leaving the US several days before. My body and mind have no idea what time it is: 19:00 on 6/20 in Shanghai, 7:00 on 6/19 in New York, or 13:00 on 6/19 in Paris, where I was the week before. In the audience are about 200 people. Elaine gives a long speech, in which I hear the words "John Cage." We do a free improvisation. Then we take turns explaining what we do.

Temporal harmony makes textures of relative instead of absolute time, since listeners can choose which beat to follow, if any. In a field of 3:4:5, for example, they can hear 4 and 5 in terms of 3:

3 and 5 in terms of 4:

or 3 and 4 in terms of 5:

In each case the composite rhythm is the same.

Rich achieves a similar effect with his layers of metrically offset rhythms whose perception is analogous to that of Moiré patterns.

A pulse field resolves to simultaneity at the lowest common denominator of its component beats. For example, 3:4:5 resolves after sixty beats. Fields of three or more pulses have multiple points of simultaneity. In 3:4:5, the field 4:5 resolves three times, 3:5 four times, and 3:4 five times. These points can be used structurally to change the parameter(s) of your choice.

Rich's wife Anna recites a poem in English and Chinese about her mother, who died when she was four. The poem relates how, when she turned thirty-eight, her father showed her a photograph of her mother, taken when her mother turned thirty-eight, forty-three days before her mother died. It's lovely, except she botches the Chinese, which makes her giggle.

We accompany her with bowed sounds: Rich bows cymbals with a violin bow. I bow piano strings with a copper bar. Piano strings all lie in a plane, so bowing makes clusters that vary with bar pressure and placement, motion angle and speed, and damping strings by sustain pedaling or silently depressing keys.

We improvise to a video by André Vida, which Rich brought and I'm seeing for the first time.

We take questions. They ask a lot. Their questions are intelligent.

This morning we fly to Beijing. The smog is horrible, compounded by sand blowing off the desert. Billboards all over town read, "Only 400 days to Olympics 2008." To clear the air, the government plans to shut all the area's factories three months ahead.

We visit Tiananmen Square and the Forbidden City. On the way we're accosted by a hat vendor. A bicycle cop charges and tries to kick him. He runs into the street.

In the square someone offers to drive us to the Great Wall for what seems like a good price. We accept and arrange to go the next day.

There are 9,999 buildings in the Forbidden City. Ten thousand would be unlucky, because the Chinese words for ten and death sound the same. In between are vast, vacant spaces paved with stone slabs. The oldest buildings date to around 1400. Inside one is a display of musical instruments from the Qing Dynasty (1644–1912). They're beautiful but covered with dust.

We dine on Beijing duck at a restaurant where Mao hosted Nixon and Kissinger.

6-23-07 @8:30

This morning, we're driven to the Great Wall two hours from town. En route we stop at a jade gallery. We weren't told about this when we signed up and have no choice but to go. The parking lot is full of buses. A woman gives a long talk and then ushers us onto a vast selling floor teeming with uniformed sales people.

Late morning we reach the foot of a mountain with the Wall on top. After a long debate we decide to cable car up and toboggan slide down. We want to take one cable up and another down, but this is forbidden.

We set out along the wall, which rises and falls steeply from peak to peak as far as the eye can see. This is far despite the smog, which is as bad here as in town. It's a workout! Eventually I reach a tower, beyond which it is forbidden to go, though the wall divides and continues, overgrown and in ruins. It's actually several walls and, contrary to legend, not visible from the moon. This part was built in the Ming Dynasty (1368–1644). It's also called the Great Cemetery, because so many workers died building and were buried in it.

6-25-07 @8:55

Day before yesterday we fly to Chongqing, population 28 million. It's autonomous, like Beijing and Shanghai (and Washington, DC). It sits at the confluence of the Yangtze and Jialing rivers, which it spans with seventeen bridges. Enclosed by mountains, with a 2-stack power plant or incinerator in the center, it's the most polluted city we've seen. The minute we get off the plane we're handed bottled water, which seems odd, until minutes later our throats are burning. Rip Hayman, composer, sea captain, sinologist, and naval historian, tells me later he declined a job offer there for fear of poisoning his family, and that satellite photos show Chinese smog wafting over the Arctic to America.

Compounding the smog, there's fog, so much so that Chongqing is also known as Fog City. Fog is even said to have prevented the Japanese from invading. Compounding the smog and fog, there's the heat. Stepping outside, I'm sweating in seconds.

We're greeted at the airport by a throng of Anna's relatives. She was born here in 1940, left at age six after the Japanese War (World War II) and returned in 1992 for the first time, so this is only her second time back. She tried to go in 1989, too, but was thwarted by the uprising in Tiananmen Square. A bus takes us to our lodging, the Foreign Guest House of the Sichuan Fine Arts Institute.

Chongqing is celebrating its tenth anniversary as autonomous. One way it chose to celebrate was to invite students of the Institute to paint the facades of buildings. Every building around is covered with murals. They're skyscrapers! It's spectacular! Unfortunately the art is obscured by smog and smudged by soot.

Walking the streets, I'm met with stares, giggles, and occasionally hello, the one English word every Chinese seems to know. As a lone Caucasian bobbing in a sea of Chinese, I cut quite a figure.

We dine with Anna's relations at a hotel in a private dining room with a large, round table with a Lazy Susan. Rich and I get the seats of honor, the ones farthest from the door. The table is so laden with food that dishes are piled on top of each other. The wheel spins. A dish appears before me. I take some. After one bite, my mouth bursts into flame. Debbie quickly makes tofu and cucumber appear before me.

Toasting begins. Everyone says something like, "I'd like to welcome you to Chongqing. We look forward to your magnificent performance." With each toast, all rise, bow, clink, and drink from tiny glasses of beer quickly refilled by hovering waitresses. When my turn comes, I say I feel at home, although I live on the far side of the world.

After supper we set out on foot to visit the homes of Anna's relatives. Her second cousin's son lives on the tenth floor of a seedy high rise. His wife beckons us to admire the view. Laundry hangs out the window. Laundry hangs out every window in China, it seems. The smog and fog are thick. It's dark. I see nothing. Their young son studies piano. He shows me his exercise books. They don't have a piano, so I whistle the tunes. He sings them in solfège. He cuts me!

In the home of the oldest relative, we sit in a room dominated by a desk. I ask what he writes. He shows me the third edition of his history of Chongqing. The frontispiece is a photo of him and Mao, followed by twenty pages of photos and 700 of statistics.

Like every Chinese city, Chongqing is booming. It's also girding for a massive influx of people displaced by the Three Gorges Dam. Cranes hover over skyscrapers shrouded with bamboo scaffolding and green, gauzy tarpaulins. Apartments in unfinished buildings are already occupied. Laundry hangs from what will be windows but are now just gaping holes in grids of concrete. Slip putting out the wash, and plunge thirty stories to your death!

Yesterday begins with a long bus ride to Anna's birthplace, a village in the mountains, largely in ruins, through which a new road is being plowed. A brook tumbles through a ravine. Old sheds and houses crawl up the sides. A few new houses have electric gates and Astroturf lawns. In one drive sits a Lexus with a Buddha on the dash.

We explore on foot. Chickens squawk. Cats fight. Debbie, in shorts, is attacked by mosquitoes. Anna points out caves where she hid from Japanese war planes. The heat and smog stifle, yet I crave sky or sun.

We lunch in a restaurant by a lake near another village. Joining us are two professors from the Chongqing Institute of Arts and Sciences, where we'll perform that night. We're in another private dining room with round table and Lazy Susan. Toasting begins again, full of thanks for our coming and praise for the concert we've get to give. Dragons of polished yellow stone are presented to us. Having no anuses, they signify plenty. Plenty goes in. Nothing comes out.

The concert hall is on an island called Green. Out front a sign, like several around campus, reads, "Music is a kind of soul gymnastics. It makes spirit honest, conscience pure, emotion and faith proper. Solzhenitsyn." The acoustics of the hall are good, but the decor is ratty. A sound man sits at the mixer smoking. It's 3:00, and the sound check is at 6:00. Debbie says Chinese have time on their hands.

We go to the university entrance to be photographed under a 20-foot red banner that proclaims, "Welcome to the Musicians from America!" My 15 minutes have arrived!

We go to the student union, where students are playing mahjong and watching TV. This is supposed to be a place to rest. I go for a walk. The others get back on the bus, which idles to keep the AC going.

The next activity is a cultural exchange with music and dance faculty. We sit at four tables set in a rectangle with potted plants in the middle. Clearly the room was set this way for the occasion, though we had no idea it was happening. Also in attendance are the Institute's Director of International Affairs and a Party Secretary. Denman in China! What an honor it is to have us! What a wonderful concert we're going to give! Two music faculty members regale us with Chinese folk songs that sound to me like ersatz European art songs.

Now, would we please explain our music?

I favor Messiaen's modes of limited transposition. First with two transpositions is the whole tone scale, 02468A in integer notation. Messiaen discounted it, saying Debussy had beaten it to death. Monk proved him wrong! Second with three is the 8-note 0134679A, third with four is the 9-note 0234678AB, and fourth with six is the 10-note 012346789A. There are more, which I confess I haven't learned well enough to use. Like Messiaen, I like to mix them up.

Messiaen also liked what he called non-retrogradable rhythms, which sound the same backward and forward. He said they reminded him of God, because they're symmetrical. Temporal harmony is symmetrical, too. Pulse fields are palindromes. Maybe that's why I like Messiaen's modes. I don't need to be reminded of God but do agree with Ayler that music is

161

the healing force of the universe. In 1969 I even tried to use being a musician as grounds for conscientious objection to the Vietnam War.

At 5:45, the hall is half full, though the concert is at 7:30. Sound man is still at his station smoking. He has wireless microphones but won't turn them on for fear of running down the batteries. I turn them on. We get a sound.

At the symposium we're asked to include American folk songs in the concert, so we do a blues, *Mysterioso* by Monk. In another nod to folk music we open with a tune I remember from a Charles Lloyd LP:

I don't know if it's authentic but hope it helps lead the audience to the space we like to fill. The place is packed! Maybe 1,000 strong! We're introduced. We think it's time to play, but no, it's time to introduce more honored guests, including the University VP and another Party Secretary. Speeches follow every number. We field questions, mostly bemused. On cue, all rise, applaud, and leave as a unit. More photos are taken. Thanks to the heat, stage lighting, and playing, I feel faint.

It's dinner time. As usual there's a round table and Lazy Susan, and Rich and I have the seats of honor. But also at each setting is a hole in the table with a flame heating a bowl of oil. It's Hot Pot, a Sichuan specialty. The Lazy Susan is laden with raw meat, fish, poultry, entrails, brains, mushrooms, celery root, etc. As a guest of honor, I get a fish head plopped in my bowl. When cooked, it floats. I fish it out and dip it in another bowl of sesame oil with garlic and MSG. Our little beer glasses are instantly refilled. The hosts smoke, drink, and get drunk and loud. We toast around. I thank them for having us and say when I saw the food I was afraid but then liked it. They guffaw.

6-27-07 @21:20

Two nights ago, after Hot Pot, we meet with three professors: two photographers and a sculptor. They ask more penetrating questions than the music professors. We drink tea. I get indigestion. Now I've got diarrhea. The Hot

Pot's to blame! I spend the whole day yesterday in bed. Outside soft rock plays loudly from speakers hung in trees. Two men sit on a bench talking. It doesn't seem to bother them, but it drives me nuts. Rich gives me Imodium. We go out to eat. Anna's cousin Peng Yu orders me boiled apple and tofu. Nothing helps.

This morning I'm still sick, but we're off to Jiuzhaigou. I fall asleep on the plane. Waking I see mountains out the window. I recall the *Twilight Zone* episode where a plane descends to a landscape of palm trees and dinosaurs instead of runway. We skirt high peaks to reach Jinhuang Airport, the second highest in the world after Llasa. From there it's two hours to Jiuzhaigou on hairpin turns through spectacular scenery.

We stay at the Noah's Ark Orphanage for Disabled Children, actually a foster home for Tibetan children. In an inner courtyard, children dance for us in costume. They're beautiful! Rich and I play for them. There's no piano, so I play a drum. Debbie does gymnastics. She's good! Anna does Tai Chi.

The home was founded by Anna's grandfather, a wealthy landowner before the Revolution, which found him on the wrong side. It's an outgrowth of a school that fled here during the Japanese War. The home's doctor, a co-founder, was once the personal physician of the Dalai Lama. I ask him to prescribe me something. To my disappointment he gives me a pharmaceutical. It doesn't help.

There's another American here named John Paul. He's studying ethnography at Harvard. He wants to make a documentary about the home, but they're reluctant to let him. It's the only privately run institution of its kind in China. They have to be careful not to offend the government. That would be easy. The public orphanages are factories teeming with children and the elderly. Here there are only twenty children and no elderly.

Debbie and her husband Jon were here once before. Anna told the home the couple wanted to adopt a child. The home had never released a child for adoption but decided to in this case, since Debbie was related to the founder. But Debbie and Jon didn't know this and wouldn't have considered adopting a child from there anyway, because the children are so well treated that to take one away would be like wresting it from its family. Thus they found themselves having to decline an offer they hadn't solicited.

6-28-07 @18:30

The school that preceded the foster home was founded a century ago in memory of missionaries from Oberlin who were murdered. In the Japanese War the school took refuge on the estate of Anna's grandfather. The original idea was to make an orphanage. The founders went looking for Tibetan orphans. Having found some, they couldn't part with them, so the orphanage became a foster home.

Today we visit Jiuzhaigou National Park. The scenery is spectacular. The air is sweet. The sky is blue! It's a big valley like Yosemite. Buses shuttle people up and down. Our guide shouts factoids: Peacock Lake is multi-colored by mineral deposits. It's five meters deep on average and 20,000 sq. meters in area. I take pictures of people taking pictures of people posing before a big, wide waterfall.

6-29-07 @20:45

This morning I go back to the park by myself. I follow a trail by a tropical blue river rushing through a deep valley with a canopy of conifers and beds of fern. The sky is as blue as the water. About an hour in, I reach a meadow where the river widens and slows. Tall peaks frame the scene. A boardwalk goes up the middle. Where it crosses the river, I stop to eat a peach and wash my face. It's idyllic. For the first time on the tour, I'm completely alone.

The plane to Chengdu, our next stop, leaves four hours late. The air at the airport is so thin I get a headache. Anna gives me Shiatsu. At midnight we finally reach the Sichuan Conservatory of Music, where we'll perform the next evening. We stay in a dorm. There's a piano in my room!

The concert is organized by another relative of Anna's who teaches composition at the Conservatory. He hasn't bothered to publicize our concert but does give us a nice lunch. Attendance is predictably sparse. There's no projector, so we just play. Anna recites. The audience is enthusiastic. They crowd the stage for demonstrations.

I'm asked to show how I get my timbres. This has to do with what object I use. Those of plastic, rubber and wood pass lower overtones, and those of metal pass higher ones. A piano string isn't stopped completely when an object is applied, so it sounds on both sides of the contact point. Its division into fractions of length (e.g. 1/4 and 3/4) produces reciprocal pitches (4/1 and 4/3, a double octave and a perfect 4th). Here (in just intonation) are the reciprocal intervals of the chromatic scale:

The number of strings tuned to the same note varies by register: one in the lowest octave, two in the next two, and three in the highest five, more or less, depending on make and model. When an applied object is rotated, the corresponding intervals are detuned to different degrees. If a long enough object is rotated far enough, the intervals invert. This is disorienting at first; it feels weird to play CDE and hear EDC.

Peng Tsu, Peng Yu's brother, asks me to accompany him as he recites a Tang Dynasty (618–907) poem. About as long as a haiku, it tells of a man who looks at the moon, sees moonlight on the floor, thinks of frost, looks back at the moon, and thinks of home.

7-2-07 @9:45

Yesterday we quit the dorm for the supposedly 5-star California Garden Hotel. The lobby has a four-story ceiling encircled by meter-wide columns, but it's seedy all the same.

Our host is an administrator at the Film & TV College of Sichuan Normal University, where we'll play that evening. He's also dean of the foreign language department. He thinks he speaks English. He talks all right, but he doesn't understand. He tells us 100 million people live within 50 kilometers of Chengdu. He takes us to a reconstruction of an old city street. It feels like a mall. For lunch we have dim sum.

The venue is a cinema. The piano is a Steinweg, not as nice as the Steinway the night before. I ask the sound man to tweak the EQ. This is a mistake. From the booth he can't hear it. I get him to reset it to flat. We get as good a sound as we can hope for. Then, while setting levels for Anna, he throws ours off. We have to start over. Once again I'm running back and forth between the piano and the board, which is two flights up. By the time we restore the sound, it's 6:55, and the concert is at 7:30.

The publicity is together this time. A big banner at the university entrance reads, "Warmly Welcome American Musicians Denman Maroney and Rich O'Donnell!" People are pouring in. Backstage Debbie whispers, "It's the last time."

The 1,000 seat hall is full. People pay little attention at first, but eventually we win them over. Backstage afterward, three local musicians ask us to play *The Girl from Ipanema* with them. Rich is indignant. "We don't do that kind of thing," he says. I say to one, "Do you play piano?" He says yes. "You play," I say. Rich doesn't escape.

More pictures are taken. Among us is a man someone says is a pop star. He does act like he graces us with his presence.

As Rich packs his drums, a crowd of people in costume suddenly comes on stage to rehearse. Rich gets flustered.

Back on the bus, we think we're headed for the hotel, but no! It's time for a reception with the university president. Denman in China! A state visit! Lots of rhetoric is spouted about the value of cultural exchange and how the college aspires to be tops in its field. A woman asks why I play inside the piano. "To imitate nature in her manner of operation," I say, quoting Cage. The president admits missing the concert but says it was great.

Free at last, we dine alone at the hotel. Rich and Debbie discuss why China has so few great composers. Debbie says the Chinese were still wearing Mao suits and riding bicycles well into the Nineties, and China has been in constant turmoil for a century. I don't buy either argument. What environment is best suited to great composition?

7-3-07 @2:30

I'm up, because at 1:30 I soil myself in bed. Luckily I don't soil the sheets. I take a long bath. I can't sleep. I'm dehydrated. I'm scared. This is the fourth time I've been sick since getting back to my room at 21:00. I have to go down to the restaurant for more bottled water. It goes through me like a bucket with a hole. With what shall I fix it? Do I have cholera? Will I die in China? In the morning, to my amazement, I'm hungry. I go back to the restaurant. A man is scrambling eggs. I order some. He adds way too much sesame oil. I eat them anyway and resolve not to eat again today.

We go to the country to visit the memorial to Anna's grandfather, the founder of the foster home. We visit a 90-year-old relative who lives in a nearby hamlet with a courtyard, garden, and several barns, which turn out to be inhabited. This is poverty as grinding as we've seen. Peng Tsu points to carved wood panels that used to be gilded but were stripped in hard times.

The memorial is in a bamboo wood. The epitaph says the man was one of a long line of charitable men. I learn from Peng Tsu that his skull and thigh bones were later found elsewhere with his name carved on them. Rich says this was traditional.

Our next stop is the grave of Anna's father's grandfather's grandfather, as she puts it. It's at the foot of an embankment at the edge of a cornfield. We get mud on our shoes.

We visit the birthplace of Peng Yu's mother. It's in another hamlet, even more impoverished. A man and woman load a pile of bricks into a wheelbarrow. Another man paws listlessly through a pile of garbage. People play mahjong. Around back is a courtyard. This is it, says Peng Tsu. He points to another screen stripped of gold leaf. In the courtyard are stumps of trees cut for fire wood and a hand pump for water. A woman peers from a corner. We bow. We go to an old barn with what appears to be a loading dock but once was an opera stage. In the Forties some 500 people lived here prosperously, Peng Tsu says. When the Communists came, everything was destroyed or confiscated. Revolutionaries from the cities had no idea how to live in such a place.

We stop at a sake factory. The owner, another relative, takes the lid off a large earthenware jar and invites me to put my head in. The smell is overpowering. In one room, rice is hulled and fermented. In several others, wine is aged in jars for five years.

We go to a really wretched village for dinner. I won't eat, I say to myself, but as usual they put us in the seats of honor and set food before us, which we can't refuse.

ROCK HEMIOLAS

BRAD MEHLDAU

When I was in 6th grade, I had a band—a power duo with my best friend Bill who played drums, called The Rolling Pebbles. Bill did most of the singing, but I had a couple of vocal features, and one was *Subdivisions* from Rush. Bill and I were nuts about Rush, and that was the title track of their latest record at the time, and the first single. *Subdivisions* was the first song I played that used the odd time signature of 7/4. It planted the seed of all things "7" in my brain and I followed up much later, exploring that rhythmic meter in the jazz format with my trio.

For the non-musicians: Much of Occidental music is rhythmically written and felt in continuous groups of 2 (TUM-tum TUM-tum), 3 (TUM-tum-tum TUM-tum-tum) or 4 (TUM-tum-tum-tum TUM-tum-tum-tum) beats. Other rhythmic groupings—like 5, 7, 9 or even 11—are common in folk music from the Balkans, Indian ragas, flamenco music, and other music, but are not the norm in western classical, jazz and pop/rock music. "Odd" rhythmic meters, as they are called, do indeed crop up in those genres: 20th century composers like Bartók and Prokofiev use them, and jazz musicians like Dave Brubeck popularized them. For me though, the portal into that rhythmic world when I was ten was Rush.

The appeal of *Subdivisions* for me is the way it simultaneously has a "large" and "small" 7 feeling. (The whole song is not in 7; it switches between the odd meter and a straightforward 4/4 meter throughout—a favorite device of prog-rockers.) We could write the opening synth-bass figure that drives much of the song like this:

or like this:

How we write that should depend on how we feel the song. The figure itself is 7 beats long; so one might ask, why write it the first way? Why put two of those seven beat figures in one bar, subdividing the bar awkwardly in the middle? (I wonder if the double-entendre of the song's title was intentional on lyricist Neil Peart's part.) Why not simply let the length of the figure dictate the meter, so that it starts logically at the beginning of the bar, as with the 7/8 meter of the second example?

I myself favor the first notation, though, because it corresponds to what I'm feeling, which is two things at once. On the one hand, I'm feeling these groups of seven that continually repeat. On the other hand, I'm simultaneously feeling a larger, slower seven—I'm feeling the quarter notes of the 7/4 in the first example. That is for me what makes the groove not merely complex but also pretty fat. There is symmetry at play: The large 7 is split into two smaller groups of 7s. Because seven is an odd number, though, it must split *between* the third and fourth beat. This rub of something resembling a downbeat landing on an upbeat gives a very cool feeling in the body.

This phenomenon has a name in classical music—it is called a *hemiola* (yes, it sounds like a blood disease). Brahms loves them, and will keep them going for a long time, creating wonderful rhythmic tension. A hemiola in classical music is usually understood as a repeated pattern of four in the context of a meter of three or six—for instance, in a 6/8 meter, groups of phrases that last four beats. But it could involve more unorthodox, odd numbered patterns. One of my favorite hemiolas is at the end of Brahms' *Capriccio,* the fifth piece from the Opus 76 *Klavierstücke,* when he places five-beat groupings into the 6/8 meter:

The effect is great and full of drama, like a big wheel that has fallen off its axle, careening wildly towards some poor soul. This piece of Brahms is huge for me. It's chock full of hemiolas and 2 against 3 patterns; one could say that hemiolas are the "subject" of the piece. Note the more traditional hemiolas in groups of two as well in the right hand.

When I learned about fractions and their common multiples and denominators, I think in 3rd grade, we had rectangular blocks of different colors and different lengths. If you lined them up, two longer red ones would be the same distance as three green ones, or four shorter blue ones, etc. The fun of hemiolas is not just where the overlap, but also where they meet again, and when my teacher, Ms. Hurwitz, showed me what they were for the first time in a piano lesson, I thought of those colored blocks.

This phenomenon has a name in rock too: *Kashmir*. Led Zeppelin's classic groove on that song from *Physical Graffiti*, demonstrates why its members are truly rock gods: We usually think of Led Zeppelin as proto-heavy metal, leading the way for head-banging, but with *Kashmir* they instigated a solidly prog gesture, one that bands like Rush would expand upon, and later, prog-inspired metal bands like Dream Theater will exploit. Here is the grandfather of modern rock 'n' roll hemiolas, the vamp on *Kashmir*:

Even though drummer John Bonham plays a relentless rock beat in 4/4, no one would say that this song is simply in 4/4, because the riff played by the guitar, mellotron, etc. is in groups of three. That riff unto itself, though, is twofold: It suggests a quicker 6/8 meter, as it repeats that ostinato rhythm every six 8th notes, but also implies a larger, slower 6/4. The single D that ends each bar above is subtle but very important—it makes us feel the end of a bar; it wordlessly instructs us to feel the 3-note ostinato in groups of two, and thus ultimately hear *Kashmir* as a slow, strange 6/4. So there are really *three* implied grooves at once: the quicker 6/8 meter suggested in the figure played by the guitar, the 4/4 of the drums, and the final marriage of the two—the 6/4 as it is written above—or at least that's how I feel it.

As with Rush's *Subdivisions*, the play between quick and slow meters in *Kashmir* is a big part of its design. In both the Led Zeppelin and Rush, the drummer is holding down the fort, so to speak, providing the slower backbeat that passes over the barline, like a cement roller smoothing over cracks in pavement. This approach pays off for the same reason in both songs: Both of them shift to a regular 4/4 groove, making an actual time signature change, but when they do, there is no hiccup—the drummer is already there, grooving.

The metaphor for the feeling that hemiolas give is often one of physical motion, and with *Kashmir*, I'm led—undoubtedly by the back story of the song as well, which was inspired by a journey through Morocco—to visualize the way a camel and its rider move across a desert—slowly, stately, powerful, but with a bounce and a shake on each step, with a constant funky jerkiness that mingles with the backbeat of the camel's slow trudge.

When I went to write *Boomer* for my trio with Jorge Rossy and Larry Grenadier, which we recorded on an album called *House on Hill*, both *Subdivisions* and *Kashmir* were informing it: Jorge, a la John Bonham, plays a slower rock beat in 4 which passes through the barline and then meets up again with the quicker meter, and the 7/4 bar is split into to equal halfs of eight 8th notes, like in Rush's *Subdivisions*. Here is the piano ostinato figure of *Boomer*, the bass root-motion, and a simplified sketch of the drum beat under it:

A little more of that 3rd grade math will tell us that the first common multiple between the 7/4 meter and Jorge's implied 4/4 is twenty-eight. So it takes twenty-eight quarter-notes—or four bars, like the four bars shown here—until Jorge's bass drum cycles around to land on the downbeat of the bar, as it does on the following bar.

Larry, Jeff Ballard and I explored this idea a little further on our version of Oasis' *Wonderwall* a few years later. On that one, Jeff and I played in regular 4/4 meter, but Larry played a truncated bass line:

That line would immediately repeat itself starting on the 8th note upbeat of beat two of that fourth bar, and similarly thereafter, giving us a repeating pattern that was twenty-seven 8th notes in length, against the backdrop of the 4/4 meter. Did we all meet up eventually in the right place? I'm not even sure anymore!

PROCESS, CREATIVITY AND
PLANETARY RETURNS

JESSICA PAVONE

Process, by definition is, "a systematic series of actions directed to some end." All of the tiny rituals we perform throughout the day that enable us to accomplish anything and everything; the first things we do in the morning when we wake, how we go about feeding ourselves, cleaning our homes—these are some simple routines and practices that make us efficient in life. They are necessary for us to be functional. While some routines (brushing our teeth, doing dishes and making our beds) figure themselves out quickly, others (a yoga practice, learning an instrument, or composing music) take longer to settle into and need constant adjustment. These can take a lifetime to develop and there is always potential for deeper understanding.

Although I began playing music when I was very young, I did not begin to compose music until I was in my early twenties. I joined an instrumentalist/composers' collective that met once a week and we played each others' pieces. The instrumentation was different every week so this lent itself to composing in a very open way, which was a really great place for me to start. From there, I began to formulate clear ideas of what I wanted to hear in sound and began forming my own groups, with more specific instrumentation to compose for. I began with bowed string instruments because, having played all of them at one point in my life, they were the instruments that I most naturally understood. Fresh out of conservatory, to write music, meant to be a "composer." Feeling like I needed to be more "well-rounded" in order to truly be a "composer," the next step for me was to write beyond just string instruments. I wrote for piano, bassoon, horn section, rhythm section, sine waves. I wrote music that incorporated improvisation and indeterminacy, as well as pieces that were completely composed in western notation.

This period of trial and error lasted for years. I learned just as much from what didn't work as from what did. There were certain compositional devices that I began to favor, and after a few years of handwriting scores, I invested in music-notation software. I would sit at my desk, working for hours straight, moving through sleepless nights to find the muse, or waking up at the crack of dawn in search of the same. I would often not allow myself to take a break or think about anything else when I was "composing." My approach was rigid. My intention of well roundedness was practical. For all this hard work, I began to ask myself, is my process really just trial and error? Although those years were essential for honing my craft, there was a sweeping undercurrent of dissatisfaction that induced some intense reflection.

During the re-evaluation that followed, I pondered my deviation from string instruments. I didn't at all regret the years I spent broadening my compositional palliate. I had learned a great deal and if it wasn't for that, I wouldn't come full circle to later be reminded that my relationship to music began with a violin. Aside from my speaking voice, string instruments were and are my voice—why deny it?

Music made the most sense to me with a bowed string instrument in hand. The previous self-imposed pressure to incorporate other instruments became irrelevant. Everything was right about doing what came naturally to me. I also thought a lot about music I'd spent time with throughout my entire life, not just what I was presently giving attention to. I focused on how different musical forms resonated with me, and their purpose in my life. This allowed me to become fully aware of how different musics made me feel, what they reminded me of, how much they made me want to dream, what songs I wanted to listen to over and over. All of these observations occurred, appropriately so, during the time of my Saturn return.

According to astrological belief systems, Saturn return is something we experience between the ages of twenty-seven and thirty and its influence manifests for close to a year if not longer. This is when the planet Saturn returns to the place in the zodiac where it was at the time of one's birth. Being an outer planet situated far from the sun, Saturn takes approximately 29.4 years to make one rotation. Closer planets like Jupiter take approximately twelve years, Mars, twenty-three months. Every time there is a planetary return, a new cycle begins based on the energy themes the planet possesses. When there is a return of an outer planet, like Saturn, its significance has a greater impact on our lives because these returns happen less frequently than say, a Mars return, which happens almost every two years. Saturn brings life lessons. It is associated with restriction, limitation, and defines our boundaries. It gauges our physical and emotional endurance during hardships. During a Saturn return, we reconsider our past and devise new structure for the future.

A person's first Saturn return marks an entrance into adulthood. It is common for people to experience major life shifts around this time. Some people marry, have a child, experience their careers come to fruition, or simply understand the purpose of their lives in a clearer way. It is not always an easy ride, but most often when it is over, a person gains a new level of maturity.

My Saturn return arrived around age twenty-nine. Although it wasn't obvious at the time, the return was intimately connected to my compositional process and creative intuition. This largely had to do with Saturn's placement in the fifth house of my natal chart. A natal chart is broken up into twelve equal parts or houses. Each house bares topical significance concerning fields of life activity. The house placement for each planet in one's chart is determined by the exact time and place of birth. The fifth house in astrology pertains to creativity and self-expression. For me, that translates to music and composing. Therefore, it made sense that the energy during Saturn's return manifested for me this way, a deeper understanding of my compositional process and a clearer sense of the meaning behind the art I was creating.

During that assessment, I recognized that some of my most satisfying music-listening experiences have been of replaying the same side of a record over and over, or more intensely, just one song. The more I'd listen to something ad infinitum, no matter how simple it would seem initially, an increased depth of understanding and attention to subtle detail surfaced. Sometimes what entranced me were the words, sometimes the music, other times subtle, strange intonation or inflections.

With that type of listening, I go through a cycle with a song. One would catch my attention and be with me for few weeks. At first, I'll listen to it over and over, sometimes varying it with listening to the whole side of the record it's on. After maybe a week or so, its playtime dwindles to just a few times throughout the day, but its first play would always feels like coming home.

Eventually, the compulsive listening fizzles out, maybe because I move on to another song, or simply because I get busy and don't listen to

175

music for a few days. After a song runs through this cycle with me, it is banked in my body and becomes part of me, almost as if we're friends Many of the songs that I've had this experience with are 2 to 5 minutes long, achieving great depth in a relatively short span of time. I am attracted to the conciseness of these wonderfully crafted songs, the idea of saying a lot with a little, or only saying what is essential.

At that time, I had already been incorporating elements of folk songs to the various pieces I had been composing—utilizing verse-chorus structures and deriving chords from the voicings that fit naturally when strumming a guitar. I was also becoming interested in the idea of creating collections of songs as a body of work as opposed to isolated pieces unrelated to other isolated pieces. Taking all these things into account with my new re-acceptance of bowed string instruments, a song cycle for strings seemed like an honest artistic expression for me and was what I decided to work on. With an intention to shake my trial-and-error approach to creating, I entered this project with a much more deliberate and clarified intention. Logistically, I set out to write one song a week.

The project produced some strange routines. Almost inevitably, formulating ideas seemed impossible at the beginning of the week. Instead of "working" while sitting at my desk, I would end up sorting through piles of papers that were sitting around for weeks, even though I otherwise deemed them unimportant. Then, I'd start re-alphabetizing my records, mess around on my piano, make drawings, listen to music, etc. I'd feel quietly panicked toward the end of the day, as my procrastination prevented me from getting any music written. Sometimes, a whole day would pass with nothing on paper and I'd go to sleep feeling frustrated. But then, more often than not, the following day I would wake up, sit at my desk, and a flood of music would come out, effortlessly. Inevitably, by the end of the week, there was always a finished song on paper. This made me question whether what I perceived as procrastination was actually part of my composition process.

Rolling with this idea, I became more accepting when I'd get stuck. Rather than force myself to sit more, think more, write more, I would get up, take a shower, drop off the laundry, water the plants. I was starting to find that what I was searching for would sometimes arrive when I stepped away from the desk. I'd be washing my hair, and the next logical progression of a song would come to my head I'd go back to the desk and jot it down, elaborate on it a bit, and then maybe get up again and sweep the floor. I started to flow with the idea of working in short spurts. Not only was my apartment getting cleaner, but I was beginning to feel like the songs lived in me all week, the way my favorite songs would. I'd be out bowling with my friends and something about the ball or the pins would make me think of a chord or a rhythmic pattern. I'd be in a conversation with someone and something that was said would somehow solve a musical problem I'd been thinking about all day. This is because the work stayed with me even when I left my desk.

Working in shorter spurts matched my natural attention span, and this eventually led me to be more productive. A short attention span was something that I always struggled with. When I finally accepted and learned how to work with it, I became much more efficient. This awareness reminded me of a similar experience I had regarding practicing my viola. Once I learned better practice techniques, I could achieve in one hour what used to take me four. For me, the potential problem of a short attention span was, in the context of composing, no problem at all because that was my nature. Rather than fight it like I'd done in the past, what actually made sense was to just do what came naturally to me.

The consciousness and experiences that took shape during the time of my Saturn return helped me realize that a deeper understanding of the process in which I create is just as important as the creations themselves. Not just so that I can be efficient has a composer, but also so that my music can be a more authentic expression of myself. For me, making music is not just about the end result—it's equally about enjoying and identifying with the rituals involved in the act of creating. When I write music, I am inventing a puzzle for myself to decode. I enjoy creating the puzzle just as much as I enjoy solving it, realizing it, recording it, and playing it for others. I consider all of the music I make to be songs rather than pieces these days. This is not just because of the forms I chose to work with, but also because, even though some lack lyrics, they all tell a story. Like a musical diary, I can remember the place in my life I was at when I revisit a song. This is because they've all lived with me and are a part of me. I also recognize that although currently, this is where I am at with my creative process, it could change again. I keep a small note on the wall by my desk that says, "as long as we remain open, we continue to grow." Whether triggered by a revaluation of taste, process or a major planetary return, being open to change is important. Regardless of how my process or interests may change in time, my intention is for the music I create to be wholly integrated in my life. I'll always want my creations to live with me the way my favorite songs do.

A short list of some of the songs that live with me:

Laurie Anderson: *Sweaters*
Blondie: *The Tide is High*
Born Heller: *Big Sky #4*
David Bowie: *Queen Bitch*
Chicago: *Does Anybody Really Know What Time It Is?*
Leonard Cohen: *Two of Us Cannot Be Wrong, Tonight Will be Fine, Lady Midnight, So Long Marianne*
Electric Light Orchestra: *Can't Get it Out of My Head*
Elizabeth Cotten: *Oh Babe it Ain't No Lie*
The Cure: *Boys Don't Cry*
Dinosaur Jr.: *Freak Scene*
Bob Dylan: *Boots of Spanish Leather, Desolation Row, It's All Over Now, Baby Blue, I Shall Be Released*
Marvin Gaye: *Inner City Blues (Make Me Wanna Holler)*
Al Green: *How Can You Mend a Broken Heart*
Jimi Hendrix: *Bold as Love*
Tommy James and The Shondells: *Crimson and Clover*
Leadbelly: *Goodnight Irene*
Love: *My Little Red Book*
The Main Ingredient: *Everybody Plays the Fool*
Nirvana: *Dive, Sappy, Drain You*
Jim O'Rourke: *Memory Lame*
The Pixies: *Hey*
Iggy Pop: *The Passenger*
The Pretenders: *Show Me*
Pure Horsehair: *What It Kills To Grow In*
The Ramones: *I Want You Around, Listen To My Heart*
Otis Redding: *I'm Coming Home, That's How Strong My Love Is, Come to Me*
Smokey Robinson and the Miracles: *Save Me*
The Rolling Stones: *Wild Horses*
The Shirelles: *Baby It's You*
Elliot Smith: *Pitseleh, Between the Bars*

Sun Ra: *Chicago USA, Interplanetary Music*
The Supremes: *Love Is Here And Now Your Gone, My World is Empty Without You*
The Talking Heads: *Heaven*
The Velvet Underground: *Pale Blue Eyes*
Neil Young: *Till The Morning Comes*

OLD AND LOST MUSES

TOBIAS PICKER

Looking back forty years, it seems clear to me that in choosing to study composition with Charles Wuorinen, Elliott Carter and Milton Babbitt, I was definitely not interested in composing tonal music at that time.

I started out a twelve-tone composer. And, while I worked hard at learning techniques for disciplined composition, I worked harder at developing my own techniques adapted from the ones I'd learned from my teachers. I wanted to devise a more flexible system for myself that was at the same time twelve-tone but one from which I could wrest allusions to tonality. I was impelled in this direction by deep-seated tendencies from my earliest musical memories and training.

I began studying the piano when I was eight. That training centered on the standard 18th and 19th century piano literature given students at the Juilliard Preparatory Division in the mid-1960s. I loved all of this music and I still do—Brahms perhaps even more than anything. I listened closely to Baroque, Classical and Romantic music and I practiced that steady diet every day.

At the same time I was discovering Lead Belly, Josh White and Bob Dylan, the Beatles, the Stones and Zappa's Mothers of Invention. Such memorable albums as *Uncle Meat* and *Hot Rats* featuring *Peaches en Regalia*, the Stones' *Birthday Cake Album*, the Beatles' *White Album*— while opening my ears to a world apart from Bach, Beethoven and Brahms still kept me firmly rooted in the tonal world. The first time I heard Stravinsky was in a live televised concert with the master himself conducting. The sounds I heard made no sense whatsoever to my limited ear. I dismissed it and turned off the television. It was just noise.

When I was fifteen, my piano teacher gave me Szymanowski *Mazurkas* to study and these were my entrée into a new sound world— an escape from the endless tonality I was beginning to feel suffocated by.

Still, while technically difficult to play and written in an extended tonality, it was relatively tame stuff. "Modern music" and I did not meet again until I was seventeen and looking at composers to study with in college. That is when I first discovered Wuorinen's music and my life changed. Somehow this rich and strange music, cut across and through everything I'd ever heard and it all made perfect sense to me. His *Concerto for Cello and Ten Players* was a revelation to me.

The summer before my freshman year at Manhattan School of Music, I went up to Tanglewood to hear the world premiere of Wuorinen's *Concerto for Amplified Violin and Orchestra* played by Paul Zukovsky. I remember well how it opened with the violin sustaining (VERY LOUD) the highest E on the instrument and how that sound soared above the orchestra—above the clouds—above the heavens... As I sat there listening to this stunning and vital music, I thought I felt God Himself communicating through the music. Soon I realized that God speaks to us through all great music.

Around the time I first began my studies with Wuorinen in the fall of 1972, I read that Schoenberg had said: "There are a lot of good pieces still to be written in C Major." This vision of Schoenberg's stuck with me throughout my early years as a composition student and eventually, rather than leading me back to C major led me a half step away—to D flat major.

When I improvised *Old and Lost Rivers*, twenty-five years ago, I wasn't thinking about "being in" D flat major at all. It wasn't until some time after I'd transcribed the whole thing—with accidentals in front of every note and a million ledger lines instead of octave signs, as I'd been taught to do—that I realized it was all in D flat major. Even though I was writing something "tonal"—it's harmonic rhythm came out of the work I'd done in twelve-tone music. Each pitch was in a "class" of its own and not conceived pre-packaged in any key. And yet, the key signature came in very handy—even though it was an afterthought.

Old and Lost Rivers was an improvisation that took 3 minutes to record in real time, a few days to transcribe from the recording and it became my most performed piece.

I gave the piano version to Ursula Oppens as a birthday present in 1986, leaving it in an envelope with her doorman. Last spring when I was finishing up my Piano Quintet—LIVE OAKS for Sarah Rothenberg and the Brentano Quartet, I asked Ursula to have a look at the piano part.

It was very difficult to play and I wanted to be sure I hadn't written something technically unreasonable. As she looked at it, I was relieved that she felt it was playable but that some of the accidentals should be respelled enharmonically for ease of reading. The music was full of sharps and flats. Just a few adjustments said she would make Sarah's task in learning it a little less arduous. When we'd gone through the entire movement, I suddenly realized that it was all in D flat major! When I put in five flats, most of the accidentals went away.

The piece turned out very well. And, I thought; D flat has always been good to me.

CHAPTER 24

DREAMY BITS

GYAN RILEY

In 2001, I went to London to perform at a small festival. The entire trip had a dream-like quality to it, so much so that I often wonder if it really happened. (And the fact that I wrote about it in my dream journal doesn't clear things up much.) I flew on Halloween night, and the San Francisco International Airport was all but deserted. It was only six weeks or so after the 9/11 terrorist attacks, and apparently people were still quite afraid of flying. I was one of about twenty-five folks on the large plane heading east. That afternoon I'd had quite an unpleasant argument with my girlfriend, and as soon as the wheels lifted off the ground, I leaned deeply back into my window seat, feeling a welcome wave of peace and tranquility wash over me—all of the pre-travel stress slipping behind and below.

I had recently written and recorded a new solo guitar piece, but hadn't yet come up with a title for it. I often find that titles are difficult. Unless a piece has some sort of theme from its inception, ascribing words to it in the form of a title rarely makes sense to me, as the music tells me everything I need to know. I must have dozed off for a few hours, since it took me awhile to figure out where I was when I awoke. When I was finally able to focus my eyes, I discovered that all the clouds had disappeared to reveal a beautifully clear night. And shining in full view directly outside my window was the constellation Orion: confident, powerful and glorious, with its shimmery stars gracefully suspended from the heavens. Particularly striking were the stars in his head, like fiery eyes gazing off toward the Pleiades. I must have stared out at him for at least a half an hour, captivated by his gaze and the way he seemed to be looking perceptively into the distant future. I suddenly felt a fresh sense of confidence and inspiration to bring about positive change in my life. I decided to dedicate the new piece to my starry friend—*Eyes of Orion*.

The following evening, I opened up my performance with an Indian *alap*-ish improvisation, the general idea for which had popped into my head that morning nearly immediately after stepping out into the brisk North London air. The sound in the hall was beautifully resonant and inspiring, enhanced by a state-of-the-art ambisonic system. But not more than a minute into my performance, a prominent pounding sound rattled down from above, adding yet another spatial element to the already broad sound system. Its rhythm was steady and quite conspicuous. It seemed that the noise wasn't going to let up, so I began to play along to the rhythm of the pounding. I noticed that some people had begun to glance around, trying to locate the source of the incessant percussion. Others seemed to be just closing their eyes and swaying back and forth, as though it were an intentional and harmonious collaboration. But before long the noise subsided, and I began to wind down my improvisation. I noticed one of the staff members leaving the room, presumably to try and prevent any further pounding. If that was indeed her mission, it proved unsuccessful—as soon as I began the next piece, my faithful percussionist resumed, this time with even stronger persistence, and dead on the beat. I was amazed with their accuracy—could it be happenstance? I thought certainly they couldn't have heard the soft-timbre of my classical guitar projecting through the high ceiling. But then their pace began to accelerate, and I had no choice but to go accelerate with it. The tempo continued like a runaway train, and just when I reached my technical speed limit, the pounding abruptly stopped. I thought of the staff lady who was still gone and began to worry about her well being, wondering if the absence of the pounding was somehow connected with her absence. It was turning out to be a rather strange concert.

At intermission, I walked out into the hallway and discovered a few dozen people slowly and ceremoniously descending the stairs, all dressed in long black robes and ghoulish masks. One extremely tall and ghostly figure seemed to float rather than walk down the stairs, wearing the mask of what appeared to be a bizarrely ornamented raven head. At that moment I recalled the date: November 1, Day of the Dead, Samhain…and noticed that gently dangling from the apparitional figure's hand was a long and knotty wooden staff. They paused to momentarily hold my gaze, and somehow I got the feeling that this mysterious creature was not entirely oblivious to the concert, or of our spontaneous collaboration.

Here are a few other brief scenarios, these being of the literal dream variety:

          ✳   ✳   ✳

I was on my way to an interview and audition for a guitar professorship position. I walked through the front entrance to the building, and found myself in an old European bank, with marble floors and high vaulted ceilings. There were signs with strange names I didn't recognize pointing every which way, and in my confusion I approached the nearest teller window. A woman directed me to where I needed to go, but by the time I arrived, I noticed that I didn't have a guitar with me, and my clothes were very dirty and stained, and much too small for me. I asked a man at another teller window if there was a guitar I could borrow, but he was too busy umpiring a little league baseball game, and the kids just kept running around the bases. The interview never took place…

          ✳   ✳   ✳

Last night I met Jimi Hendrix. We were riding in the back of a van together when he produced a big brown grocery bag full of pot. Everyone seemed to agree that his pot was the best. We then stopped and some of the people went into a bath store, one where you could apparently try out any bathtub you liked, simply by running the water and pulling a rubber sheet over the top up to your neck for privacy. The store was huge, and several people were having a cocktail party in there. I suddenly remembered Jimi, and realized that he hadn't followed the crowd into the bath store. I left to search for him, and soon found him at a hole-in-the-wall taquería down the street. At first he didn't appear to remember me, but we talked a bit nonetheless. He described to me how he wanted to create a completely transcendental form of music, and that some people "do a creative thing here and there," but his whole intent was to take the audience to another place for the entire duration of his concerts. It didn't occur to me until I woke up that Jimi had died nearly thirty-five years ago. But when someone is so influential for so many people, do they ever really die? Conversely, if someone else goes through life without ever really influencing another person, were they ever really alive?

*   *   *

I was warming up late one afternoon for a house concert in somebody's living room. My program was to feature the premiere of sixteen incredibly difficult new works, one of which involved playing the guitar left-handed. I realized that I had never tried this technique before, so I busied myself with this new challenge, nervously noticing the composer sitting in a large leather armchair in the far corner sipping sherry. I was exhausted. The next thing I knew, I was waking up, slouched over my guitar, and it was dark outside. It being summertime, I knew several hours must have elapsed. Nicole had just awoken too, sitting in the front row. She mentioned that the crowd had arrived but did not want to wake me, so they quietly left. They would return the next night, she said.

*   *   *

I was on an airplane watching a movie. It was somewhat sad and not particularly memorable, and featured some well-known actors. I felt bored and about to nod off when I realized that the current scene, shot from the perspective of looking out through the windshield of a moving car, was entering the driveway at the Sri Moonshine Ranch where I grew up. I was surprised, as I never knew the Ranch was featured in a Hollywood film. As I floated up the driveway, all memory of the film receded, and I became aware that I had traveled decades into the past. The hill above the house was covered with vibrant purple lupine flowers, and the whole place shimmered with an almost underwater illumination, as if bathed in the hue of a yellowish cloud cover. The Ranch also teemed with birdlife, more than I've ever seen in a single place. There were many species I didn't recognize, and some of them curiously followed me around to the back of the house. It was then that I began to hear the music, and saw that Dad was sitting at an upright piano in the grass near the top of the house, facing away from me and up the hill. He was deeply engaged in a composition in raga Bhairavi,

186

singing and playing with his head bowed in trance-like concentration. Although I was outside and still quite far away from him, the sound was impressively loud and full, pouring out into the entire atmosphere. It was as if we were inside a snow globe amphitheater, the acoustically perfect sonorities richly reverberating throughout. I had not seen my Dad for a long time, and he was not expecting me, so I approached slowly as to not startle him. Before long the music wound down, with a long, clustery chord ringing out all the way into silence. I gently laid a hand on his shoulder, and for a moment it looked as though he was waking from the trance, his head about to turn to face me. But in the next instant he only sighed, bowing his head, and resumed playing.

As I lie in bed, the dream replaying in my now conscious mind, I wonder where my friend Solomon is. It was only two days ago that he passed away, his soul lifted from this earth, embarking on the ultimate unknown adventure. Is he traveling the world, hovering around his loved ones, as is often portrayed in films? Has his soul landed in a new bodily form? It's the great mystery, but a secret that is to him no longer confidential. Much as I can only speculate, deep down, one thing seems certain to me—that the universal tone continues…Ooooooooooommmm, ad infinitum…the music plays on…

LINES IN RED SAND

JON ROSE

A Few Neuro Fence Posts

Descartes articulated the fence *formidable* with his irreducible separation of mind from matter, subject from object, self from other, and in doing so, arguably set up the major concerns for the Enlightenment. The *thinking* homo was going to have to spend a lot of energy working through the checks and balances of separation and hierarchy; cementing the consequences of all Abrahamic religions into proof of superiority—us, lording it above, beyond, and over the riff-raff of the evolutionary also-rans, the environmental rest of (*Genesis 1:26*). Cartesian duality has recently been debunked by a number of philosophers such as John Searle. He argues that consciousness exists in the physical and chemical reality and we should just get on with it. For the irreligious amongst us (and I count myself in), the brain is the bastard child of the body, of all living things from all times—get over it! God the father is not going to help.

But try as some of our species may, duality maintains its grip through a plethora of human perception—scientific method versus artistic practice, heterosexual stereotypes, yin and yang, black and white, the two-sided battle metaphor of team sports, and despite Westminster parliamentary systems, politicians preferring to sit on the fence of public discourse.

Paul Hegarty (2007, 144) shows that although duality is trashed by philosophers, it still maintains its power in everyday thought and action. It is the basis for social structures, hierarchies, and relationships through all historical political and social trajectories. The rational mind demands "mind over matter," human control over all flora and fauna. In relevance to this piece of writing, duality demands distinctions between the personal and the public space, the theirs and ours of ownership; it demands the physical defining of friend or foe, the enforcing of the domestic and the foreign, the reciprocity of the certain and the uncertain, and the separation of the wild from the tamed.

Iain McGilchrist goes further, suggesting that the divided brain (the two physically separate hemispheres) is the root cause of the duality problem; it is, in fact, the species problem—the filter through which we perceive and create most artifacts, including the millions of miles of fences erected in the last 150 years. As he points out in the introduction to his book *The Master and his Emissary* (Yale University Press, 2009), neurologists have yet to understand why the brain evolved in two distinct hemispheres, whether in the bird, beast, or human bastard. The fence, then, is a classic metaphor for all those working at the final frontier—how the brain works and the big question, "What is consciousness?" It's also a great musical instrument.

Hold these thoughts.

The Road to the Fence

I'm a violinist, have been for fifty-four years. Gave up my classical education when I was fifteen and then, after ten years of assorted musical activities, went to work creating a *Gesamtkunstwerk* for the instrument. To put it simply, creating a body of work that would include everything on, with, and about the instrument that my imagination and skill could come up with. Part of this story included building string instruments and some radical hacking of dozens of cheap Chinese violins (The Relative Violins[1]). One investigation led to the creation of a violin that could define a piece of music in terms of distance as well as duration—with help from the inventors of the wheel (The Double Piston Triple Neck Wheeling Violin[2]). Another particular line of inquiry led me to consider what happens to the sound of strings when they get long—and even a lot longer. In the sense that Paul Klee described the process of drawing as "taking a line for a walk," so it was for me with a string. Violins appeared with very long necks, violins appeared with many necks and many strings; a number of mechanisms for string excitation were tested. By 1983 I was using fence wire to string up whole gallery spaces. Two years later, the penny dropped. Why was I making string installations when the continent that I was living on was covered with strings? That became the conceit:

1. The Relative Violins: http://www.jonroseweb.com/d_picts_rel violins_describe.html

In the late 1970s, I discovered that my instrument hacking had a genetic precedent. In a Japanese POW camp, my father had built a two-string cello and had started, optimistically, to build a piano at the request of a concert pianist. After several months' work, he had two keys and strings functioning, but then the camp was ordered to move. The beginnings of the upright piano were lashed onto the underbelly of one of the trucks after bribing the guard with a box of Red Cross cigarettes. The piano fell off en route to the new hell.

2. http://www.youtube.com/watch?v=Whj mI-it4Ig

Australia was not mapped out with millions of miles of fences; it was hooked up to millions of miles of string instruments.

Unlike the USA where barbed wire is the ubiquitous material of choice, the fence men of Australia in general go for a more economical five-wire fence, of which only one strand is barbed wire; the rest are plain wire of varying gauges and quality (the amount of carbon steel hardened in manufacture determining the resonance and purity of tone). For years, I bowed the accessible plain wire, thinking that the barbed wire was beyond excitation, indeed beyond any musical worth. Wrong[3]. In the inspirational words of T. S. Eliot, "Only those who will risk going too far can possibly find out how far one can go." Barbed wire (in good condition) turned out to be a broadband noise modulator of dangerous intensity. It also turned in exponential stepwise ascending scales (with the health imperative to be accurate) never considered in any musical language that I've come across. Barbed wire is certainly hard to control—laterally challenging, you might say. The looser the barbs, the more rattle and roll (is this *Klangfarbenmelodie* or what?). Non-violin-playing people have often suggested that the violin is a tough instrument to play because, unlike the piano, you can't see where the notes are. With the barbed wire, it becomes quickly clear where the "notes" are—and if you miss em, quite painful.

3. http://www.youtube.com/watch?v=uU ARc6ufZAk

It's an extraordinary invention dating back to the 1860s—the French and Americans still argue as to who was first. Over six hundred patented designs are registered. As a basic principle, barbed wire utilizes two strands of wire instead of one and automatically adjusts itself to changes in temperature. When heat expands the wires, the twist simply loosens, and when cold contracts them, the twist tightens, while barely altering the overall length of the wire. Quite an idea, almost beautiful. Brahms was still trying to finish his first symphony when the genius of barbed wire construction entered the history of string music.

More Life Threatening Danger?

Other unexpected sonic wonders revealed themselves over the years of fence playing. For example, some outback fences are electrified by primitive DC batteries, the power often produced by a large plastic bucket full of rotting grapefruits strategically placed by a corner post. By utilizing contact microphones and amplifying these specialized hazards, the snap-crackle-pop of DC becomes audible—the ghosts of Edison and Westinghouse haunting the Australian outback.

Most improvisers have at some time had to deal with an unsympathetic audience, or even a darn right violently aggressive one. But even a propelled beer bottle (Nickelsdorf Konfrontationen, 1988) or tossed firecracker (Exiles Gallery, Sydney, 1982) mid-performance is nothing compared to the malevolent onslaught of the Australian bush. This continent takes out a significant number in the world top ten of life threatening snakes and spiders, let alone the unrelenting wind, heat, sand, and flies that wish to inhabit any available orifice. Let us also not forget the possibility of encounters with a "salty" when on fence expeditions in the crocodile-infested northern reaches of the "Territory." The American violinist, composer, and ornithologist Hollis Taylor has been my collaborator on most of the fence expeditions since 2002. Her book *Post Impressions: A Travel Book for Tragic Intellectuals* lays bare the full implications of empirical research in the Australian bush[4]. Altercations and direct conflict with the young military men who patrol the border fences of the world's hot spots and in so doing wish to shorten your life are beyond the scope of this essay, but reports of these fence encounters are available at: http://www.jonroseweb.com/f_projects_israel_fences.html or http://www.jonroseweb.com/f_projects_mexico-usa.html).

4. Taylor, Hollis. *Post Impressions: A Travel Book for Tragic Intellectuals*, Twisted Fiddle, 2007. A book/DVD of forty fence performances, eighty-eight color plates, notation.

Rabbit Stew

Ordinarily the why questions are not useful and lead to that existential barrier beyond which it is extremely time wasting to proceed. Probably like Everest, once discovered, it's difficult to avoid the challenge of fence music. But there are other more demanding types of why when the curious start to investigate the short, violent, cockeyed colonial history that is Australia. The how, where, and when lead us to the bunny rabbits.

Thomas Austin had grown tired of shooting kangaroos on his Barwon Park property in Victoria, Australia; he wished to shoot something that would remind him of home sweet home—England. In 1886, he imported a dozen pairs of rabbits into SE Australia and thought no more about it. The rabbits did what they do so well and by 1900, millions of them were to be found thousands of miles away on the borders of Western Australia, eating their way through native flora that the white colonials had earmarked for other imported species—sheep and cattle.

The rabbits would have to be physically stopped in their tracks; government officials declared war on *Oryctolagus cuniculus*. And so it was that in 1901, four hundred men set forth from the glumly named Starvation Bay on the south coast of Western Australia. Their mission: to survey and then build a 1,200 mile long rabbit-proof fence through the outback and desert to an equally bleak place on the northern coast—Cape Keraudren. As they wired up their fence posts, they could see across the denuded plains, that it was already too late. Laboring under the humorless sun, the rabbits were happily springing into Western Australia before the fence could be finished. But this (may I remind you) was the British Empire, and so despite the hopeless, useless, pointless action plan, the project had to be completed for crown and country. And it was, in 1907. Since the rabbits were already at home inside the fence, two other rabbit-proof fences were built to contain the invader. But a total of 2,050 miles of fencing couldn't contain bunny. More distance warping fences were built, eight in all. That's a lot of fences for a state the size of Western Europe and a then population of a few hundred thousand.

By the beginning of the 20th century, fence mania was well under way in Australia (even after the gold rush, the population was still only three and a half million). *Fence-ologist* Dr. John Pickard has estimated that by 1892 there were over two million miles of fences just in the state of New South Wales, and that did not include the now famous Dingo Fence. Conceived in the 1880s to keep the wild native dog away from the sheep flocks of South East Australia, The Dingo (or Dog) Fence, at 3,500 miles long, is probably the longest fence in the world; maybe even the longest man-made anything, being twice as long as the Great Wall of China. And then between these mega fence constructions are all the station (ranch) fences—countless miles upon miles of musical instrument.

One of my favorite points on this map of insanity is Cameron Corner. It is the Mecca of fence lines in Australia. In 1880 John Brewer Cameron started walking west in a straight line along the 29th parallel, at the 141st meridian, for no really sane reason, he turned left, and kept going for an awful long time. Actually, he stuck the corner post in the wrong place, but what's a few yards in the middle of a desert? Three state border fences meet here and combine with the Dingo Fence. Cameron Corner is psychic territory that gives agency to anyone who hears voices or who doesn't believe their map. The thermometer is regularly stuck at 120 Fahrenheit in the summer months.

Quality Control

Not all fences are created sonically equal or even interesting. But as most improvising percussionists will tell you, any object that makes a sound can become musically relevant. And so it is with fences; they are sonic resources. A brand new or recently restored, fully tensioned fence will reveal a pure, almost comprehensive, accessible harmonic series when bowed—complete with 1960s style spring reverb unit. At the other end of the musical spectrum comes a rusty, rattling, collection of transient envelopes that defy category—just hit the thing! The double bass bow, with its slip-hold-slip methodology is the weapon of choice, capable of building and manipulating complex structures over time[5].

Sometimes a tapping screwdriver is the required tool from box; sometimes a primeval clutch of stones will do the simple trick. But it remains a conundrum to me just what massive amounts of tough metal a wad of tightened horsehair can excite. Unlike short strings designed to trigger a response through a resonator (e.g. violin), the plain wires of a fence become both trigger and resonator, audible sometimes for up to a mile on a well-tensioned straight section.

5. http://www.youtube.com/watch?v=_1V5zFGZnGo

Barbed wire does not have the same distance reaching resonance, but a sharp clip of a *col legno* bow stroke can set in whip-like motion dozens of loose fitting barbs, like so many miniature, independently sprung tambourines. Our species has come up with a plethora of fence design, not all of it so obviously musically user-friendly, but all of it capable of sonification.

Technique

Fence music in general is not loud (about the level of a muted violin), and the experienced use of amplification reveals yet more jingle jangle songs. I have utilized both contact microphones and electro-magnetic pickups to lift fence sound to reinforced volume levels, or on to levels of howling feedback. Cheap contact mics (bought or homemade) present the possibility of amplifying the resonating properties of wood and metal fence posts as well as the fence wires themselves, providing the piezo is kept under as much pressure as possible via the use of G-clamps and/or the weight of the fence wire, all without breaking the crystal. The main problem with using electro-magnetic pickups is that the resulting sound tends to the reductive timbral characteristics of the electric guitar—definitely not the sound of a fence.

Pretty well the whole gamut of bowing strokes can be brought into play on a fence. The traditional *détaché*, *martelé*, *portato*, *collé*, *legato*, *louré*, *staccato*, *flying staccato*, *ricochet*, *jeté* are all useful on the fence. *Tremolo* is arguably less so, as the bow needs time to snatch the wire for excitation—but still it always looks good! Over the years, a grab bag of non-legit tech-niques have offered themselves, some directly taken from my work on the violin. In classical pedagogy, the assumption is that the left hand (the pitch controller) and the right bowing arm (the tone generator) are brought together in synchronous harmony. With my autodidactic re-education, however, I set about creating independence between these two basic com-ponents of string technique. One set of chops was a kind of *on-the-spot-spiccato*, developing rhythmic patterns more akin to a drummer's training than a string player's. This area of technique lends itself well to fence music, especially when armed with a bow in each hand, which permits polyrhyth-mic bowing.

The notion of dividing a string into two sounding parts has attract-ed me since a harpsichord maker lent me a clavichord to hack around on in the early 1970s (the first thing I did was take out the damping cloth which dampens the "non-sounding" part of the string that the tangent has split). Two tones for the price of one action is very appealing in string music, where it can be a lot of work, as a novice, just to get one decent sounding bowed event. This line of investigation led eventually to two quite versatile instruments, a 10-string double violin with double bow to match, and a two-string pedal board designed to be played with the feet at the same time as *musicking* on the violin.[6]

In fact, using the feet gives the fence player the option of pitch bend by applying foot pressure to the bottom cable; wide vibra-to can also be accessed by this means. A fence set up in a gallery or factory space with the bottom cable set only an inch above the floor can give new meaning to the "walking bass" as a literal incarnation (foot as hammer-on dividing the wire). And if you wish to be paid an adult fee for your fence work, reconstructing a fence in the urban space is probably the only option; the chattering classes in general don't like

6. http://www.jonroseweb.com/g_rosen-berg_double_violin.html

http://www.jonroseweb.com/d_picts_10_string.html

to get their feet dirty in the outback.

Lateral bowing between fence posts (in effect bridges) maximizes the potential for longitudinal vibrations within the fence wire over distances of up to thirty feet, causing phasing-like effects from the bow hair and the upper partial of a 12th (or higher octave equivalent) to ring out like a ferry horn. At times, I have substituted the lateral bow with an upside-down violin. If the violin is fitted with a flat cut bridge rather than the normal concave shape, all four or five violin strings can be engaged in scordatura chord mode on the fence wire.

The sheer size of the fence as a musical instrument allows not only the finger to split the wire on a harmonic or stopped tone, but the grabbing hand, arm, knee, or body can be brought into action for stopping and muting the wires or allowing access to both parts of the divided wire. The scale of the physical components also enables a vast sonic pool of harmonic resources, unleashing piled up partials and sub-harmonic modulations through *sul ponticello* (close to fence post) and *sul tasto* (away from post) positioning of the bow(s). On some fence wires of a certain tension and length, I have witnessed phenomena that interfere with the very hold-slip-hold-slip process of the bow stroke: a kind of macro hold-slip-hold-slip superimposes itself on the fundamental bow hair action, two sawtooth wave patterns for the price of one. It's the investigative equivalent of slowing down a recording to half speed, except this is all in real time.

Fences come with such a host of impure noise-making faults and attached buzzing, pulsating, clattering, muting artifacts (brittle degraded plastic bags, cigarette packets, tires, hub caps, tin cans, dingo bones, underpants, condoms, spider webs, sign boards, stabilizing droppers, and even the remains of previous fence posts swinging in the wind); the notion of a "prepared" fence (as in the "prepared" piano) seems self-defeating and anathema to me. Humans or weather have already prepared most fences.

Pick a fence—chances are no one has played it before; never ask permission. It is significant that in all the hours or miles of fence playing, no one in Australia has approached with an aggressive posture. On the contrary, even the police know the captivating Aeolian qualities of wind-on-fence, and on one occasion at the Dog Fence near the mining town of Coober Pedy, they suggested a better sounding fence 100 miles down the road at a vacated former US military base. Warning: discussing fence music aesthetics at international border fences is asking for trouble.

Fences, Football, and Painting

The Aboriginal town of Naiuyu, about 200 miles S-SE of Darwin, presented my fence-playing partner Hollis Taylor and me with another kind of quality control. Here, half the year is "The Wet." Naiuyu is cut off, surrounded by water and crocs. In a historical paradox (one of many that pass in Australia as normality), we were invited to perform fence music at the town's annual Merrepen Arts Festival (in "The Dry"). At this Festival, the women sell their paintings and the men have a football (Australian Rules) tournament, with teams driving in from similar towns. Now the fence is the artifact by which much of Australia was stolen from the Aboriginal peoples, so to be asked to perform on a specially erected fence in the middle of an Aboriginal town, was, to invite a few white nerves.

As the three fence posts were lowered into their holes in the center of town, a group of women assembled with very troubled looks. When I asked what was wrong, they explained that the fence posts were dead and that we couldn't possibly make music with dead fence posts. Not quite up with their logic, and fearing interracial meltdown, I asked how we might solve the problem. "Them posts dead ones. Them dead posts gotta be painted up—bring 'em back to life." Everyone nodded heads in solemn agreement. We couldn't believe our luck. This seemed less like a problem and more like an intercultural bonus scheme. Tjingling, Yambeing, and Diyini took it upon themselves to bring the fence posts back to life by painting them with seasonally appropriate motives. The next day we played the scheduled concert. Then the local children played their hands-on fence music, after which the fence posts were auctioned off as art works to a commercial gallery and the cash from the sale added to the town coffers. Not a bad day's music, I thought to myself.

Mapping

A fence line is not a songline; it doesn't come close, as the imposed superstructure of European ownership makes little reference to the geographical features—maybe a river will be noticed and incorporated into the grand plan of conquest, but little else. In Aboriginal terms, land cannot be owned; the tribe belongs to the land, and they are the land's guardians through a network of kinship and totems—it's not negotiable. With that comes the function of music in the nurturing and reciprocity of the complex aural mapping. These sentient relationships have to be "sung up" to bring each and every part of the network, the massive memory bank, into existence— the continuum that verifies the mystic ancestors, the cross-species kin, the signifying stones of the perceived universe that are indelibly linked to the human component, all kept through music and dance in a living sustainable present tense. (Music without dance, or dance without music, is inconceivable). It's a tough gig, but this genealogical and aural mapping is key to knowledge. If the elder no longer knows the right song for a particular species or geographical feature, the people have not only lost that connection, but the feature/animal/ancestor no longer exists on all the necessary levels necessary for the people's survival. The songline is broken. For just over 200 years, we have stumbled and blundered around (intentionally to exploit and sometimes simply without thought), destroying these ontological links—these are the first principles of music: music embedded in sound, time, and place.

Fence music only exists as a spin-off from the industrial revolution—the mass production of steel wire and cable. You would think that industrial process would have little luck in summoning up sonic images and psycho-history of outback Australia, but you'd be wrong. Everyone gets it. No explanation is required when fence music is heard—it's the sound of the fifth continent. We are there, and it's vast ... unfathomable. It's also the sound image of Australia's internment camps where "illegal" immigrants are locked up behind barbed wire, often in remote locations. The epistemic evocations of fence music can transport you to any wide-angle panorama: to sci-fi moonscapes, to the trenches of the First World War, to the gates of Auschwitz, and even to edgy items of fashion.

Redeeming Moments

There are compensating features in the practice of fence music, apart from getting unhealthy musos (musicians) more out and about. It may not ever attain the spiritual connection to land that indigenous Australians developed over more than 40,000 years; that's unlikely to happen again, short of the deinvention of electricity, but here are some thoughts. First, revealing beauty in inherently ugly structures does find a function for music that could be considered worthy. Secondly, the notion of instrument as conduit to the land could have currency.

Performing on fences places the musician in an area where terrain, map, score, and instrument are physically connected and signified, if not interchangeable—the map of the fence marks out (on a scale of 1:1) the geographical entity of itself. The distance and regularity of fence posts determine pitch fundamentals, although sometimes these underlying frequencies are at the edge of our hearing range—a slow, earth-bound, sub-harmonic rumble. The audible degree of harmonic series that is available indicates condition and state of tension within the instrument. The nodes on a fence wire correspond proportionally to any string instrument. The midpoint between the posts (the bridges of this chordophone) give the performer the octave; split that distance in half and you have the second octave, and so on in true Pythagorean proportional logic, on through all the scientifically proven partials—into the world of just intonation[7]. My personal aesthetic is predisposed to leaving any fence in its initial condition—I never consider tuning (in the broadest sense of tuning—for function as well as pitch)—so it's the sonically unknown *objet trouvé* that attracts. This music can only be conjured into existence (can only be produced) by standing on that piece of the land on which the instrument exists. As the real estate man says, "location, location, location."

7. Colleague and friend Ellen Fulman has spent decades exploring just intonation systems and relationships with her Long String Instruments. http://www.ellenfullman.com/

Despite the ruthless inevitability of fence posts positioned across the plains, temporality will remain a feature of fence music. A well-built fence will give you ten years of optimum musical instrument and at least thirty years of a standing although sonically failing artifact; after that, gravity eventually wins. Even if fence post entropy takes its time, the wire is the first thing to go, eaten by the countless salt lakes that colorfully pockmark the continent's surface. Geography determines history. It is now illegal in Australia to build a fence using wooden posts. Quite simply, the colonial fence-building spree ripped the eucalypt forests asunder, and they have never recovered. New fences with metal posts will survive Australian conditions for even shorter durations than the harvest from the pioneer's folly. However, the original hardwood posts are made of stern stuff, and all across Australia the casual observer can note the wireless, silent ghosts of fences on salt pans, the traces of white man spooking the horizon.

According to some *Homo sapiens*, our present demise (or overwhelming global triumph!) is due to the domination of the grasping, language-based left hemisphere of the brain over the holistic right hemisphere. Why do we have a divided brain anyway? We find ourselves now in a situation, maybe too late, where we are trying to reconnect with an animate planet full of beings, whether flora or fauna, that we have treated as "not us" and trashed to the edge of extinction. OK, it's time to get away from the misanthropic tendency, or is it?

More Struggles

Assuming you have a well designed and inaugurated musical instrument strung up, is that all the maintenance required? Unfortunately not. The Dingo Fence employs over 200 men to keep the construction in top condition. It's an impossible task as fences move—a lot. On the stretch south from Cameron Corner, the Dingo Fence lines up with huge red sand hills. The fence is always in a state of being pushed over and buried, and needing to be dug out; or the wind is blowing away the sand in which the fence is footed, leaving said fence waving around rather forlornly in mid air and requiring a forced gravitational lowering back to terra (less than) firma. In conversation with Len in 2004, the district manager and fence runner responsible for this section, he spoke of the eternal struggle against the dunes, in heroic terms of last-ditch stands, man versus nature. Len's voice was dry, as if sand had permanently lodged in his throat, as he described the drought conditions—"bloody hell!" he gasped between every sentence.

Maintaining this musical instrument is an expensive proposition, but still considered a worthwhile one. Floods send debris against the Fence, which takes a toll. The enemy can have a detrimental effect. Despite the ur-utility of many Australian fences, rabbits burrow straight under, weakening the wooden posts and causing soil erosion. Emus, in their desperate search for water, fracture the bottom wires with their iron toes. Kangaroos and feral camels travelling at full speed can fail to see the rabbit-proof mesh, punching huge holes as they crash into it. Wild pigs and dingoes push and squeeze their way through the barest of openings. There's plenty of punishment for the fence: wear and tear as compositional structure.

The violin is an awkward and perverse instrument to play in terms of its physically demanding contortions. The fence by comparison can be plain exhausting. Apart from *Musca Vetustissima's* interest in fresh flesh[8], the fence's sheer bulk requires some getting around, climbing over, exploratory walks up and down, and schlepping of PA gear if a human audience is expected. Post outback performances often witness the musicians heading back to the truck in quite a wrecked state, seeking neutral sanctuary.

The Fence is an open system instrument. Unlike a contained system like a violin, where there is a high degree of reliability in the sense—that if you repeat an action exactly, the resulting sonic event should sound much the same on each repetition—the fence is just not like that. Once interfered with (i.e. played, excited), the fence does not return to its former state of equilibrium. In fact, it exists in a state of continuous transformation. Nodes have a habit of moving incrementally up and down the wires as the posts are disturbed, impurities in the cheap fence wire declare their authenticity at irregular intervals, "droppers" beat to their own tune and can be relied upon not to do "that thing that worked so well in rehearsal," and if your colleague starts bowing the same wire as you, there *will be* issues.

8. Along with music, the origins of dance tend to be lost in the mists of time. But we can surmise that dance punctuated the various critical parts of our ancestors' lives such as birth, death, marriage, the arrival of something good to eat, the return of the warriors, etc. I would like to add to this list of fundamentals that dancing is a time-honoured method of keeping the flies at bay, hence the expression "no flies on him" for someone who can dance fast enough. It seems clear to me that here in outback Australia the Aborigines have been dancing for over 40,000 years not only for religious ceremony or because it keeps you fit but because of the flies.

Bogged down for two days as we are in our less than hermetically sealed four-wheel-drive, we pass the time killing as many flies as possible—mostly using the splat technique. But eventually one is forced outside the defensive ramparts to attend to the calls of nature (becoming more frequent, I'm afraid, the longer we are trapped here).

Leaving the car is not a major problem. The manoeuvre is carried out with precision and with an element of surprise. They are just not ready for that car door to suddenly swing open and a fly-netted warrior to leap forth with an angry cry. As the door slams shut, perhaps ten flies in the front line get in, more by accident than battle campaign design. Getting back in, however, presents a formidable problem. After a matter of seconds beyond the keep, one is covered with hundreds of flies. Looking at my arm, I see there is no landing space left on my airport; the next wave circles above in a holding pattern, genetically programmed to know that wherever their mates are, there must they also be.

Community Music

"In the best of all possible worlds, art would be unnecessary …the audience would be the artist and their life would be art." —Glenn Gould[9].

Well, in our only possible world, we have already reached the time where the professional musician has lost his function (as indicated by worth) in western society; the

9. Gould, Glenn. "The Prospects of Recording" in *Audio Culture: Readings in Modern Music*, Continuum, 2007.

eradication of specialised roles is not so much the prerogative of art as it is a result of technology and hard-assed economics. Everyone these days can slip past quality control and invent themselves as a filmmaker, a journalist, or a composer through the mixing, cutting, and matching of sound files—all positions vacant, only the unskilled need apply. But I suspect that online communities cannot really replace the close proximity of an integrated social group (as you might find in a small town in outback Australia), anymore than improvising musicians are totally satisfied with an intercontinental Skype concert—it might be of passing sonic interest, but in the final analysis, the animal requisites of physical proximity are missing.

In many non-western societies, there is no word for music—the vital integral *content* of its transmission deemed more important—the antithesis of Marshall McLuhan and his medium as message. Our current take-it-or-leave-it music culture might be comfortable and palatable to consume, but its transformative power compares unfavourably to earlier (pre-enlightenment?) praxis.

Fence music does lend itself to the visceral and the community. In fact, I have often suggested that fence playing should be a national pastime, if not the official music of the modern state of Australia—outside of the indigenous traditions, pretty well everything in the mainstream is an import. Normally there is a long pause after this suggestion, followed by an unsure laugh as to my sanity.

It's very rare after a fence performance in front of a small group of *Homo sapiens* (other species are always present although not necessarily engaged with the art) when someone doesn't come up at the end and reminisce about a time in childhood when they tapped out rhythms on the fences around the homestead. Fence playing can be that simple, or can incorporate the kinds of chops picked up from a lifetime of avant-violin playing. There is, however, a big jump from the fringe to the unmotivated community. Let's face it, outside of the Arab Spring, a community event normally means people standing around shooting video on their iPhones.

How to get back into the castle without bringing a battalion of them with me? Dance. I'm not at this stage suggesting a waltz or foxtrot—I'm recommending something post-Sarah Bernhardt, post-Martha Graham, post-Pina Bausch, post-contact improvisation, first-past-the-post dance. No, I'm indicating here total unrestrained free form, maximum waving around of arms, jumping up and down, running this way and that, and the occasional loud scream. Don't worry, the flies are fast learners, they pick up on your moves quickly. You have to invent new moves all the time, or it gets boring for them. However, flies are never bored to death—they like death, the smell of death, the smell we will all have one day when we buy the farm. By creating total confusion you get one chance, when you are about two feet ahead of the pursuing army, to open the door and jump in. This must be done in one move; otherwise, all is lost, and you have a carful of flies.

The dance-and-in method works about 65–70%, which means you will spend the next two hours hunting down 200–300 flies. Oh, I nearly forgot the prisoners. The fly net is never 100 percent fly-proof, not if you want to breath and see without choking to death. So, carefully take off the net, sealing the hole quickly. You have perhaps twenty to thirty prisoners caught while infiltrating your perimeter. Slowly screw up the fly net and place it on the dashboard; a pleasure as old as life itself wells up inside you as the entrapped little shits make their last twitching free-form gestures (Taylor, ibid., 160).

201

Later this year, I will attempt to get the inhabitants of White Cliffs, New South Wales (population currently eighty-four, according to the town postmistress) to play a particularly sonorous fence on their approach road. We'll see what happens. Significant is the fact that the nearest town of any size to White Cliffs is the former mining rush of Broken Hill. In 1912, it was home to no less than thirteen brass bands and a town orchestra. Broken Hill, as with many other regional towns, was historically alive with home-made, do-it-yourself music until quite recently. These days, there is just a single brass band, one with a depleted line up. When I worked with them on a piece for the Melbourne Festival a few years back, a senior tuba player remarked to me that it used to be a "professional outfit." I think he may have been referring to the attitude of the musicians, because I'm sure all the bands used to be staffed by union members who worked for their living in the mines; to belong to the union band, as well as ensuring a functional *Gebrauchsmusik*, was a privilege and honor. I'm not sure that writers on music such as Attali really get this; I hear it as both sides of the paradigm that was colonial society[10].

I started this section with a quote from a pianist. Here's something from another pianist, Oscar Commettant:

10. Attali, J. Noise. *The Political Economy of Music*, Manchester University Press 1985.

"I do not believe there is a country in the world where music is more wide-spread than in Australia. Certainly there is none that has more grand pianos per head of population. 700,000 instruments have been sent from Europe to Australia since the vast territory became a centre of white settlement. Everywhere here the piano is considered to be a necessary piece of furniture. Rather than not have one of these sonorous instruments in the drawing room …they would go without a bed.

"…Custom demands that there be at least one piano in every Australian home; even in the most distant shacks, away from the centre of population, the humblest farmer will have the inescapable pianos. Way out in the country they are not very expert in music, and the piano that adorns the humble dwellings will be cheap and nasty…constantly going wrong, but the main thing is that they look like a piano, with vulgar moulding and ostentatious double candle-brackets; they make a noise when you strike the keyboard, and often that is all that is required[11]."

11. Commettant, Oscar (1890/1980). *In The Land of The Kangaroos and Goldmines*, Adelaide: Rigby, 136–137.

The figure of 700,000 imported pianos by 1890 is unsubstantiated, but musicologist and researcher Alison Rabinovici has sent me the records of piano imports from just the Port of Melbourne Authority, and it is certainly several hundreds of thousands of imported and locally manufactured pianos by the first decade of the 20th century.

Otherness Along the Fence

Although the fence is a recognized force of negation, well over 30,000 miles of exploration have led me to exciting domains of *musicking*, including chance meetings with original artists whose work almost guarantees omission in any book on Australian music. They play what could loosely be described as folk music, but folk music is accepted as part of the mainstream culture, so it can't be that. I'll relate just two examples, one from our species and one from another.

Auntie Roseina Boston is a Gumbayungirr elder from the Nambucca Valley. She was born under a lantana bush on Stewart Island. Her Aboriginal name is Wanangaa, which was given to her by an Aboriginal elder and means "stop" (she's still hyper at 77 years old). Due to an early demonstration of facility, she was given by her uncles a special dispensation to play the gumleaf, which is traditionally a male preserve. Her grandfather's brother Uncle George Possum Davis was well known for his Burnt Bridge Gumleaf Band in the late 1800s to the early 1900s.

So how does Auntie Roseina sound on her gumleaf? With that wide vibrato, this free reed instrument reminds me of the soprano saxophone of Sydney Bechet. Her repertoire consists of an impressive range of birdcall mimicry, popular songs, and hymns.

Gumleaf playing may well go back thousands of years. According to musicologist Robyn Ryan[12], it was documented first by pastoralists in 1877 in The Channel country of Western Queensland. The gumleaf was used by Aborigines in Christian Church services by the beginning of the 20th century and reached popularity in the Great Depression of the 1930s when the desperately unemployed formed 20-piece Aboriginal gumleaf bands like Wallaga Lake, Burnt Bridge, and Lake Tyers and, armed with a big Kangaroo skin bass drum, marched up and down the eastern seaboard demonstrating a defiance in the face of the whitefella and his disastrous economic hegemony. The

12. Ryan, Robin *A Spiritual Sound, A Lonely Sound: Leaf Music of Southeastern Aboriginal Australians*, 1890s–1990s. PhD thesis, Monash University, Clayton, 1999.

Wallaga Lake Band played for the opening of the Sydney Harbour Bridge in 1932. This is the New Orleans jazz of Australia, and it has completely vanished or been "disappeared."

As is common with Aboriginal peoples, Auntie Roseina is a polymath and all-around artist. You cannot enter her world without taking on her total continuum—her storytelling, dreamings, dog, gumleaf, copious collection of shells and badges, and paintings—punctuated by her constant refrain: "It's beautiful!" (For a transcription of one of Auntie's stream of consciousness raves, go to The Australia Ad Lib Site[13].)

My further example of "other" belongs to the species *Canius lupus*, although Aboriginal peoples have many names for the dingo, depend-

13. http://www.abc.net.au/arts/adlib/stories/s914726.htm

ing on what action the dog is actually doing (before white settlement in 1788, it is estimated that there were over 600 Aboriginal languages and distinct dialects, now there may be fifty, of which only a few dozen are in first language use). The dingo is a relatively recent immigrant in Australia and has probably only lived here for 6,000 years.

14. Dinky and Jon Rose improvising together at Jim's Place.

http://www.youtube.com/watch?v=mr0SGd4qChY

Dinky[14] could be the envy of most struggling musicians that I know: he works five to seven nights a week. At Jim Cotterill's Roadhouse, just south of Alice Springs, Dinky packs 'em in, entertaining bus and carloads of tourists from around the world. The hardline view might be that Dinky is yet another exploited species, while the anthropomorphic view frames the dingo as cute pet. My examination of Dinky is that he is neither; music is his primary means of communication and expression. He is a fellow musician (albeit from another species) making the most of what fate has served him up. Dinky's parents were exterminated, not by the Dingo fence, but by the particularly heinous and widely distributed poison sodium monofluroacetate (known popularly as 1080)—banned in most countries except Australia.

An entry in Wikipedia describes how the poison works on the carnivore's last twenty-one hours:

"…excessive salivation; abrupt bouts of vocalization; and finally sudden bursts of violent activity. All affected animals then fall to the ground in teranic seizure, with hind limbs or all four limbs and sometimes the tail extended rigidly from their arched bodies. At other times the front feet are clasped together, clenched or used to scratch …This tonic phase is then followed by a clonic phase in which the animals lie and kick or "paddle" with the front legs and sometimes squeal, crawl around and bite at objects. During this phase the tongue and penis may be extruded, their eyes rolled back so that only the whites show and the teeth ground together. Breathing is rapid but labored, with some animals partly choking on their saliva."

Dinky's sonic vocabulary is based on melismatic contours spanning about one and half octaves. He is extremely *loud*, with a projection that today's batch of over-boiled opera singers would do well to study. Dinky has an intuitive understanding of phrasing. It's uniquely his thing. My partner Hollis Taylor and I accompanied him in two quite different genres of music to see what he would make of the material. One piece was a Lutheran hymn (quite common to Central Australia). The dog placed his lazy glissandi firmly in the cracks between the black and whites of the piano and phrased impeccably. Dinky had decoded the diatonic nature of the music immediately—easy stuff. Then I tried some free improvisation. The canine coloratura was a little suspicious at first, but within a minute he got the idea and by the end of the session, he was trading phrases like an old paw (sorry). Like all those performing in an oral tradition, Dinky has the odd cliché—he ends every piece with a little endearing sigh—it seems that he has to have the last word. Dinky also likes to be physically connected in his art form, hence his preferred position actually standing on the keys of the piano. It's his territory. This does reduce the comfortable options for the pianist, but how often do you get the chance to immerse yourself in interspecies music? (Taken from The Australia Ad Lib web Site[15].)

15. http://www.jonroseweb.com/f_projects
_australia_ad_lib.html

Final Post

What began as an occasional diversion and deviation from improvising on the violin has led me to out of the way geographical places and metaphysical spaces of contemplation. The fence project started simply as conversion of material into sound. It was a few years before I looked up and glimpsed the ramifications of what I was tangling with. The contemporary world of culture is all flotsam and jetsam; our lost tribes have created a rootless megaculture—some of it very seductive, even brilliant. I relish cultural collision too. But our brains still demand to function within basic ancient principles of duality and hierarchy that are corporally and environmentally based. Seems to be no way to climb over that.

Gary Scott owns a sheep station that butts up against the Rabbit Proof Fence in Western Australia. One day after he'd heard me play the fence, we stood looking at the red sand on both sides of the fence—irreducibly the same material we agreed, beyond argument. Then Gary said:

> "All of a sudden, you're stepping over this line, and it's a little bit more remote or something, there's bad things out here—that's what this Fence is about, you can feel it as you go through the gate, you're sort of stepping into somewhere different, crossing over; a fence can change your feeling, where it's actually not my lease and I'm outside the Fence, it really feels like you're in the middle of nowhere."

Jon Rose and Hollis Taylor playing a fence on The Strzelecki Track, Australia, 2004.

TO A GATHERING OF PERCUSSIONISTS

STEVEN SCHICK

Gathering.

It's such a beautiful way to describe what we aim to do here.

I imagine you assembled out there, young percussionists like so many I have met over the course of nearly forty years of making music. You gather in my imagination like a corroboree, a composite of my individual memories of you. For the most part you don't know each other, but I know you and think of you often. I think of meeting you in Sydney on my first, idealistic trip as a guest of the Synergy percussion group in Ultimo. Or, I remember you from one of a hundred of master classes I've given to college-aged percussionists in Albuquerque or Dartmouth or the Manhattan School of Music or the Regional Conservatory in Paris. You've been there to say hello after concerts from Taipei to Sao Paulo. I hear from one of you at least weekly in an e-mail that asks about mallet choice in *Psappha* or set-up in *Six Japanese Gardens*. Our encounters have made a deep impression on me. With how many of you have I ridden from a regional airport to your university and talked for 30 or 45 minutes about career choice or graduate school? I remember meeting dozens of you at the Chopin Academy in Warsaw on a 1989 tour to Eastern Europe. You drove through the pale white night of mid-June to arrive exhausted and optimistic in the bright sunlight of a pristine Polish morning. You came with questions; I came with new music to share. And now I have assembled you here in my mind for a serious and in-depth conversation.

Yes, I imagine that "gathering" is just the right word for what we are doing. "Conference" has the unseemly air of academic heaviness. "Convention" brings with it the baggage of commercialism. Even "conversation" seems wrong, too little and too light for an evaluation of where we are and where we want to be. But "gathering" seems just right: a coming together, a confluence of energies. It is a term of optimism and of sharing, which are qualities perfectly suited to this moment in the history of the percussive art. Now that we are here, what will we talk about? Nothing less than the state of our art, which is another way of saying the state of our lives! What will follow are my thoughts and my questions. To the extent they overlap with your thoughts and questions, then I will take pleasure in our common cause. But if they don't, well, you know how to reach me[1].

Now that we are gathered, let me start by introducing myself. My name is Steven Schick, and I am a percussionist.

1. sschick@ucsd.edu

But before I was a percussionist I was a farm boy. I grew up in a small farming town in Iowa in the United States. That town, Clear Lake, is as far from the great cultural centers of the world as it is possible to be. Clear Lake is not New York, Tokyo, Paris, or Vienna. It's not Brisbane or Florence. It's not even Des Moines. When I was a boy I believed certain things to be true about the world. I believed them strongly enough that they formed an unshakeable view. The world I knew then could be constructed—it could be grown, literally—within a tightly bounded spiral of laws governed by seasons and weather, work and sacrifice. The beauty of farming is that at the center of a fenced square of dirt lies the remarkable freedom to grow whatever can be grown. The land may be limited in its size and shape, but what can be grown there is nearly infinite. The world I now know as a musician is remarkably similar to that. Musical freedom is also to be found at the center of set of meaningful limitations. These limitations may be the tightly scripted set of rules set forth by the scripture of the score, or they may reside in the more flexible framework of an improvisational context. However one constructs one's limitations though, in music as in farming art is propelled by the friction between structure and freedom, between the fixed and the flexible, between where we are and what we are doing there.

I would like to tell you that I have always seen this. I would like to begin by telling you a mythical story about how I arrived at a life in music based on the rules of the earth. But that would not be true. No, when I was old enough to leave home I simply left, and turned my back on the farm with its sundry promises of a future in the dirt and a life at the mercy of the elements. I left home to study music.

I became a percussionist by accident because that was the decision my mother had made for me. And who doesn't become a percussionist or clarinetist or organist through some kind of odd accident? I was at dinner recently with the wonderful percussionists of "So Percussion." We were drinking "Lime Rickeys" and eating Korean food on the Upper West Side of New York City when we started swapping stories of how we and our friends became percussionists. Somebody became a percussionist because he was in a group of friends and as one raised his hand when the music teacher asked who would like to play the drums so did all the rest. Sticking with your friends seemed like a pretty good reason to play the drums to us. Another thought he was signing up to play trumpet but got in the wrong line and became a drummer by mistake. So like nearly everyone else, I became a percussionist by a pure stroke of luck. My mother checked the box next to "drums" because the school didn't require the drummers to buy a drum, just the drumsticks.

In a second fantastic stroke of luck I began my studies of percussion at the University of Iowa in 1973 at a time when the university was in full creative swing. A Rockefeller Foundation grant in the mid-1960s made Iowa City a magnet for all kinds of innovative artists. There was a thriving "Center for New Music"—the concert I attended on the day I arrived at the university was of William Parsons and James Avery playing Karlheinz Stockhausen's *Kontakte*. The Writer's Workshop had been spearheaded by the poet John Berryman and Kurt Vonnegut. Vonnegut was still living in Iowa City when I showed up. We used to see him eating breakfast or lunch in the student haunts. And, everyone knew where he lived. When the light was on in the bay window of his Victorian house on Dodge Street—reportedly his writing room—a crowd of want-to-be-writers and hangers-on, occasionally including the stray percussionist, gathered below in hushed reverence.

That period, the early 1970s, was also the moment, more or less, when the academic percussion world developed a sense of itself as a community. In essence percussionists of many different disciplines looked at each other and saw their similarities more clearly than they saw their differences. The ability to recognize similarity within a large and turbulent world of diversity underwrites the very notion of community and has paved the way for large gatherings of percussionists like PASIC (the Percussive Arts Society International Convention) and even smaller events such as the imaginary corroboree we are enjoying here. This commonalty set the stage for the third great stroke of luck: my discovery of the "Great

Problem." The Great Problem consisted of my attempt to cultivate an unexplored region wedged between two relatively known areas. One of the known areas was "percussion," an increasingly unified set of practices, and the other was "music," as I knew it at the time, a collection of pieces by mostly male, mostly dead, mostly European composers. The Great Problem as I saw it was to explore and expand the unknown ground between "percussion" and "music." There was an enormous imbalance—I see that it's still there—between a rich source of sounds created by literally thousands of percussion instruments coming from every corner of the world—and a serious repertoire in the realm of contemporary percussion music that numbered fewer than a couple of dozen truly worthy pieces. Count them for yourselves: in the early 1970s we had *Ionisation, Zyklus, The King of Denmark, Amores, Interieur,* and a bare couple of handfuls more. We had "percussion" and we had "music." The Great Problem was that we needed "percussion music."

Remarkably, one of the first things I learned in Iowa City was that not all composers were dead. As a kid, I knew the famous names from the past, and not knowing any living composers, nor even being able to conceive of a living composer, I briefly feared that there was something very dangerous about the composition of music. Why else, I wondered, would they *all* be dead? But discovering living composers in Iowa City, including my classmate David Lang, who has become a lifelong friend, was revelatory. There are many ways of making new music, but for my part creating percussion music has meant commissioning new works. Therefore only a few years removed from the farm, I willingly re-entered a remarkably similar world in which friction between the known and unknown governed everything. In the realm of percussion music this meant balancing the concrete, rational, and permanent qualities of a newly composed musical score with impermanent and often intuitive interpretations of that score. Again I was seeking the inevitable friction between the bounds of form and the freedom of choice. Between *the* world and *my* world.

Let me pause here in the interests of accuracy: I was certainly not the first nor only percussionist who saw the need to commission new music for percussion instruments. The many pioneers in our field are well known to us precisely because they commissioned or championed new work. Some of them are good friends—Michael Askill who participated in many of the Australian premieres of classic percussion pieces and Fritz Hauser the great

Swiss percussionist. I also think of Christoph Caskell and his ground-breaking performances of Stockhausen's *Kontakte* and *Zyklus*, which are some of the earliest pieces of western solo percussion music. There is Jan Williams as champion of the percussion music of Morton Feldman, Robyn Schulkowsky—a classmate of mine in Iowa City—and her advocacy of Kevin Volans, William Winant with John Zorn and others. And of course there is Sylvio Gualda, to whom we all owe a great debt as an interpreter and champion of the music of Iannis Xenakis, a gifted teacher and a true artist who still lives in a world of pure music. There are others: Amadinda, friends whom I met at the Darmstadt Summer Course in the early 1980s; the great Mexican group Tambuco, also old friends. The Percussion Group Cincinnati, So Percussion, *Les Percussion de Strasbourg* and many others. We are brothers and sisters in important ways. Our debt to these artists and others can never be repaid. It is to them and not to concert presenters, instrument makers, or professional organizations—however worthy they may be—that we owe the vitality of our art.

I always was and still am a bit player in a large historical moment. I moved forward not along a carefully plotted path but by blind reckoning. Starting by working with composers I knew and respected, I commissioned new pieces. At the same time I set out to learn existing pieces that spoke to me. I worked one side of the problem against the other. I knew what music was (or thought I did), but had a less clear vision of the future of percussion. Thus I was guided by more by music than by percussion. I loved Brahms and Stravinsky and Stockhausen and Beethoven and Varèse. My initial interests in new percussion music were therefore in passionate, complex works that leaned towards the virtuosic. My first real commission, beyond the work I was doing regularly with fellow students at the University of Iowa, was to Charles Wuorinen in 1979 for his *Percussion Duo*. This commission represented a lot of money to me at that time. I owe the existence of this fine piece to my former wife Wendy who took me by the hand and led me (on cold feet) to the bank where we withdrew half the money we had in the world and handed it to Wuorinen. Following that I commissioned solo pieces from Kenneth Gaburo and from David Lang. Later came commissions to Brian Ferneyhough, Roger Reynolds, and John Luther Adams, along with the American premieres of Xenakis, Kaija Saariaho, and others.

I recite this list not to document my *bona fides* as a contemporary percussionist, but to show you how I conceived of new percussion music. I saw each piece as a stone laid along a path towards a meaningful and complex musical experience. A meaningful and complex experience with a piece—both by me as interpreter and by an audience—was the Holy Grail to me. Complexity was important because it provided multiple pathways of perception to a listener and required skill and patience from the performer. I wanted both!

Gradually I began to conceive of these new percussion pieces as vessels to be filled with music. The dichotomous rapport between container and the energy that fills it seems, now so many years later, to be the same thing as a field and the life that fills it. By embracing a binary structure of equivalencies—that is to say a vessel and its contents, a piece of music and the experience of that piece, a field and its crop—I also embraced the ultimate binary in which a performer's and composer's contributions were equivalent. I never subscribed, and still do not, to a view in which the composer's contribution to music is lasting and spiritual, while the performer's is workmanlike and transitory. In new percussion music, the energy and intelligence that fills a piece at the instant of its performance is indivisible and belongs properly to both. Every conversation I have had with a composer about a new piece of music, now numbering in the hundreds, was some kind of variation on the theme of a deeply interconnected binary relationship consisting of discrete but equivalent rights and responsibilities. When this conversation is fruitful a worthy piece results, when it is not we go our separate ways.

My conversations with composers in advance of a commission almost always drift towards an understanding that a new percussion piece consists of a dynamic interplay between a contained space and the dynamic questing energies that fill it. This was hardly a new idea—the aesthetics of the late 18th century onwards were built on similar ideals. In percussion music, as I had done as a lover of orchestral music, I allied myself with the fundamental musical-social equation of the Enlightenment. This is found most easily in the late symphonies of Mozart and the early ones of Beethoven: that great music is aspiration in the face of struggle; that great music is the most immediate and potent form of social currency; and that it not only can but must change lives. And adding another dichotomy I learned from Takemitsu, that great music is by definition both joyous and melancholy. Anyone who sees great classical music as property of the Elite, the enfeebled soma that is served up with dinner at an up-scale restaurant, has never really listened.

Over time my alignment within this equation has meandered. In my student years, in line with my affinities above, I was more attracted to the energetic contents of the vessel than I was to the vessel itself. The pieces that I commissioned and chose to play show that clearly: Lewis Nielson's *Connections and Moments* and Stockhausen's *Aus den Sieben Tagen* are examples. Later after my long exposure to Xenakis and in particular to *Psappha* I began to see the huge Bernoulli multiplier to be found in the formal aspects percussion music—that the more constrained the vessel and the narrower the aperture to the outside world, the greater the pressure of the energy contained within it. If you want to experience this in real-life terms open the tap on a garden hose and look at the accelerated rate of flow as you close off the end with your thumb. In the end I never became the formalist that some of my friends became but I have a healthy respect for the salutary contributions of boundaries.

The fluid, plasmic aspects of music—the energy within the vessel—demonstrate repeatedly that it is the most ineffable and fragile of the arts. Sculpture, painting, and even writing have gravity. They are *things*, things that you can literally hold in your hand, things that have edges and content and are made with the concrete materials of canvas, paper, or clay. But music is weightless. It seems to have no edges and as for material, well...clap your hands and hear for yourselves. There it is: sound. It rests in your hand for an instant then is gone forever. And yet to this weightless and most fleeting of arts, this "un-thing," we attach enormous emotional weight. It is moving to me that for all of our materialism we humans ultimately give greatest value to the least concrete of the arts. We love music not in spite of but because it vanishes, just as we love our fleeting and rapidly vanishing lives. So is it a wonder to you that I began to value the complex energies of performance? Is it a wonder that I value the experience of music above a piece of music?

I have referred a few times to the complexities of performing percussion music, but you will note that I have given only vague definitions of the term complexity. Complexity is, well, complex! We can know a few concrete things though: Complexity is not a question of musical style and it certainly is not a synonym for complicated. Maybe complexity is like falling in love or the early stages of the flu. It's hard to describe but you know it when you have it. I can tell you this: for me complex music means the presence of open options and a resistance to category. It means that we are faced with choices rather than a controlling script. As a side note, I try to embrace the same philosophy of openness in my teaching. I try very hard not to tell my students anything concrete or categorical. I do not tell them what I think they should be playing or recording. I want them to walk the length of their own fields not mine.

But a new problem has arisen—one that challenges the inherent openness of musical complexity in percussion music. Perhaps we are victims of language, but when you name something it becomes some "thing" whether you like it or not. Now, eighty years after *Ionisation* and nearly fifty years after *Zyklus*, "contemporary percussion music," a veritable mother lode of the complexity, has become a well-defined genre. There is a repertoire, performance practice, recordings, books, signature mallets, and academic programs. Complex percussion music has become to some large extent classical percussion music, respectable and acceptable in the mainstream, and many of us have helped make this so. Much of this is welcome and all of it is inevitable, but we should be careful of what we wish for. With every step towards respectability we have taken a step away from the beautiful ineffability of the original. And with every step we have lost a bit of the inherent friction of complexity when the freedom of creation rubs against the constraints of form. The beauty of a Great Problem is slowly becoming the flatness of an everyday dilemma.

Our dilemma—that we are rapidly de-complexifying percussion music—has become increasingly apparent to me as I tour and meet students and young percussionists just like you. Student after student tells me that they see the big beautiful openness of the origins of our art not as an invitation for exploration but as a series of tasks to be mastered. They—we, I should say—are stressed out. Instead of seeing a cymbal or triangle or a brake drum as a door to an unknown world they—we—increasingly see it as a skill to be learned. We try to do our best by buying just the right book or finding just the right teacher to learn how to play the triangle or brake drum just right. But there are limits to everyone's capacity for "just right." And so we begin to see the thousands of percussion instruments not as thousands of possibilities but as thousands of tests to be passed, to be executed "just right." I am fearful. Is this really what we want the world of contemporary, complex percussion music to be? Do we really want Iannis Xenakis's vibrant *Rebonds* to become just another test of skill? *Zyklus*, just an audition piece? Roger Reynolds's *Autumn Island* no more than the required repertoire of a competition? Do we really want the gauzy sound of bowing a wood block or the ear-shattering roar of Stockhausen's *Mikrophonie* tam-tam at the apogee of its orbit to become the grist for juries and debut recitals? Well, I am sorry to say we are not far from that. So while my original problem was how to combine "percussion" and "music," I believe our current dilemma might in part be rooted in "percussion music!"

Ours is such an odd historical moment. Here I am in our imagined gathering of young idealists and what it seems like I am saying is that one of the biggest hurdles we percussionists face today might be percussion music itself. So let me hasten to add that I am not turning my back on percussion music. I will play *Bone Alphabet* and *Zyklus* and new pieces yet to be made until the day I die. I am not arguing against percussion music but rather arguing for a way to sustain it. And its sustenance depends on retaining the openness, the sense of experiment and, yes, the complexity out of which it was born. As the quidity—the "this-ness"—of percussion music becomes increasingly set in its ways, looming issues of scale and sustainability have arisen. Regrettably for the most part we do not even know that they exist. In one example, I am fearful for our art when so many young percussionists today seek to follow a "star" model of commercial success in classical music. This world dictates that celebrated classical soloists appear as often as possible in the most desirable venues. Such musicians cannot afford to engage in experiments or in commercially unviable music. They cannot afford to do so. So at their demand, more and more pieces are made to conform to the predictable tastes of the marketplace. Many of them are well made pieces of music, but they are guided perforce by the time-honored principals of musical consumption. They use readily available, mass-produced instruments. They always show the performer in the best possible light, usually as heroic virtuoso, and they pose the fewest number of impediments to the listener. In the case of percussion concerti, ideally they should be capable of being learned and rehearsed within the parameters of union scale—no overtime allowed! In this world, music is all product and no process. As such it becomes the musical equivalent of over-harvesting: we are overly invested in the outcome and too little invested in how we arrive there. Music becomes just another commodity, something we expect on demand like cheap oil, airline tickets, or downloadable video. In this world of over-harvesting, we often say we value openness and

215

creativity (note nearly every acceptance speech of a major award), but what we actually value is an extensive set of pre-existing options. And then when we have arrayed these options before us, we are content to choose the same ones over and over again. Alas, we say that we want a journey but what we really want is a map.

I fault commercialism here, but to be as clear as possible I am not pointing a critical finger at commercial music. Popular music, movie music, top forty radio, marching bands, and other commercial forms are honorable ways to make music. Furthermore they do not try to deceive us: they claim to be commercial! I am pointing a finger in fact at contemporary and experimental percussion music, at the world I represent and to some extent even at myself. I point a finger at music that pretends to high-minded altruism but is in fact highly commercial. To the extent that we, the world of academic percussion specialists, have followed the quirky experiments of Cage, and have followed the feverish dreams of Harry Partch, and have followed the luminous sonic canvasses of Morton Feldman with the paltry offerings of mass produced concert pieces that parade as innovation, we will face a lot of difficult questions from the percussionists of future generations.

A further aspect of our dilemma results from the way we senior members of the percussion establishment serve as stewards of our extant repertoire. This problem is especially insidious because it threatens to taint the attitudes of younger players. A short list of the most important and foundational composers quickly indicates that they are dying: Cage, Feldman, Stockhausen, Xenakis, Grisey and others. Still more are in advanced age. But the percussionists who were their collaborators and acolytes are still alive. The very great danger is that these percussionists will assert a kind of ownership over the music that is unwarranted. I already hear it being said: "I knew him. This is what he told me. This is what you should do."

If you replace all of those "him's" and "he's" with "Him's" and "He's" you have language that sounds very much like the early Christian Church. Here we might reflect upon a very public altercation between Saint Peter and Saint Paul at Antioch. Very briefly, as outlined in *Acts* and *Galatians*, the Apostle Paul publicly rebuked the Apostle Peter for his insistence on maintaining old Jewish law among early Christian believers. The circumstances surrounding their falling out dealt with the laws about circumcision and Peter's unwillingness to dine with uncircumcised Gentiles. At best the reasons for their fight seem opaque to this early 21st century reader. But, the relevant issue here is the difference of their perspectives relative to the establishment of a new doctrine. Part of it was personal. Peter knew Jesus and thought of himself as a living representative not just of Jesus's ideas but of the Man Himself. Paul's faith, however, was based on a conversion after the fact. His faith was ignited not by personal loyalty to Jesus, whom he never knew, but by the fire of a new and pure ideology. The Peter/Paul split played out over the course of centuries as the bifurcated history of the Christian Church. Peter, always mentioned first among the apostles, founded the Church in Rome and fostered a conservative view of canonical law that dominates the Roman Catholic Church to this day. On the contrary, the apostle Paul—passionate convert, tortured intellectual, and in the view of many the first gay man of the modern Church—becomes the major protagonistic force in the second half of the *New Testament*. Paul represents the transformative power of the spirit, and personifies the desire to revisit the old laws in the service of accommodating new generations of believers.

In the world of percussion we are now very close to the Peter/Paul schism. Many members of my generation who worked directly with the foundational composers of our art play the role of Peter. You, the younger idealists of our art are Paul. I knew Xenakis, met and talked with Cage and Feldman. Likewise, Allen Otte speaks often of his long relationship with Cage; Jan Williams with Feldman; Bob Becker with Takemitsu, and so on. I mention these percussionists and their relationships with famous composers because they, importantly, have refused to become the current-day spokespeople for recently-dead composers. For example, I have never heard Bob claim ownership of Takemitsu by saying, "I knew Him and here is what He said to me." To the contrary in the numerous coaching sessions I have observed with Bob Becker and students, he assiduously passes the responsibility of decision making to the students themselves. But he might be in the minority. Many of today's percussionists trade on their acquaintance with famous composers, just as Peter did on his discipleship at Antioch, as a strategy to acquire power and curate influence.

And though I often warn myself not to participate in this process, it can be difficult to resist. Of the important late 20th century composers I was personally closest to Iannis Xenakis. We were not friends, but I played all of his important percussion music for him, and have a fair personal collection of Xenakis quotations and anecdotes. When a student is searching for authenticity in a performance of Xenakis's music it is hard to resist deploying the stories. To my chagrin I once stopped myself in mid-sentence as I found myself saying: "Iannis once told me…" I was talking to student talking about *Psappha*, a piece he intended to play on an upcoming recital. He urged me to continue, sure that what I was about to say was going to be a pearl of interpretative wisdom. In any event it was bound to be the closest thing to a conversation with Xenakis that student would ever have. But equally surely whatever I was going to say next would be taken as absolute Gospel. Whatever it was—that Xenakis said to use only wooden sticks in this passage, or Chinese temple blocks in that one, or never to play from memory—would probably have been accepted without question. An important question would be answered for the student, but with that another small realm of openness would be replaced by a small bit of dogma. I refused to finish the sentence. And my student played a very provocative version of *Psappha* without the advantage of any messages from the grave. Behold the tight-wire act of a maturing art form. The more percussion becomes an established practice the less fluidity it has. So to those in the mainstream percussion community who wish we were as established as concert pianists or solo cellists: be careful what you wish for!

Obviously our dilemmas are manifold. But there are many pathways out, and they all start by asking interesting questions. I urge each percussionist to find questions for him or herself: prickly and uncomfortable questions that threaten the acquired comfort of respectability and move a performer's heart towards uncharted territory. For me personally recent questions have mostly been about the relationship between the sounds on the inside of a concert hall—the ones we call music—to those on the outside of a concert hall—the ones we call noise. Such a line of questioning begins simply enough by following the trail that John Cage left. Is there musical wisdom in the random noises of the outside world? How do we contemporary percussionists apply our musical intelligence to the outside world? Do we hear everyday noise differently because we know the sonorous and vivid music of Grisey, Varèse, or Stockhausen? Five years ago I walked 750 miles along the coastline of California to listen to the sounds of waves and cities to test this idea. I still walk, more casually of course, about 20 miles a week along the trails of San Diego County. I walk in order to listen, and what I hear seems to me be the foundational sounds of our art. I respectfully disagree with those who identify the spiritual basis of percussion music as playing Bach on marimba, or even playing Cage on tin cans. I love the music of Bach and of Cage, but the roots of percussion music are not found there. They are to be found in the noises of the outside world, and in the beating of our hearts, and in the echoes of our footfalls. So put down your Cello Suites and Cage *Constructions* and take a walk. Listen to the wind as it hisses through a stand of Lodge Pole Pines at 10,000 feet, or listen to an old Renault backfire when you start it on a cold morning. These are our sounds; this is our art.

There are other questions. I also wonder about the role a sense of "place" serves in our newest music. As we become increasingly a global civilization, I often think of my friend the Alaskan composer John Luther Adams who has said that his music used to be about place and now it has become place. In a world of YouTube and GPS, being lost and anonymous has become a state harder and harder to find. But in pieces of music like Adams's six-hour long *Veils* or Morton Feldman's four-hour plus *For Philip Guston* you can still get blissfully lost. The questions continue: What kind of musical world will we leave to future generations? (Answer: a rich and surprising one, I hope.) Will I ever commission another well-crafted 12-minute solo piece for drums and woodblocks? (Answer: extremely doubtful.)

I also ask myself what I believe to be the most difficult question of our time. Is music a tool for the betterment of the human condition, or is it only something that distracts us from the realities of our condition? Perhaps this question is too grand to address here. However, I confess that I would like to see that the interlocking spirals of Stockhausen's *Zyklus* might help us understand the pervasive cyclical nature of much of the world from political fortunes, to stock prices, to storm systems. And, perhaps the superfluity of musical information to be found in Brian Ferneyhough's *Bone Alphabet* amplifies the need to make choices within a saturated system. When dozens of sounds vie for our attention, certainly they cannot be equally important. Answer such questions of priority in *Bone Alphabet* and you have a head start on a welter of real world options. If the relationship of the one to the many in Steve Reich's *Drumming*—the musical version of the age-old question of balance between individual rights and group responsibility—can be solved with bongos then perhaps it need not be addressed using smart rockets and road-side bombs. With more recent music, how differently do we now hear Erik Griswold's prescient piece *Spill* in the year or so after the deep water "Horizon" rig began spewing oil into the Gulf of Mexico? How much more clearly do I see the culturally inter-penetrated and socially co-relational lives of the early 21st century now that I have disentangled the density of George Lewis's *The Will to Adorn*? There are many who doubt that music can "inform" us, but having personally experienced the agency of music in illuminating life's problems, I must say that I have faith it can. I have faith that we can use the music we make to understand the lives we live. And I have faith that can we use the music we make to *change* the lives we live.

I would like to finish here with a brief anecdote: In June of 1988, I found myself sitting down with the American composer Kenneth Gaburo to a post-concert midnight meal in the small Warsaw apartment of Józef Patkowski, who had been president of the Polish Composers' Union through the darkest days of the Soviet occupation of his country. The enor-mous storm clouds of political upheaval that were just beginning to gather on horizons all over Eastern Europe that summer were ominously mirrored by flashes of real lightning clearly visible through the window. I sat quietly by as Patkowski and Gaburo talked about contemporary music in Poland and how an uncompromising Polish avant-garde gave Poles a real voice even when all other freedoms of expression had been strangled. I had just flown in from California, arguably the most unconstrained culture in the history of the planet, and yet I was stunned by the way contemporary music—yes, thorny and complex modern music—was being *used* in Poland for the common good, to understand and to change lives. There was a pause in the conversation as the storm approached and I began to wonder towards what quality of the common good I was using the music that I played. Suddenly Patkowski slapped his hand on the table. The food was ready he said. Let's talk about life now, not music. He laughed then as though such distinctions were absurd, and the rains came.

So even today the questions pile up and clouds heavy with hard rain lie just over the horizon. Out of the Great Problem of my student days has come my credo. I believe that the roots of percussion music are found in the noises of the world. I believe that through percussion music we can understand our lives and make them better. I believe that, at its best, per-cussion music is not a set of skills but a system of knowledge acquisition, a way of reading the world. I value sounds over instruments. I value music over sounds. And, I value being a human being over being a musician. Yes, the path continues. It is the same path that has led from the known to the unknown; from the categorical to the complex; from the rational to the poetic. In the truest and most beautiful sense it is a path away from refinement and respectability and towards the beauties of the unknown. It is the path of ignorance, as the poet Wendell Berry has described it. And strangely as I go forward along this path I am led back towards the fields of my childhood and to the mysteries of creation that await anyone who stands in an empty space and feels the need to fill it with something that grows. I am led back through the mists to my father on a day in late March as he strode onto the mile square section of black earth that was our farm. He crumbled a knot of dirt absently between his fingers, sniffed at the warming breeze, and in the first virtuosic performance of solo improvisation that I ever witnessed said, "It's time to plant." After a moment he added, "Now."

LELEWÅ: MEMOIRS OF A BONE AND VOICE TRACER

JEN SHYU

3/6/03 *4:30 the space between San Francisco and Taipei*

> *Now on the plane to my past*
> *Father's land first*
> *Flying forward and back and seeing the sun rise*
> *The beauteous.*
> *I am not a poet. We are all poets.*
> *We hear thoughts in our head and keep them in*
> *2003*
> *Flee from unknowing, having to know there*
> *The sound of there.*
> *Must trace the faces of the basement photo*
> *above dad's old desk*
> *with my real eyes*
>
> *The gun in my side is a farce. Can you hear the other voice?*

✻   ✻   ✻

3/19/12 21:52 Jajar, Surakarta, Indonesia

It is March again, nine years later. Surakarta, Indonesia. I arrived in Jakarta on Sunday, September 25, 2011, 1:05 PM to begin thirteen months of a Fulbright scholarship. That same morning at 10:55 AM, a suicide bomber attacked Bethel Full Gospel Church, also known as Gereja Bethel Injil Sepenuh, in the Kepunton district of Surakarta. Also known as Solo, the city that was to be my research base for the next year plus. Context. And don't forget it, mbak Jen. The work for me as an artist and human being is already laid out before me: to continue to serve as the link, to build the peace, to bring people into the unknown so that they might know themselves better.

Language is one way of linking. This is now my seventh, hundreds more to go. Three months of one-on-one Indonesian lessons in Yogyakarta, eight hours a day, six days a week at an excellent language school called Wisma Bahasa. On my days off, I would take the Prameks train, short for Prambanan Ekspres, to Solo and begin to learn *sindhenan*, the improvisational singing of Javanese gamelan music, with Bu Cendhani Laras and Pak Darsono "Vokal." They would be my main teachers when I moved to Solo in January of 2012. This was at least the time map I had drawn for my Fulbright tenure, but already in the five months here, the map has become varied and complex and multi-dimensional.

I first began studying with Bu Cendhani. I corralled friends to help translate my first two lessons with her. Bu Cendhani's voice was so clear and strong without pushing, so consistent and relaxed. How do I get my voice to approach that unforced clarity that can cut through the whole gamelan? She answered, "Suara kecil," which means "small voice." It is far from small, but it is so focused and steady–this is what she meant. By my third lesson, I was able to speak enough Indonesian to learn without a translator, and this changed everything. Our two-hour lesson became three or four hours, as we took time between singing to drink tea and eat her delicious snacks which she had lovingly cooked or baked. At that third lesson, she taught me the macapat melody Pangkur. She described how one night when she was feeling heavy-hearted, she sang 40-some verses of Pangkur on her rooftop, from midnight until 3-something AM, in a quiet voice to the wind, but loud enough for her neighbor to hear when he awoke in the middle of the night. She told me how singing Pangkur brought her inner peace and helped lift her spirit from the everyday troubles that intrude. That night when I was practicing along with my recording of her, I discovered one way I could "meniru" (Indonesian for "imitate") her *gregel*, or her ornamentation. In a way, she was almost whipping her voice and landing on the specific pitches which made up the melody of the ornamentation. Before discovering this, I was just singing the quick notes straight on as I would for any melismatic singing (say in a Bach Cantata), but it was lacking something essential, the mystery that lay within the *gregel*.

I realized that this whipping of the voice toward a destination was not far from what I had learned in Beijing, China, when I was studying the ancient opera form of Kunqu in the summer of 2009 and again in January 2010. To me, it was almost the same technique except that to execute the *gregel* in *sindhenan,* the landing notes were much faster, like a carefully controlled vibrato, where each wavelength (if you broke it down as such) was a different note. And almost each of those notes was weighted differently, some lightly touched, some heavier, some held straight, some held longer, shorter, etc.

In Beijing, I was learning Kunqu as well as *shuo-chang,* or literally *speak-sing,* from a young master, Zhang Wei Dong, whom we called Zhang Laoshi, which means "teacher" in Mandarin. I had to push hard and prove how serious I was in order to receive private lessons from him because he refused to accept money when teaching. He was adamant about this, as he believed the exchange of money corrupted the passing down of the tradition. *Shuo-chang* involved more whipping of the voice, but of a different sort. The focus was more on retaining the contour of a line of text as it would be spoken normally—following the contours of the Mandarin tones, but then fitting the text into pentatonic melodies. Almost as if *shuo-chang* quantized the speech into pentatonic scales.

Before studying *shuo-chang,* I had already a done a great deal of transcribing text spoken in Mandarin (not unlike what Hermeto Pascoal and many other musicians have done with spoken language). I then developed melodies and thematic material out of that process. But *shuo-chang* was an entire tradition built upon ancient texts and generations of singers and interpreters learning the same songs as an oral tradition. It was not just one composer writing a song using a "system" of transcribing text for the purposes of a composition. The focus was on the text. My friend Liu Yu, who had already been studying *shuo-chang* for a few years, criticized me for "singing" the melody too much and that I needed to "speak" the melody more than sing it. Of course, this really required much better fluency in Mandarin, which I might have been able to acquire with more years of living in Beijing.

Zhang Laoshi was from another era, as if he were visiting our present day world from the Tang Dynasty. He was very charismatic, his group lessons full of young men and women who hung on his every word. He spoke deliberately and slowly, like a character from a Kunqu scene, and usually wore a white traditional Chinese blouse. His emails to me were cryptic and poetic, strictly adhering to rhyme and meter of Chinese poetry.

At the end of my stay in Beijing in 2009, myself and two friends—Wu Na, a guqin virtuoso and Zhang Jian, of electronic music duo FM3 fame—took Zhang Laoshi to dinner at a restaurant known for its Peking duck. It was here that Zhang Laoshi proclaimed that my destiny was to learn 一萬首歌 (*yi wan shou ge* or 10,000 songs) during my lifetime and share them with people around the world; and of course, in his explanation, he played with my Chinese name 秋雁 (*Qiu Yan* or Autumn Goose), which my parents so appropriately gave me. The autumn goose in ancient Chinese poetry captures not only the concept of seasonal migration, but also the cycle of departure and return, the inevitability of both, and the longing that accompanies the one leaving and the one left behind. So in the course of two months in Beijing that summer, I memorized as many *shuo-chang* songs as I could along with the song 原來 "*Yuan Lai*" from the Kunqu opera, *Peony Pavilion*. Zhang Laoshi claimed that this song was the first step, a window into understanding the whole art form of Kunqu. I am eager to return to Beijing again, but until then, I am indeed on the path to learning 10,000 songs, a process that will cease when I cease to be.

Cut to November 2011. As I shuttle between Yogya and Solo, I begin studying Javanese dance in Yogya from my dear teacher, Bu Tiyah, the widow of the late gamelan master and dancer, Rama Sasminta Mardawa. I met Bu Tiyah in June of 2010 during an 11-day break in Yogyakarta and Bali in the middle of three months of fieldwork in East Timor. It was my first time visiting Indonesia as well as the first time meeting a friend of Steve Coleman's, Sani Dumonde, who was also an Aries, born exactly three days after me in the same year. She has become one of my closest friends. She took me to meet Bu Tiyah, who was the first to teach me macapat songs, even though she is mainly known as a legendary dance teacher. It was Bu Tiyah who said in her sweet way that I should come back for a year or two to learn the song and dance in Java. I took her seriously and applied for the Fulbright based on that short week visiting Jogja and three days in Bali en route to and from Dili, the capital of Timor Lorosa'e, otherwise called Timor Leste or East Timor, where Mom was born. This is confirmation of my belief that even a short time in a place is better than no time. Even 5 minutes.

五分鐘—*wu fen zhong—5 minutes. 9 am, Christmas day, 2007, Taiwan.*

Tina, the passion woman, came for the ride
Cab ride to Jingpu, the Amis village she knew
Just before Taidong, where the mountains dropped steep into the sea
On a curve of the road where the grass grew high

She spotted the boy
Da Niu! Big Cow, he was nicknamed
Young and tall, teeth stained red
Betel leaf and areca nut cherished here
We're looking for the elders who know the true songs
Can you take us there? He led us behind a house
Ocean below, mountains above
Cement clearing, elders sitting, waiting for the day to unfold
Christmas Day
The sound of chickens, birds, pigs, waves, wind
Cement cracked, plastic tables, chairs, worn, broken, rusted doors
A half-built house
Pots and pans, coats, hats, helmuts hanging
From the same metal fence
Tina explains, she came all the way from America
Her father, born in Tainan. She's looking for the true songs
The women shy, at first refuse
A song from Jen, a song from you, Tina makes a game of it
Silence
Finally, a man to my right offers a song
His voice blends with the wind
Iya o hoi yan hei ya o hoi yai
Iya o iyo yan hoi yin hoi yai
Iya o hoi yan, iya o hoi yan, iya o hoi yai
Iya o iyo ho yan hoi yin hoi yai
The melody repeats, the women join, and the songs flow from there
The village leader who had been sitting quietly then decides to sing
Call and response, his voice wild and weighty
Please stay for lunch, they say. We oblige
We present a donation to the village
A pig was cooked and served with rice and greens
A car pulls up, commotion, homecoming
Marason, the blind masseuse, has arrived from Taipei
Back to his village on Christmas Day
Oh, he has a good voice, he has good voice! his village claims
Marason is seated and served the sweet liquor
He holds my hand lovingly as Tina explains

She came all the way from America
He clears his throat and sings an arpeggio under his breath
mi mi mi *mi* mi mi mi
He sings a Japanese song, or rather
a Japanese melody with Amis words
He forgets the words in mid-song, and everyone laughs
Meanwhile, Tina is talking to Kapah, the man who drove Marason
Kapah is kind and soft-voiced. He stands up and everyone listens
She came all the way from America
So we should show her our harvest ceremony
It should be July, but we'll do it now. The tables are cleared
The chairs are set in a cluster in the middle. The eldest will sit here.
Marason also
They clothe Da Niu, Tina, and me in traditional dress
Reds, whites, greens, yellows, feathers, bells
The sound in the air is loud and loose, voices cracking into laughter
A circle of hands forms around the cluster of the eldest
Everyone clasping and stomping and stepping
in time, in motion, call and response
The sweet liquor is offered around the circle
The steps are simple but strong together
Late afternoon arrives
Tina and I must catch the last bus to Shoufeng
No, no, you can go with Marason by car
Kapah will take him back to the city
We agree to follow Marason
But let's visit some of my friends before we leave, he says
Our first stop invites us to eat their home-cooked Christmas dinner
五分鐘—*Wu fen zhong* says Marason. 5 minutes just 5 minutes
We start drinking soup. 5 minutes become thirty
On to the next home 五分鐘—*wu fen zhong*—5 minutes just 5
Tina and I realize that we must take the bus
if we are going to get home
We leave Marason in the hands of his village which loves him

I see this circle of hands again. Timor Lorosa'e, 2010. *Lorosa'e* is
Tetum for "East," though from somewhere I remember it also means the

sun, rising. May 10, 2010: I meet Nelson, a Timorese photographer, singer, and drummer. He takes me to the mountains. First, by ferry, to the mountains of Oecusse, the lone district within West Timorese territory. A sacred house was rebuilt in the village of Tumin, thanks to monies from the US Embassy and the initiative of then US ambassador Hans Klemm. Before we arrive, the ceremony has already begun with music, the women standing, playing the hanging gongs, and the women gathered around the drum, taking turns beating in fast, even hits, alternating hands. The ceremonial instruments are always played by the women. David has come with us, a filmmaker from Spain, with the desire to build a school for culture in Timor. A team of three, we document all. We witness the slaughter of a pig as the offering. The screams frighten, but I do not flinch. Perhaps the video camera in my hand, a shield.

The speeches end, the officials fly home, and everyone relaxes. We stay on and chat with the villagers of Tumin and the many who came from other villages to witness the ceremony. I hang about the gongs and play with the children who are fascinated with my digital camera. They love how they can see themselves immediately after their photo is taken. They laugh at their own funny faces, when suddenly David and Nelson call me over. They've asked the group of villagers who were relaxing on the small hill to sing a traditional song. At the top of the hill is an enormous banyan tree, and they sit terraced on the slope under the tree's shade, most of them chewing betel nut. Her mother was born in Dili, Nelson explains. They peer into my face in search of Timorese blood. Nelson explains further that Mom's parents were Hakka from China. Ah, they say. So what to sing? They argue amongst themselves for a while, then finally settle. Nelson, another charismatic figure, gets everyone's attention and counts down in Indonesian. Tiga. Dua. Satu. And they begin to sing the song to the Bonet dance. Many of them hold their fists in front of their mouths, as if ready to cough, and I realize that they are doing this to amplify their voices. After many verses, they say I must see the dance that goes with their singing. They gather into a tight circle, shoulder to shoulder. Only some of them hold hands while most of them link arms.

Circle dances and choral songs with people harmonizing in octaves and 5ths exist in so many cultures around the world, like this Bonet dance. Melodically, speaking in Western music theoretical terms (which is NOT how the villagers are thinking about music), the complexity and variety of all the fieldwork from Taiwan and East Timor was immense and distinct. Still, I heard similarities between the music of Taiwanese indigenous groups and the music we heard from each district in Timor. The connection makes sense as they are both territories of Austronesian-speaking peoples.

They both had songs which used syllables without literal meaning. Take just the songs from each culture that, when there is no text, connect vowel syllables with "h" like "hei, hai, hoi." Indeed, you might have trouble determining which culture each song is coming from, unless you've studied or know that particular tradition very well. With just these syllables, you hear so clearly the connection between cultures, and the connection between human beings, especially the further you go back to when most of us were living closer to nature. One type of song I learned in Timor Lorosa'e used these syllables, what they would call *xu zi* or "empty words" in Taiwan—meaning that there is no literal meaning attached to the syllables, but it is these syllables which carry the most emotion and power. They say maybe the shamans knew the meaning before, but now, just the song has been passed down.

May 24, 2010. This Timorese song was accompanied by the bamboo instrument called the lakadou, a special instrument usually played by two people. Nelson and I drove to the mountain village of Fahisoe in Aileu, the district directly south of Dili. We followed his bandmates who were already working with the PLAN NGO in teaching traditional music to the youth there. They had told Nelson about a teacher and master musician who lived there, Mestre Marsal, whom we should hear. We met Mestre Marsal upon arriving that day, but had to wait to hear him sing when he had a free moment. We spent the day with the children, helping them rehearse and record some old Timorese guitar songs. I sometimes wandered, walking alone along the main road. Fahisoe sat up high between two valleys, the sky wide on all sides, the air hushed. I did not want to blink and miss an instant of this vast beauty. The most striking thing about Fahisoe, which translates into "land rich with pigs," was the redness of the landscape, the earth a red-orange clay.

Later, Nelson's friends and the young Timorese men working for the NGO set up a white screen outdoors in front of a school where the kids had been rehearsing and recording music all day. When night fell, parents and children gathered around to watch the film *Balibo* about the killing of a group of Australian journalists called Balibo Five in 1975 before the

Indonesian military invaded. We began to watch, when Mestre Marsal walked along the red road toward us, wearing what looked in the dark to be a bathrobe. He warmly invited us to his home and we followed him, our path lit by the movie playing behind us. When we arrived at his house, I realized that we were unprepared for the lack of electricity in the village. The film was being run by a generator which the boys had brought just for that. We had only our weak head lamps to provide light as we recorded Mestre Marsal. It was so quiet outside, only his dog barking occasionally. His home was small. He began to sing in the dim light. The way his voice filled the night was so powerful. He switched back and forth between singing an improvised virtuosic wordless phrase, with "o, hei, ho" syllables, and then a verse of his poetic lyrics. I was happy he played the same song a number of times, both alone and with his brother-in-law. Hearing these different versions, I began to understand a little about how he was improvising the syllabic section. Each time was different, but the cadences were almost the same. I noticed later when listening back that the whole syllabic section was only as long as his breath—he never interrupted the phrase with an inhalation. This to me was a beautiful constraint, and I never asked him if he even thought about the breath that way. After recording, we went back to the screen and caught the last 30 minutes of the film, and experienced the trauma dramatized.

5/23/10 11:22 Dili

> Had a nightmare last night that people tortured my mom, but my mom looked different—looked like a white woman. The torture was that they pressed her face against a flexible or maybe stiff plate with spikes (the thorns that Naldo was talking about as they dragged his body along the ground, tied to the back of the truck?), and then I tried to heal it with ice, and it seemed to help. But then they pressed her face into the spikes again. I thought she was dead, but she came back to life later…I wish I wrote this down write [sic] after I woke up. But I was crying when I woke up, sobbing

On May 21, 2010, I met the Timorese author Naldo Rei who wrote an autobiography called *Resistance*. I began to read his book on this day. He was born in 1975, the year of the Indonesian invasion. He was just three years older than me.

Song For Naldo

Intro: Lakadou song in Tetum as taught to me by Mestre Marsal, from Fahisoe, Aileu:

Hori uluk beala la rai buat ida, rai netik kultura, hanesan osan mean

(In the past, our ancestors just left us culture, and it's like gold. "Red money" means "gold" in Tetum. Translated from Tetum to English)

Bo'ot bele, bo'ot ba, riku bele, riku ba'a, tau netik kultura iha nia fatin eh

(transl: You can be big, you can be rich, I don't care; just practice culture from your right place)

My friend was a weaver of words
and he began to write
His voice was young, with the soul of a sage
He wrote of our motherland
and the violation
by a bigger nation

My friend was a weaver of dreams
I read his words one night
Then fell asleep, my cheek upon the page
with his images haunting me
and my transformation
by his etched reflection

And I dreamed of another time
and I saw her there
My mother
But she looked different, with white skin and short golden hair
but in dream I knew it was her
In a colorless cell
surrounded by guards with guns
torturous questions

when finally, they pressed her face
into a shield of thorns
a silver shield of thorns
Mother!

Then I appeared
like an angel unheard and concealed
and I ran to her
To lay her face
in a veil of ice
Mother!

to heal her bleeding brow
I thought she had died
but she survived
to sing the Timorese woman's sorrow:

"I saw mutilation of our organs
including insertion of foreign things
into our bodies' hollows
They burnt our nipples and sacred sex with cigarettes
Such violence power begets

I witnessed the torment of women
who had their hands and feet handcuffed
and who were blindfolded
In some cases women who were bound in this way
were ravaged till lifeless they lay

I saw the forceful harvest of sacred hairs
In front of male soldiers. I saw the rape
of pregnant women
including once when a woman was raped the day
before she gave birth
To a child of this troubled earth

I watched us thrown into tanks of water

Our heads submerged eternally before being raped
They used a snake to instill terror
And the threats to us that our children would be killed or tortured
if we resisted
Couldn't count the multitude of men
Counting wouldn't do any good again"

Silenced again never again never again

O la seluk ida be, be la le'et, ida be, ita mesak feton deit, na'an nian deit
(We are not strangers, we are not separate beings, we are brother and sister only)

—*August 23, 2011, Yaddo, NY*

Music and lyrics by Jen Shyu, based on text from *Chega! The Report of the Commission for Reception, Truth, and Reconciliation Timor-Leste, Executive Summary*. Song dedicated to Naldo Rei, East Timorese author of *Resistance*

3/22/12

I have performed this song in Indonesia a few times, and the response has been surprisingly positive in a strong way, but I realize that I should translate it into Indonesian for non-English-speaking audiences. I would love to have it translated into Javanese, perhaps I can work on this when my Javanese is good enough.

There is a Javanese concept called *Lelewå*, which according to Pak Darsono means "the character of the song." He talks about how I must learn the character of the song as sung by him "completely, one hundred percent;" and by whoever is a good example to learn from, like Bu Ngatirah; only then I will be able to learn *sindhenan*. Bu Ngatirah is one of the greatest pesindhens now, aged sixty-seven, who lives nearly in obscurity in Semarang. I've visited her twice, such an amazing woman. In order to learn each person's different style, I need to internalize each *Lelewå*, all aspects of the song and how it is sung. I take it further to mean capturing the song's and singer's most minute details, seen and unseen, far beyond surface imitation and dealing solely with musical elements. This process of learning *Lelewå* is not new to me, but the term is. In finally hearing a name for it in another language, I realize that this process—this attempt to reach into a living tradition and trace, and in turn make that connection to a new land and its people—is the foundation of my current creative approach: the transmission of knowledge from masters young and old in their home environment; the transformative act from internalizing the song and the singer's way; the gestation period and alchemical process within; and then the output or offering in whatever form needs to be expressed at a given time.

These might be the steps, though it is the silent, sensory impressions and human interactions in between which are the most fundamental and give everything life. That's why learning from recordings, though useful in its own right, is just a fraction of an inch of the thing itself. In terms of learning *Lelewå* and the creative process throughout, there is no formula and no predictable timeline. Music and memories from my first trip to Taiwan in 2003 are still gestating; on the other hand, I have just arranged a famous Javanese song called "Bawa sido asih," five months after the innovative *dhalang* (puppeteer) Ki Slamet Gundono first taught me the song in October of 2011. I composed the arrangement for Taiwanese moon lute accompaniment just last week before I flew to Vietnam, and I will sing and play it in an upcoming performance with the renowned dancer and choreographer living in Solo, Eko Supriyanto. I had no idea then, the impact that learning *Lelewå* of all my influences would have on my creative, compositional, and improvisational processes. That includes the time I have spent with Von Freeman in person and learning his solos on recordings, especially when I first started singing with Steve Coleman, who introduced me to so many giants and got me to squeeze the most I could from a recording. It also includes all the Taiwanese music, songs from Timor Leste, my studies in Cuba, Brazil, and films like *Opera Jawa*, directed by Garin Nugroho, with whom I've had the fortune to meet and begin to collaborate. I saw this movie before coming to Indonesia. Seeing this sublime marriage of tradition and contemporary art made me think, yes, this is where I could be for a long time. To create *sambil* learn (*sambil is* Indonesian for "at the same time as") new modes of expression through tracing, absorbing. The act of tracing the voice and movements of an elder remind me of a time I do not really remember—the time when I learned how to speak my mother tongue and also the time I learned how to walk.

When Craig and I were in Bali, he advised me to try and walk behind a Balinese man and match his slow pace that pervades this entire archipelago. I am trying to match fully to this Javanese vibration, but even away from New York City, the City of Ambition, I find that ambition lives within me, mostly in the sense that I feel there is so little time. I am reminded of this fact every time I grab onto the arm rests in my plane seat when the bottom falls out from under me, and I wonder at that moment before possible death (like last night flying from Kuala Lumpur to Solo) whether I had done enough, left enough for the next generations, made enough of a contribution…there is so little time, in fact, to make everything that I wish to make, to fulfill the desire to share, perform, collaborate, experiment, create, and travel to as many lands and sit before as many masters as I can before we all transition into the next realm of existence.

Example. Just five days ago, I sat before Kim Sinh in Hanoi, Vietnam, on a night off during a Fulbright-scholars-in-Southeast-Asia conference, at which I was presenting the next day. When Fulbright had invited us in January of 2012 to this conference, the first thought that entered my mind was whether I could find Kim Sinh, the great Vietnamese *Cải lương* singer and instrumentalist whom I first heard on a King Records World Music Library recording, the whole series of which I had bought in Taiwan in 2007. Perhaps it was destiny that Kim Sinh happened to live in Hanoi, and by some miracle, within two days through two Fulbright connections and a local classical musician in Hanoi, I was able to find him. Before January, I would never have dreamed that I would get the chance to meet Kim Sinh while here in Indonesia let alone in my lifetime. What I've learned is that one search grows exponentially into infinite searches, and my job is to remain open and receive these gifts from the universe.

I took a taxi with Lan, the kind young woman who was the key link to Kim Sinh and happened to be the concert master of the Vietnam National Symphony Orchestra. She was a friend of a Fulbrighter who did his research last year in Hanoi on *Ca trù* (pronounced "ka-choo"), an ancient vocal chamber music of northern Vietnam, which might be the next tradition I delve into, after studying Pansori from Korea.

The taxi driver slowed down to search for the address we had for Kim Sinh. Lan and I spotted a gray-haired woman who might have been in her 60's, standing, waiting, in front of what was approximately the building number we were looking for. We paid for the cab and walked toward her.

With no formalities and barely a word exchanged, this woman hurriedly waved at us to follow her into an alleyway and through an open door.

We followed her up spiraling, uneven wooden stairs. The sound of leaking water echoed distant in the stairwell. It was too dark to see the colors of things. We squeezed past a young woman who faced the wall, standing above a plastic tub on the first landing. She seemed to be waiting for us to pass her so she could walk down the stairs, but when I looked back at her, she didn't move even as we continued upwards. There was no time to solve this mystery, as we finally arrived at another open door. We took off our shoes at the entrance, and I felt the floor either cold or wet under my bare feet and quickly stepped onto a rough, woolen mat. It was a tiny room, and there was a smiling Kim Sinh shifting toward us from a cross-legged position, warmly murmuring a welcome. I recognized the same soft, warm, slightly nasal voice of his, and I also greeted him with a long sigh, so delighted to meet the source of that idiosyncratic music I had only known on record, music that was both familiar and unpredictable, and altogether romantic.

He wore knitted everything—black knitted tights, beige knitted sweater, green and yellow knitted scarf, brown knitted hat, and white knitted socks. The room felt unheated, and we quickly saw that Kim Sinh was quite poor, or at least appeared as such. He reached forward and I took his hand, for he was blind. He apologized for the small house and for being blind, and I told Lan to translate that *please*, he shouldn't apologize. His hands were so soft, like unworn satin. We sat and talked, and he explained that the woman who had led us up the stairs was his third wife named Lei, pronounced the same as my mother's family name no less, and how she was much younger than him. He didn't know if she was beautiful (we confirmed that she was), but he could feel her beautiful spirit. He soon took in his arms his *đàn nguyệt*, a long-necked, moon-shaped instrument that was very much like my Taiwanese *gat-kim*, or "moon lute" in Taiwanese. The frets were placed differently, giving it a different mode—his was pentatonic whereas my moon lute's frets are basically tuned diatonically except for having both the minor and major 3rd as the chromatic addition.

Lan had told him over the phone that morning that I wanted to learn from him, so at one point he took my left hand slowly and silently and pressed my finger under his onto a string between two frets. He talked about how vibrato is used only on some notes in Vietnamese folk music, and he demonstrated this effortlessly on both the *đàn nguyệt* and with his voice. There was so much beauty in his simple explanation for such a deep and unique sound, which could at once carry in it his life experience and give voice to a nation, his motherland.

> *Maubisse*
> *There is an opening of land off the Flecha road*
> *Where the earth spreads wide its grassy skins*
> *'Til it breaks and reveals red clay*
> *Flesh where the wild horses graze*
> *Just beyond*
> *From afar their exhales fluttering*
> *Sighs in the expanse*
> *I knew not where I was, who I strove to be*
> *It was cold*
> *Mother, I give you the sign*
> *I grabbed the first warm hand*
> *I rush home, and I see*
> *I was home all the time*

FLUKEY CONCATENATIONS

DAVID TAYLOR

The bass trombone is a relatively new instrument, and when I was in school there wasn't a rich tradition of individual personalities performing on it. Great low trombone writing began in the Renaissance, and for me, reached a very "high" point with Mozart's Operas and Masses. Orchestral writing didn't explore the very low register of the instrument until Hector Berlioz, who is generally given the credit for introducing the modern bass trombone in *Symphonie Fantastique*. Jazz big bands didn't use bass trombones until the 1940s, and it took until the 1950s for the horn to achieve an individual voice. In the early 1960s the bass trombone had a major breakthrough, it went from one valve, which left a gap, to two valves, which made it totally chromatic. I was very lucky to be in the right place at the right time, because the new chromatic instrument's use and repertoire increased exponentially. I've been trying to find my voice with the instrument since then, and it's been happening in stages that coincide with lucky breaks in my career.

If I had a concept of personality or vision, it came in the form of maintaining a sense of independence by not caving into peer pressure at school. I chose my first instrument because it felt good to play, not because it was the "proper" sound. In the conservatory, and classical orchestral arena, there is an accepted sound and a sound that just doesn't fit. I didn't buy into that mentality. I needed an instrument that had a more immediate response for my articulation, which also meant there were more high over-tones in the sound, causing it to have a more buoyant quality. Although the sound was big, and had a very rich core in its tone quality, it also had more sunshine in it than the orchestral folk were going after. When I started play-ing in big bands, and brass quintets, this tone quality helped my approach and function to include time keeping to support the ensembles. Quick, clear articulation helped "push" the band around and free the musicians to float in and out of time. With the added dimension of more brightness and clarity to my tone, the sound projected through ensembles even at soft volumes. This might have been the first stage of developing a personality on the instrument. I was always heard.

I saw every offer to perform as an opportunity to learn and grow. When I felt insecure about the style of a musical genre, I threw myself at the mercy of the court. I'd ask the more experienced musicians to help me. I was in my early 20's and the older musicians saw my genuine desire to "be there" and learn. I wanted to develop a career on a high musical level, with the upper most thought of being in the moment with the music, and being able to "climb into the sound around me." I wasn't aware of it, but by being successful in small doses, going to all the rehearsal groups, and gigs I was called to do; I was networking. I never showed up late, and I was always warmed up. Playing in jazz groups while studying classical music in the '60s was going against the grain. The Juilliard School didn't even have jazz recordings in the library, and the students had to put on a drive on to make that happen. I found myself between a rock and a hard place because I wasn't just focusing on classical music. It literally affected some of my schoolmates' and teachers' thinking about me, but I was fortunate; employers in all areas of musical performance heard something special; even if it was just my enthusiasm. I ran into a friend recently, and he reminded me of something I offhandedly said to him years ago. We saw each other in the street, and he asked me, "So? How's it going?" While shaking my head side to side, my response was, "I think I'm too loose for the tight and too tight for the loose!" And, that's how it was for years. It's still that way in many situations. Many people have specific categorical concepts of what music is and isn't. Palastrina's ability to write Secular and Non Secular music, and J.S. Bach's ease of crossing into the German, French, and Italian Styles is a wonderful example to me of "genre-jumping". That inspired me. I had the desire to take my performance practice a step further by commissioning solo pieces. I wanted to learn how to phrase, and to perform standing in front of the general public. I felt this would add personality to all areas of my playing. I went to composers who were looking for an individual voice, and who understood how to bring their music to the general concert going public in concert halls. It was easier for me, because I met most of the composers I commissioned while I was playing in their larger ensemble pieces. After composers saw how seriously I took their music, and had success playing it, I was sought after by other composers, and developed an extensive repertoire. Perhaps that was visionary, being with people whose drive was similar to mine, and getting wonderful music to perform in front of non-musicians. I knew this would force me into realizing a style "of the street". At this point I was already playing in a lot of high profile engagements in all genres. I played in Leopold Stokowski's orchestra while I was still in school, and recorded with the great Duke Ellington when I was in my 20's. I knew it was necessary for me to mature into a style so I could continue to be in the company of great musicians. I also knew I wanted to continue growing musically while supporting a family. Because I have a loving relationship, and strong work ethic ingrained by my Mother and Father, a wonderfully strong support system through my marriage with my wife, Ronnie, I think I've always had a good instinct about what I had to do and where I had to be. My concept of vision was more about improvising through the nuts and bolts of making career decisions. I recently asked one of my very trusted literary friends if he thought I had a vision. He very immediately and emphatically said, "No! You're an animal". I was flattered, because in the past he has associated me with William Blake's, "Tyger, Tyger" (Burning Bright). I think in terms of the moment, and how I can continue those moments.

*   *   *

The bass trombone chose me. When I was in elementary school, my first music teacher, George Saslow, came around giving "musical aptitude tests". The New York public school system had a wonderful music program in the 1950s and '60s, and, I remember being in P.S. 233's auditorium; seeing him, hearing him, taking the test, and can even remember some of the basic questions. I don't know why I was chosen for the class—an amazingly lucky break that came my way. I was one of those class clowns that the teacher made sit by her side so she could keep an eye on him. The following year in junior high, we all started on Trumpet. Mr. Saslow told us to make believe we were spitting. I must have spit well, because several weeks later he came out from the back room holding an instrument, and said to the class, "Who thinks they're big enough to play this big, bright, shiny tuba"—of course, being the smallest kid, my hand shot up—he wanted me on that horn, and he knew how to do it—he put me right into the senior group—put me on the fast track, made me advance quickly. The Tuba came to me.

    My brother was learning how to play the trombone. He had one in the house. When my mother couldn't pick me up from school with the tuba, I played my brother's trombone. The trombone was there. When at Juilliard, in my fourth year, a friend said he could get me a paid job if I would play the bass trombone, that's what I did. Juilliard happened to have one in their storage area. So, basically, the bass trombone was there and the opportunity presented itself.

When I auditioned for Juilliard, I couldn't read more than very simple high school "oom pah" tuba parts, and simple trombone parts, so I auditioned playing the slow movement of the Haydn *Trumpet Concerto*. Although I passed the audition, I was required to take rudimentary theory classes; including, how to read and notate music. When I was qualified to enter the theory program, my teacher, Mr. Fish, was hip enough to assign me one classical music recording a week to listen to. My family didn't have a record player in the house until I was sixteen, so I hadn't listened to any classical repertoire—all I know, is, I JUST LOVE BLOWING AIR THROUGH A PIPE!

To facilitate my reading I would take out piano scores from the library and read through the left hand bass parts, choosing notes to leave out if chords appeared, learning clefs and dealing with octaves. For technique I used violin and clarinet books. Who knew? I just thought it would be a good idea. I knew nothing about style or how to get it, but I never took the horn off my face. I played as many different genres of music possible—still do. Eventually, when my technique became pretty much an unconscious procedure, style started entering the picture. I guess my brain became a "clearing house" between my physical and mental functions. It was at that point I was really able to grasp "the total amalgamation or homogeneity of various forms of style that proved categorization of musical genres untenable." Or, to put it a little more simply: It's all just music.

I think the sooner you leave the concept of: you are you, and your instrument is your instrument, expression and technique meld; and technique becomes "a slave" to expression. A large part of technique in the classical sense of the word is the ability to play anything fast or slow clearly and in tune, while having control over the volume of your dynamics. For me, many of the musicians I think of as the "best of all time" talk to me through their "classical technical flaws". I practice very slowly, concentrating on the fundamentals. I focus my mind on my process of producing a sound; my air support (diaphragm muscles), my lip formations (emboushure and aperture), and my articulation (tongue striking the teeth or lip). Knowing what each of these muscle groups is doing, and allowing them to communicate with each other while keeping them as relaxed as possible, allows me to bypass typical brass players' syllables: tee tee, ta ta, toe, toe, taw, taw. By focusing continually on the call and response of the three muscle groups with my mind mediating during practice sessions, my body learns to respect itself and communicate instantaneously. When I perform, my mind is an empty conduit for my body's conversation; my mind is free to roam. When I began developing this process I was twenty-four. This training process was tedious and painful at first, but after a decade or two of practicing this way for hours each day, I'm now off the planet within a few moments of picking the instrument up to my lips. I guess I love breathing! By avoiding the brass players' syllables, I've cut out the communicational step that gets in the way of just "climbing into the non-thoughts and sound around me." Also noteworthy: although no-mind technique, can put you in direct contact with whatever spirit floats your way…your sight-reading skills grow and can reflect your style with immediacy while maintaining accuracy, and, your performance level music-reading can be customized to the point of rivaling memorization.

*　　　*　　　*

Each sound or note one plays has three parts: the beginning, the middle, and the end. Each part requires your attention during practice sessions, and the myriad of choices you have in producing these three segments of a sound is a major part of style. But, if I had to make the difficult decision to choosing which part of a note is the most important one, I'd say, articulation. Good and varied articulation allows you to be a Talking Trombone. It's a very positive conformation when people tell me I am one with my instrument, and that my horn speaks to them.

It's vital to find an instrument and mouthpiece that have the proper amount of resistance. If it's too free blowing or hard to blow through, you have to think too much. The mind is forced to re-enter the muscular conversation while performing, and it impedes your expression. The instrument should have the qualities of a good amplifier so you can produce the tone color you want with the utmost ease. And, the weight and balance has to be light enough for you to hold all day. Incidentally, this is the reason musicians protect their instruments with their lives!

I think in terms of language; and colors are the result. Every language has its own prosody; or rhythm, stress and intonation, and I use each of these elements as part of my musical language in a personalized way. Stress in language to me is articulation and dynamics, and for me, articulation is the most vital element in style and interpretation. Every language has countless ways to start a word. So, taking that factor into consideration, I try to not limit myself to the standard legato, marcato, doodle, slurring, or double-tonguing trombonists use to start notes. When I see dynamics on a page of written music, I think in terms of the emotion that will be transmitted in addition to or in lieu of the volume level asked for.

Intonation in language is quite different from the even-tempered, just-tuning, or well-tempered intonation that's now the standard in Western Culture. Even in recent history, you find many different, and alternative tuning systems with intervals sounding very close together or spread apart, and adding microtonal sounds. The period in musical history when the major 3rd was added to the perfect 4th, 5th, and octave, not only affected music, but the change in the ratio of pitch relationships brought a whole philosophical change to society at large. When the use of the major 3rd was being incorporated into composition, Renaissance composers, such as William Byrd, were using two tuning systems in the same pieces! The sophistication of that concept has enabled me to rethink my whole understanding of history and the musical continuum. Listening to the nuance of pitch in any Asian language is an amazing reinforcement for me to use pitch as color. The trombone is an instrument with a slide. The standardized use of the trombone slide incorporates seven positions, but really, it's a smooth sliding pitch changer with a myriad of starting or stopping places: a perfect vehicle for color. When I play with improvisers the tuning is much more "pastel" than the standard "primary black and white" tuning which is the language for many classical orchestral, or chamber music settings. To me, this pastel color not only adds more shading possibilities. It enables us to represent a larger worldly and historical framework.

I enjoy playing music as if it's a children's playground, and rhythm, allows me another way to express color in a playful manor. I like to be steady, rush/run, push, pull, jump, swagger, delay, and "place" my rhythms. There is precedence for this all the way back to Renaissance music in which musicians did not use bar lines to delineate fragments of metered rhythm. There's precedence in Jazz music when musicians "float" over steady rhythm section beats. This knowledge and experience helped me in all styles. Classical chamber musicians like to "place" beats, which is another way of entering the playground. Classical Orchestral musicians play in what I call a "European Declamatory Style". This enables the large ensemble to talk to the audience through rhythm. Speeding up speech creates excitement and slowing down speech makes a different kind of emphasis. Singsong speech can be descriptive of deep sarcasm, serious thought, and pure joy. All of these rhythmic elements can appear in any genre, and playing in many genres has taught me freedom through this overlap. Playing with click tracks in studios has taught me how to be free with a metronome while practicing expressive music.

I think the understanding of when not to use color has contributed to my being able to fit into different musical settings. Being able to "climb into the sound around you" also requires a lot of practice time and maintenance of your fundamental "classical" technique, so you have the choice of leaving it and coming back to it.

I always loved music and performing, but instrument choice came from happenstance. Trombone players weren't the inspirational force behind my becoming a musician, my main teacher Davis Shuman being the exception. Mr. Shuman was playing solo recitals in NY and around the US. He commissioned composers, wrote arrangements, played orchestral and chamber music, and produced his own recordings. During the 1940s and '50s, he was just about the only trombone player committed to that kind of work. Darius Milhaud and Ernest Bloch wrote for him. At a time when transcriptions and arrangements were frowned upon by a large segment of the music establishment, he was arranging the works of classical composers. I went to his recitals with him, and I went to his orchestral concerts with him. I remember Mr. Shuman playing to full houses in respected concert halls. He was very intense. He had a University degree in Civil Engineering, and he invented the "Angular Trombone" which had a slide that pushed off at an angle of approximately 11 degrees. Its function was to allow your arm to go out perfectly straight so 7th position was enabled with shorter arm length. I played an angular trombone for four years until I played my first borrowed bass trombone. He was a musical model for me. I commission, arrange, and compose music, customize and create my instruments and accessories, play orchestra music, chamber music, solo recitals and concerti. Mr. Shuman's favorite trombone player was the great swing era trombonist

Tommy Dorsey. He felt Dorsey elevated the virtuosic possibilities of the trombone in a way that also spoke to the people. This was a beautiful encouragement for me to include Jazz and Pop music in my search.

Two musicians Davis Shuman looked up to were the great cellist Pablo Casals and conductor Leopold Stokowski. I listened to Casals a lot, and played in Stokowski's American Symphony a few years after Mr. Shuman passed away. Both Casals and Stokowski were men whose technique was a "slave" to the music. They took their music to the people. Stokowski was the conductor known for bringing his individual sound to orchestras, and was featured in Walt Disney's movie, *Fantasia*. He premiered many new works including two Charles Ives' Symphonies. The Maestro was in his 90's when he premiered the Ives (I played on both). Stokowski always encouraged the orchestra to "do betta", and was always looking for the "other way". Many remember Pablo Casals for re-introducing the Bach *Cello Suites* to the world, and for refusing to perform on demand for two of the most heinous Dictators in European history. Casals' playing on the cello suites is so free that it feels as if he's improvising on what's written, or that he wrote it himself. For me, one of the most sterling moments on the recording occurs in the *Prelude* of the *Third Cello Suite*. Casals is in a difficult section, one where there's a quick repeated pattern with cascading double and triple stops... and he stumbles. The way he works through this struggle without losing the thread of the piece adds a drama so human, heroic, and musical, that it reveals his whole personality, and the kinship he and Bach had through the centuries. Similarly, Stokowski's spirit is strong and confident; this strength enables him to leave the performance "flaws" on his recordings. It's because of this energy the music is magical. The heaviness of Stokowski's devotion, raw spirit and energy required to premiere Ives, and to do it in his nineties has left an indelible mark on me. While at Juilliard, I was lucky enough to enroll in Luciano Berio's class for the one year he taught at the school. His music is daring and magnificent. His piece for unaccompanied trombone is iconic. Sequenza not only affected my technique, but also influenced my improvisatory vocabulary. Although he was very informative about contemporary music and its relationship with the classics, the most meaningful memory I have about Berio's class is the glee he experienced when he described the process of composition, and his relationship with other composers.

Growing up with a radio and tv and no record player in my house channeled my musical interests to radio stations featuring R&R, and R&B music. I was also addicted to old black and white movies, and comedy shows on television. The old gangster movies, featuring actors like James Cagney, Pat O'Brien, George Raft, and Edward G Robinson used "hot" music from the '20s and '30s for their sound tracks. I was totally into the rhythmic drive, and rakish melody and harmony. When I heard the film scores for early Fred Astaire, Dick Powell, and Ruby Keeler dance movies, the beat and lushness of the orchestrations were so stylish, you didn't need the screenplay. You could hear the humor, wit and sarcasm through the score. When I heard Louis Armstrong for the first time, I knew I heard brass playing at its best. The vocal quality, the time, the joyful crying expressed by the wealth and humanity of Armstrong's technique was only surpassed by the fact that you weren't aware of the technique. For me, Armstrong did indeed revolutionize and bring classical virtuosity into the 20th century. To hear Sidney Bechet play soprano saxophone is like reading the Encyclopedia of Color. I listened to these men as much as I could. When I first heard Duke Ellington's band I was already a graduate student in my '20s. Hearing a large ensemble playing so personally and intimately defined the power of modern classical chamber music to me. The Ellington Band's concept of rhythm and time was not the same as the "rhythmically perfect" Count Basie, but I related more to the looser swing of Ellington's playground; steady, slow, fast, jumping, dragging; all at the same moment with all the musicians playing individually together: great classical playing. Paul Gonsalves' big, soulful, airy tenor saxophone sound is always at my mind's fingertips. I will never forget the first time I saw Rashaan Roland Kirk play. It was an axis shifting for me. Charles Ives' piano music is a big force in my vocabulary. By playing the concord piano sonata at a snail's pace, I learned theory anew. Both Frank Sinatra's vibrato and phrasing, and Wilhelm Furtwangler's telling conductors not to over rehearse the musicians (so their interpretations have the semblance of being improvisatory and not placed in "a bottle of formaldehyde"), are totally related to me. I'm happy to have never let school get in the way of my education.

Now, add the timing, personal story telling, and deep thoughts of the comedians to the mix. The list could go on forever, but here's a few names of people I studied: Laurel and Hardy, The Marx Brothers, Martha Raye, Phil Silvers, Art Carney, Lenny Bruce, Richard Pryor, Jack Benny, Jimmy Durante (The Schnoz), Red Skelton, Joan Rivers, Sam Kinison,

Myron Cohen, Senor Wenches, Rochester, Shecky Green, Pat Cooper, Eddie Murphy, Bill Mahr, all the Borscht Belters (and on and on). Their immediate attention getting introductions, constant twisting story lines, pauses, and final cadences (punch lines) are musical gems. All Pop, Rock and R&B songs must grab the audience within the first 10 seconds. This taught me to play like there was no tomorrow. When I saw the great Mohammed Ali fight, it was like heavyweight ballet. The bass trombone had for the most part been seen as a pretty cumbersome horn, especially in the extreme low register, but Mohammed Ali showed me how to dance on the instrument: "float like a butterfly, sting like a bee" yelled Bundini Brown, cheering Ali on from his corner.

I learn spirit channeling, phasing and technique from all these places. And, they pertain to all music. In one of August Rodin's essays he says something that has had the most incredible influence on my playing. He wrote, "There is no such thing as beautiful color, no such thing as beautiful form, no such thing as beautiful line. There is only one beauty, and that's the beauty of truth revealing itself." It's for sure pretentious to say that I get to that point, but I aspire to it, and that understanding helps me get past the fears of letting go.

The word flukey is the only way I can describe my career. Flukey's definition is: done or gained by an accident, especially a lucky one. Concatenation's definition: to connect or link in a series or chain relates to my being open to events and opportunities that present themselves to me. But, when all is said and done, if you asked me "why or how do you produce your tone", my answer would be based on an early dream, "If there are Aliens in the Universe, I want them to hear my sound and know that we on Earth are friendly."

SOME MEMORIES OF JOHN CAGE

For John on his 100th

RICHARD TEITELBAUM

I

I first met John Cage when I was a graduate student at Yale University around 1962 or '63. I was studying theory and composition, and was invited by Allen Forte, one of my teachers at the Music School, to organize a series of lectures by visiting composers and theorists. We had already received a letter from Karlheinz Stockhausen's agent, announcing a U.S. tour, and Stockhausen became the first speaker on the series. Typically, Stockhausen had demanded a minimum of $150 and, as I was given only a total of $300 to cover all four lecturers, I was able to offer Cage only $50. He wrote back that if I could make it $75, he could bring David Tudor as well, and perform his newest work, but I (foolishly) replied that we could only afford the $50.

That is how John Cage, at the age of fifty, made his first appearance at the Yale Music School for fifty bucks. Unlike Stockhausen, who also demanded the highest quality equipment to play his tapes (and then took great delight in blowing out one of the audiophile loud speakers we had borrowed from the local hi-fi store—"those little impulses, they go right through the speakers!" he later boasted gleefully to us terrified students), John, on the other hand made do with three low-priced Wollensack reel-to-reel tape decks with built in speakers that he spread out across the front of the stage in Sprague Hall, and used the rather cheesy mic and P.A. system in the hall to amplify his voice. The piece he performed was the simultaneous lecture "Where are we Going? and What are we Doing?" that had just been published in *Silence* the year before.

The performance lasted quite a long time, perhaps 45 minutes to an hour. I had never heard any Cage performances previously and, frankly I couldn't quite say whether I "liked" or "disliked" it. But I recall very distinctly that I had the sense that after about a half hour or so, "something happened to my consciousness" that was unlike anything I had ever experienced.

There were a good number of people in the audience, many from outside the Music School. (Cage was then much better known in the Art and Architecture School where I think he had already appeared). The audience included a large contingent brought by Professor Paul Weiss, then the reigning aesthetician in the Philosophy Department, who had primed his students for attack. In the ensuing question period, Weiss and his students did their best to jump all over John, questioning what "rules" governed the composition of the piece and why anyone else couldn't compose this way just as well as John—to which he replied "you can, go ahead and do it!"

After that I drove with John up to the reception in his "honor", where others, including the hostess, continued to confront him ("what you do is psychology, not music" was one of the charges that I recall). En route to the reception, John said: "You know, Weiss wants me to make rules for what I do, to make a 'School.' I don't want to do that. Why, last week I heard La Monte Young hit a gong 511 times. It was magnificent, but I never would have thought of that. If I had made a 'School' perhaps that might never have happened."

It was the first of many unforgettable lessons I learned from John Cage.

II

The next Cage performance I saw **did** include David Tudor. It was *Variations II* performed at Charlotte Moorman's New York Avant Garde Festival in Steinway Hall on 57th Street. It was also the first live electronic performance I ever saw: Tudor played the piano, though never actually on the keyboard. Rather, he was crawling around under the piano with various contact mics and pickups, culling an astonishing array of sounds from the piano's innards. While this somewhat less-dignified-than-I-was-used-to "piano" performance was going on, Cage sat very formally at a table, very slowly and purposefully performing a variety of everyday activities (lighting a cigarette, taping the ashes into an ashtray, writing with a pen and paper)—all highly amplified by contact mics. After David's activities had built up to a huge roar, John slowly raised a glass of water to his lips and took a drink, whereupon a sound like Niagara Falls suddenly roared forth from behind the audience (the first time I was aware of any sound from back there) with startling and even terrifying effect. I remember spinning around and practically jumping out of my seat.

I was not the only one jumping up and down: Though I was sitting in the second row of this very small hall, and could see quite well, there was a very excited, elderly gentleman directly in front of me, who was constantly bobbing up and down to get an even better view of the proceedings. It was Edgar Varèse.

III

During 1970 and '71 I studied in the World Music Program at Wesleyan and Cage was also there as a Fellow of the Center for Advanced Studies (where I remember John organizing and leading games of Red Light/Green Light in the hallways). One night, John arranged a dinner party at a very simple but excellent family-style Chinese Restaurant in New Haven called "Blessings" for a group of people that included both the distinguished Director of the Center, who was an Arab, and myself. In a small private backroom, John sat at the head of the table and placed the two of us on either side of him. He had called ahead to order a specialty of the house that took some considerable advance preparation, about which he had been quite secretive. When the main course arrived, John grandly served out large portions to each of us (as well as everyone else) with a considerable flourish. It turned out to be mostly a kind of stewed pig fat, and John took devilish pleasure in dishing it out to the Arab and the Jew on either side of him, both of whom looked somewhat green, but were too polite to decline John's generous helpings of this great delicacy. I think John thought of it as some sort of contribution to world peace and understanding—the Arabs and Jews breaking pork together.

Among other memorable events of that year was the student strike to protest the bombing of Cambodia. I recall a wonderful lecture that John improvised on education, saying, among other things, that the kind of anarchic environment created by the strike, with students milling about freely, but engaged in small but intense discussions and debates all over the campus was an ideal one for an educational situation. A year later when I visited Cal Arts for a job interview during its first year (at the Burbank campus of the Villa Cabrini before the new building in Valencia had been completed), the free-form atmosphere was very similar.

One other indelible image that comes to mind from that Wesleyan year took place while waiting for a lecture by Bucky Fuller to begin. With some thousand students seated mostly on the floor of the large modern glass building where Fuller was to speak, John and Anthony Braxton (who had come up from New York to visit Barbara Mayfield and myself) stood, lost in a game of chess they were playing on a tiny pocket set they held in their hands. John, being a bit "tipsy" at the time, was loosing badly.

IV

In the mid-'70s, Nam June Paik made a TV program on John for public television that included a special version of *4'33"* based on performing I Ching operations on a map of Manhattan. In this way, John chose several locations around the city to record (and videotape) the sounds and sights at each spot. I drove my VW van with John perched on the front seat, and Nam June, Shigeko Kubota, and cameraman Jud Yalkut in the back. The chosen spots turned out to be at far-flung ends of the city, and the traffic was horrendous, with much sudden starting and stopping. At one point someone urged John to use his seat belt, but he declined to do so, saying: "Buckminster Fuller says, between rigidity and flexibility, choose flexibility—I never use seat belts."

While stuck in the worst and most exasperating of the traffic jams, I asked John how, in accordance with his Buddhist beliefs in the beauty of all things, he could find it in the present situation. "Well," he replied, "the only reason you wouldn't find it beautiful is because you want to be somewhere else. If you accept being here, it's really very interesting. Look at the patterns of all the flashing brake lights, listen to the sounds and rhythms of all the different car horns!"

V

Before I ever met Cage, I had heard many unusual stories about him and his ideas while I was still a student at Yale. The general line taken there about Cage was that he was just plain crazy. As proof of that, my composition teacher Mel Powell recounted that once when he asked Cage why he had made the silent piece just 4 minutes and 33 seconds long, he replied that at the time he wrote it there were only 78 rpm records, and that was the maximum length of one side of a disk. Many years later, Sidney Cowell told me that once, many years ago, when Cage and her late husband (and one of Cage's principal teachers) Henry Cowell were driving across the country, they stopped for lunch in a diner and, chagrined at the selections that were constantly being played on the jukebox, Cowell proposed that someone should put out a disk (78 of course) with only silence on it.

VI

Though I was generally very shy around John, I did turn to him for help on several occasions. Once when, many years ago, I had gotten into a very upsetting row with a colleague, I went to see him for advice. He and Merce unexpectedly, but with typical kindness and generosity, invited me to stay for dinner, and got us all quite drunk. The only thing I can recall from the evening was John urging me to "always try to be a charming as possible"— excellent advice I am still trying to master.

On another occasion, when I needed a rehiring recommendation for Bard, after much hesitation, I called to ask John to write one for me. He said that as he had need to talk to President Botstein of Bard on another matter, he would call him personally. Leon later recounted that he was so astonished and incredulous when his secretary told him that John Cage was on the line that he had replied: "Sure, sure, and Albert Einstein too!"

VII

On August 12, 1992, I went out to the swimming hole across the road from my house in Bearsville, to sit on my regular spot, take a swim, and meditate on the setting sun,—my usual routine each summer afternoon. On reaching it I discovered, much to my horror, that it was occupied by the body of a decapitated 'possum—an animal of such sweetness and innocence. Somewhat in shock on finding such a bizarre and grizzly sight exactly on the spot that I held somehow sacred, I quickly returned home, thinking to call Sidney Cowell, my neighbor, advisor on wildlife and the widow of John Cage's teacher Henry Cowell. Before I could call her, Sidney called me. My phone machine was still on, and I heard her say: "This is Sidney. I felt I wanted to tell you that John Cage died this afternoon at 2:30."

For the next day or so I lay around kind of paralyzed, in a state of sadness and shock. I couldn't decide what to do—whether to go to New York to the concert of Cage's music that had previously been scheduled in the MoMA Sculpture Garden the next night. Somehow, I had the notion that I didn't want to erase Sidney's message from the tape. I decided to fast forward the tape to the end, turn it over and use the other side for future messages. Almost as an afterthought, it occurred to me to check if anything was on that side. I pushed play, and out came John's voice, saying: "Hi Richard, this is John Cage...!" As I listened, I started to cry and laugh at the same time. Here is the whole conversation:

JC: Hi, Richard, this is, uh, John Cage. I'm at (212) 98—
RT: (picking up the phone) Hello John!
JC: Hi!
RT: Good Morning! How are you?
JC: I'm fine, how are you?
RT: Well, I'm all right. I have a bit of a cold so I have been staying in.
JC: Uh huh. Richard, do you remember when I—there was that concert up near Albany and you came, years ago...
RT: Near Albany?
JC: You were with a friend.
RT: Gee...
JC: and umm, it was out in the country? Carlton Clay had arranged it?
RT: Oh...
And they played a piece of mine, called, which was very early, uh, *Composition for Three Voices*? Do you have any memory of it at all?
RT: No, was this in Oneonta? Oh, oh, oh! Yes, yes, yes, yes! I do remember.
JC: And it was a brass piece, wasn't it?
RT: The piece of yours was a brass piece?
JC: Uh, *Composition*, it was called *Composition for Three Voices*.
RT & JC simultaneously: *Composition for Three Voices*!
JC: And it was very chromatic.
RT: Yes, uh hum! Oh yes, I do remember
JC: Was it all brass?
RT: Well now that I don't quite remember...
JC: You don't.
RT: Gee, I, I was, to tell you the truth, I was asleep John so I, I'm—
JC: (laughing) Oh you were!
RT: (laughing) so I might remember in a, in a few minutes.
JC: Oh, you were asleep just now.
RT: Yea... Yea, no, no, (laughing) not during your piece (long laughter), oh, no...(more laughter)...
JC: Weren't you asleep at the concert?

RT: No, not in the concert, I mean…(laughter)…Maybe if I was asleep in the concert I would remember it while I, now I was asleep also…

JC: Well it's nice to hear your voice.

RT: Well, you can't remember your, what your piece was written for?

JC: It was written, it wasn't written for any instruments. It was…

RT: Oh, I see. And they did it, uh huh…

JC: And they played it…

RT Yea, I think it was bra—I think they did it for…

JC: I think it was brass.

RT: Yea, I think so.

JC: But I look up the ranges of the brass and they don't fit my notes.

RT: Uh huh. Well can't we get a hold of Carlton Clay and ask him?

JC: I asked him.

RT: And what did he say?

JC: And he, um, didn't remember.

RT: Laughter.

JC: Laughter.

RT: How about Sidney, did she remember?

JC: No, I just spoke with her.

So anyway—was she along? I don't think she was.

RT: No, but I think she listened on the radio, or something like that. Huh. Well I'll try and jog my memory when I'm a little more awake (chuckles).

JC: Ok.

RT: Are you home these days?

JC: Uh huh.

RT: How are you?

JC: I'm not too well. I have an itchiness.

RT: Really, well that's…

JC: My skin. And I think it's related to a poor digestion.

RT: Oh, dear.

JC: Traveling too much and didn't eat the right foods.

RT: Uh, uh. Did the doctor give you any diagnosis.

JC: Yes, he said I should, uh, eat properly, and I shouldn't um, do this that and the other.

RT: Uh huh. So can you stay home for a while now?

JC: Yes, I hope to.

RT: Well please take care of yourself.

JC: (indistinguishable)

RT: Take care John, I hope to see you.

JC: You too Richard.

RT: Thank you. Bye bye.

JC: Bye.

JOHN HENRY

JULIA WOLFE

I have dozens of notebooks—small and large. I scribble down words for the piece I'm writing. Sometimes I draw pictures. Generally I write descriptions of the music—trying to get at the energy, the gestalt of a piece. There are pitches, rhythmic ideas, tempos, textures. But largely I jot down scattered descriptions. I worked on *Steel Hammer* in 2008–2009. Written for the Bang on a Can All-Stars and Trio Mediaeval, *Steel Hammer* is based on the John Henry legend. *Steel Hammer* is the story of the story. I listened and looked at over 200 ballads and delighted in the differences and contradictions, the universal nature of the legend, how American it is. Below are a few pages from the beginning of my notebook.

Ideas

Chest—body slaps
6 dulcimers—all tuned differently
alternate the body percussion with whistling and singing/hum
bones
just bones in the open
or just voices—dense bones near the end
whistling
shhhhh
speaking
clapping—body clapping
chimes
singers in the balcony
flashlights
metal & stone/hammers
4 dulcimers
banjo

acoustic vs. amplified
playing with the distance from the mic
covering the mouth
alternating the sound
with tunnel echo
stamping rhythms on the floor
melodica
John Henry a folk lore legend
versions of J.H. from Indiana, Tennessee, Mississippi, and Kentucky, West
Virginia, South Carolina
McCorkie says he's
a kind heart
strong & pleasant
yet a gambler
a roué
a drunkard
fierce fighter
Check out "The Yew Pine Mountains"
(a version of John Henry)

Ideas for Sections

- Where he's from—I am a Tennessee man
- When he grows up he's gonna die
- Steam engine/race/technology—"I'll hammer my fool self to death"
- Woman
- Work
- Lord
- Water (final)
- Remembering—don't want to die like JH, I'm not comin' back
- What he's like—tall, short, black, white, prisoner, worker, good, bad, 6 ft. tall

somebody dying every day
Rocks and mountain
The mountain was so tall
John Henry was so small
Woman

She wore red, she wore blue
I've been true to you
Polly Ann drove steel just like a man
left and right
size of hammers
shaker
"I've an awful roaring in my head"
to his woman
"never wear black, wear blue"
"the boy drives steel like his dad"
"the place where JH went blind"
Some said he come from Columbus, others said he come from Cain, but he
give me his name as an East Virginia man
Brinton New Jersey
Give me a cool drink of water before I die
The mountains was a crackin' all around
The rock is so hard,
The steel so tough
I can feel my muscles giving way
Take my hammer and wrap it in gold and give it to the girl I love "Julie, do
the best you can."
He laid down his hammer and cried
I believe the tunnel is falling in.
Last word "Have you ever seen cold iron run like lead?"
"Til he drove his self out of his shirt"
"That's my hammer falling in the wind"
(in response to the place falling in)
tells his son to be a steel drivin' man
tells his son not to be a steel drivin' man
til his hammer caught on fire
Desperate man
work songs tell more about the worker than documents
he drove so hard he broke his heart
he was 6 ft. tall
5 ft. tall
5 ft. 10 in.
"a big fellow"

Some say....he's from

Columbus

Cain

East Virginia

New Jersey

Yew Pine Mountains

West Virginia

Mississippi (Raymond, Crystal Springs, Jackson)

Kentucky

Alabama

(from near Bessemer and Blackton)

an old log house out a little ways from Mobile, Alabama

South Carolina

Some say he's 5 ft. 1

"My grandfather knew John Henry personally ...from Tennessee"

"I am telling you all I know about John Henry..."

Burying

they buried him in the sand

buried him in a cemetery or "burial ground"

took John Henry up the mountain

buried him between two mountains

took him to the white house

Hammer

10 lb. sheep nose hammer

Some Say

States

Destiny

He was born in Tennessee and he was a white man.

My father often told me about John Henry. There is no mistake he was a white man.

Dad worked with John Henry four years at Big Bend Tunnel. Dad says he was the hero of the world...

Amish is the new black

Starts on D humming adds C nat, below and F above

Stamps sporadic

(possible to have Mark and Evan on G and A below mid C for the humming)

Think about having dueling bones

How to build a driving section

Guitar chords and slaps

Bones—are the running basis of the section What is everyone else doing?

Evan a slow upward gliss to G and then other pitches—bell outward

Piano, Vc, C♭—cresc. chords calling out

Eventually singers come in with he's from, he's from, he's from—low and strong cresc.—possibly triggered by percussion bell.

This all builds up and leads to the states/cities he's from. Sparkling tuneful overlapping cities.

Followed by Destiny "hammer in his hand" mournful/blues like

Atmosphere with loud clank

Woman

All the names

She can hammer as good as a man

The Race

An incessant drilling on everyone's part and we go electric here. A fractured folk song that repeats itself and is driving.

Lord, Lord—prayer, moan

And water combined

It won't kill me

WOLLESONICS

KENNY WOLLESEN

The first instrument I built was with my father Ray Wollesen back in the early '90s.

It was a poor man's copy of Tom Nunn's *Bug*. (Tom Nunn is the great instrument builder and musician from the Bay Area!) It whet my appetite for instrument building and much to my father's disbelief people would pay me to play it on gigs and recordings! When Zorn asked me to make some instruments for a piece he was writing for bass flute and two foley artists, *The Prophetic Mysteries of Angels, Witches and Demons*, I really got cooking with the instrument building. Scouring the Manhattan flea markets on weekends for materials and ideas I made a gaggle of instruments of which Zorn picked three for the premiere at the Miller Theater— *The Wheary Grinder, Prepared Shot Gun and Prepared Slide Projector*.

Inspired by the concert, plus getting the gig to design and compose an all percussion score for Teller's (of Penn & Teller) stage production of *Macbeth*, I made still more instruments. One day while lying in bed playing the *Sleep Grinder*, I noticed that it had a calming, hypnotic, hallucinatory effect, so I gathered all the instruments I had built so far, taught some friends how to play them and started giving free *Sonic Massages* on the sidewalks of New York, on museum roofs, in attics in Lithuania, in art galleries, at spaghetti dinners, at the HONK Festival in Boston for hundreds of drunken marching band members...basically for any one who would listen. What's a *Sonic Massage* you may ask? It's nearly impossible to describe. It must be experienced! All I can tell you now is it's hypnotic, hallucinatory and pleasurable! Perhaps it can be explored in the next *Arcana*. For now, I hope you enjoy these instruments from Wollesonic!

1. Alvin's Spring Drum
Indian dolak, drum head, slinky

2. Angelic Grinder I
antique centrifuge, film canisters, string

3. Angelic Grinder II
antique hand drill, aluminum, string, lamp parts

4. Ball Grinder
antique piston puller, wooden balls, beads, bells

5. Balloon Grinder
antique piston puller, balloons, beads, seeds

6. Bell Grinder
antique hand drill, bicycle wheel, bells

7. Bira Biras
cardboard tubes, paper cups, string, drumheads, tape, drumsticks

8. The Bug (Wollesonic version)
wood, threaded rod, wire, metal bowl

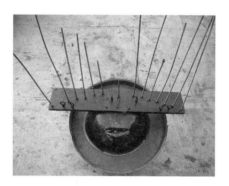

9. *Can Gopichan*
(co-built by Daniel Jodocy)
cans, bamboo, wood, guitar string, drumsticks

10. Cat Grip (off)
brief case, cat head pins, Chinese cricket boxes

11. Cat Grip (on)
briefcase, cat head pins, Chinese cricket boxes

12. Chantal's Fault
antique portable Victrola, wood, guitar string, tube, drum head, cork

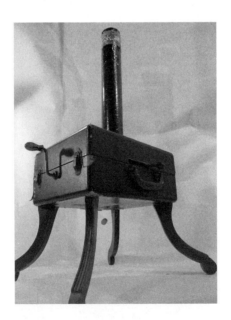

13. Chika Chikas
Nigerian seed pods, dowels, wood balls

14. Fire Cracker Rattler
bamboo, wire, beads

15. Floor Chime
clock chimes, cabinet knobs, piano pedal

16. Harmonica Grinder
antique centrifuge, harmonicas

17. High Lonesome Cycle
ready-made unicycle, fabric

18. Macbeth's Brain
ratchet, wood, African rattler, can, guitar string, spring

19. Marching Machine
(co-built by Daniel Jodocy) wood, rope, and wooden shoe inserts

20. Mini-Wind Wands
wood dowels, wood beads, rubber bands

21. Prepared Music Box
music box, wood

22. Prepared Rifle
toy rifle, slide projector parts, super 8 film splicer

23. Prepared Slide Projector
antiques slide projector, bolts, and rosin

24. Rain Carousel
antique cosmetic case, bamboo, spring, wooden ball, drumsticks

25. Rain Grinder
meat grinder, bamboo, beads, seeds

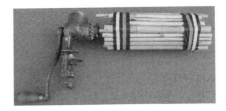

26. Seed Pod Twirler
wood, Nigerian seed pods, paper, piano parts, tape

27. Sleep Grinder
cosmetic travel case, cork, seed pods, toy accordion,
toy maraca, bell, piano parts, corrugated tubes

28. Tape Drum
(co-built by Daniel Jodocy) wood, clear tape, duct tape, bamboo

29. The Cloud
plastic bags
(in performance at a Sonic Massage on the roof of the Bonn Museum)

30. Wheary Grinder
cosmetic suitcase, gears, cooling fan, cork, saw blades,
door stop, tape measure

31. Whirly Grinder
antique hand drill, whirly tubes, metal rod, coconut
(played by percussionist William McIntyre)

32. Wind Trike
(co-built by Daniel Jodocy) tricycle, wood, rubber bands

*33. Wind Trike in performance at Great Small Works
"Rising Tide Parade" in New York City*

SMALL, STILL VOICE

NATHAN WOOLEY

I heard the phrase "listening to the still, small voice" a number of years ago in conjunction with Ralph Waldo Emerson, a writer that had a place in my romantic visions of youth in much the way I would imagine Rudyard Kipling, Robert Louis Stevenson or Jack Kerouac did for other young men and women. There was something about the transcendentalist message; the feeling that a certain brand of asceticism and self-reliance was not lonely and harsh, but a way of living that was very colorful and deep and warm, that I have always been drawn to. Over the years, although I have come to believe less and less in the present cultural relevance of Emerson (or Thoreau, another early favorite), I still carry a certain grand misunderstanding of their work that has developed into my own view on what meaning my life might have. And, my version of that phrase, "listening to the still, small voice", has become the crux of a way of living, as well as a touch point for me during my short musical career.

A little background is helpful, I think, to understand my attachment to this idea and to preface what will hopefully be a lucid explanation about what this has to do with music. I grew up as an only child. I have no ripe stories of familial discord. I was and am loved by my family and feel very lucky for that. I spent a lot of time with my grandmother who was a quiet but warm person, as are my parents. So, it only makes sense that my natural resting position, my psychic angle of repose, would be one of detachment. Ever since I can remember I've been more involved in an interior life than a social one, meaning quiet contemplation is much more natural and comfortable than almost any other interaction, no matter how pleasant and meaningful. I understand the social and career limitations of this way of living, but I've grown to accept it over time, and I'm happy with it.

This way of being opened me up to Emerson, Thoreau, and my

understanding of the small, still voice. Nothing is sexier to a boy prone to inward living than the idea of becoming the philosopher hermit. For years it was my greatest daydream to find my Walden, leave the world behind and just *think about great things*. To this day it's my "happy place" when things are going shit-fireworks around me, to imagine myself, great with beard and hair, pushing myself down a path between two giant trees never to be seen again. At my best, I laugh it off as archaic and asocial escapism. At my worst, I have to seriously start mentally tallying my many attachments to the 21st century, both interpersonal and technological. That's usually enough reality to snap me out of the daydream. It's this predisposition, however, that causes me to cling to the idea of the voice; the quiet, inner compulsion that I somehow find so important.

The small, still voice is nothing like its description. It is not small, but mighty, powerful, strong, and willful. It is often a whirling mass of activity, indecision, second-guessing, and conflicting ideas, as opposed to "still" and, lest you chalk this up to a simple schizophrenic break:

There is no actual whispering disembodied voice. (Let's make that totally clear.)

The voice is that slight quickening of the heartbeat that tells me that what I'm doing is honest and, more importantly, specific to who I am as a human being. Some people may refer to this as their conscience, but it's definitely *not* a constant beacon of righteousness, even *rightness*, not by any stretch of the imagination. It's simply a little nudge here and there, some-times illustrating how decisions can go right and how decisions can go wrong; illustrations which my mind, having a sense of what makes me unique can choose to accept or ignore depending on the reality of my situation. There are enough moments where I can truly allow myself to let go and make a choice based on what is personal and truthful that the voice is radically important as a guide to living my life.

I'm not revealing any great truths. Everyone has their version of this voice. Where these decisions are almost constantly useful to me specif-ically, however, is music. And in that sense, the one great moment of realization which came directly out of paying attention to that simple quickening of pulse was this little gem:

Music doesn't matter.

In general, the music I make is ultimately inconsequential to my individual existence unless I make it so by endowing it with my own personal qualifications, quantifications, and neuroses. This is in no way nihilistic thinking to me. It's actually freeing. It makes me realize that I am no less of a man when I play a bad concert than when I play a good one. I'm still a grounded human being that has the right to stand on two heavy feet on this earth and have myself counted by the masses.

I don't know if I can really explain that idea without feeling like a new age "game of" whatever shyster, but there it is. When I realize it doesn't matter, then not only does it free me to take creative chances, but every little wool-gathering argument over the subtleties of style, whether jazz is "dead" or not, who is the best A in the C scene and all that just becomes academic and needlessly divergent. With this knowledge I can choose to take part in the discussion (argument) as discussion without losing the rudder of who I am as a musician and as a human being. I can make music without having to feel like my existence absolutely hangs on every breath I put through the horn. Most of all, it allows me to stop being precious and no good music is ever precious.

In my musical decision making, the small, still voice gets free reign, and this contains the answer to any question that references the diversity of the musical work that I do. When I encounter a musician that is able to channel their whole being into one confined set of musical parameters, I tend to meet their work with either a sense of distrust or awe. Awe because of their ability to stay that focused on a limited set of musical language or distrust because I can't imagine someone only having such a limited set of perspectives on any topic. This is due to my upbringing, my personal aesthetic, and the chance encounters I have had with the right and wrong people over the years....in essence my history as a human being. Because of this history, I've developed a certain way of looking at things musically that is specific and three-dimensional. I'm not saying that the concept is confined to me as some sort of uber-musician (everyone is involved in the same basic processes), but my particular set of aesthetics and my way of looking at musical problems are very specific to me. They are different from everyone else and that's what makes them special. Everyone is dealing with this in their own way, which means there are enough different special takes on an idea, based on the wide wealth of personalities and personal histories that anything is open to discussion and debate. I think it's this diversity of attacks on singular ideas that make art and music and dance and THOUGHT interesting and warm and social and human. And yet, it's this kind of divergence of attitudes and views that tends to be seen as a threat to the way we perceive musical history and practice.

The natural enemy of this acceptance of divergent thinking, specifically in music, is *lineage*. For the purposes of my thinking, there are two definitions on musical lineage. The first is common to all of us, and is most likely what we think of when someone specifically uses the term "the tradition" or "the lineage" in reference to jazz music. This is lineage as a concept wholly one dimensional, linear, and prescribed from outside forces on the practitioners and audience of music through a combination of peer networks, higher education and music media. This, in terms of being a jazz trumpet player, is something we are inundated with from an early age. Buddy Bolden-the Armstrong-Beiderbecke split which somehow leads both worlds back to Roy Eldridge, then to Dizzy Gillespie, then to Miles Davis, then to Clifford Brown or Chet Baker (where the Armstrong-Beiderbecke split becomes valid again), etc. Each branch breaks off into another branch … and the next thing you know… you, as a trumpet player, are nothing more than a quivering leaf on the end of a Lester Bowie-Bill Dixon-Axel Doerner branch. (*By bringing specific names into the discussion, I think it's important to stop and say the following: This is not an attack on any player, but dissatisfaction with an idea; a completist and temporal way of viewing an artistic history.*) When talking in terms of this kind of lineage the small, still voice in me goes silent, and that tells me that something is not completely whole and personally true about this way of thinking for me.

My main problem with this way of thinking is that, to the musician, it's tantamount to saying that for someone to play *their* music they need to gather the permission, verbal or implied, of a handful of other musicians that an outside group of listeners have decided to be their progenitors, whether that is strictly the case or not. I have respect for anyone that plays music, and a great deal of love for my influences, but I think it's counterproductive to add unnecessary hierarchy and recast anyone as gods.

When you make that strange, small step that thrusts you into some sense of musical maturity, you are allowed to become a part of the social fabric of a process, a contributing member to a great open pool of ideas. I always felt that being able to join the world of your influences in a meaningful way, to metaphorically "look them in the eye" and exchange thoughts, is the payoff of years of hard work and maturation. That's what all the hours of practicing and thinking and editing and living are moving towards. To do the work establishing an aesthetic and philosophy and technique and then find out that it all comes down to an arbitrary set of cultural gatekeepers seems like a cruel joke.

Beyond my own subjective opinion, this one-dimensional concept of lineage and its tacit social reinforcement is not acceptable for a modern artistic society. How many artists have wasted time or energy waiting for permission to do their work from whomever? How many people did Bill Dixon ask permission from….or Thomas Pynchon….or Evan Parker…or Henry Miller…or Karl Marx…or John Cassavetes? They didn't. They didn't waste the energy and that's the point. Why should an artist want to place him or herself on anything but an equal footing with the greats that influenced them, knowing the level of personal commitment that these greats brought to their work? This is inspiration and energy and excitement as a creative human being, plain and simple. This is *not* the same as blindly belonging to a lineage. This is being a peer, and having the strength to enjoy it. Music is too small a field for it to be this historically stratified. Life is too short to have to ask permission (however abstract the concept is used) to say what you want to say. After all, *music doesn't matter.*

This brings me to my alternate definition of lineage, which is simply a difference of one and three dimensions. By way of illustration, my true lineage comes from a lot of musical and non-musical sources and the meta-connection that binds it into this three-dimensional mass is that my influences are the people that taught me various lesson which, when accumulated, brought me to the conclusion that I have no one to answer to but myself. These are the people that filled out my mind and my personality by slowly placing bits of themselves on me and peeling away the pieces of me they saw and knew to be false. Yes, some of them are musicians, maybe even ones that you know, but this doesn't mean that I am hanging on to their branch (nor are they hanging on mine). They're the people that at some point in time, in a positive or negative way, let me know that it's okay to drop off the tree altogether; that I had the strength to try and germinate into something different.

I want to point out, in closing and to hammer the point home, that, as opposed to the linear form of tradition most people have placed on them, using this three dimensional way of looking at tradition affirms the individual, the artist as human being. It is one thing to apply the jazz family tree to a player. It certainly narrows down the field to some extent to say someone belongs to the Miles Davis branch, but it is also a description that can apply to thousands of players. The more interesting thing is to learn the three dimensional lineage that creates the human being and letting those millions of artists float and germinate and interact in a real and meaningful way. Real influences do not exist in a strictly linear timeline. They have been prescribed to each individual through no one other than themselves. They don't even necessarily have anything to do with each other, but all of them have somehow existed in space around that person at the right time to make them who they are.

Personally, this three dimensional lineage taught me the quality I've always equated to jazz specifically and artistic practices in general: to follow the quickening of my heart, especially when that quickening pushes me in a new and frightening direction. I am letting myself be different, and the people in my true lineage are the ones that I should thank every time I play, every time I take a chance and every time I feel the happy buzzing of that small, still voice inside telling me that what I'm doing is honest and right for me.

A NOTE ON BBM

CHARLES WUORINEN

At one of the inevitable panel discussions before the premiere of my opera *Haroun and the Sea of Stories* the moderator asked me why I had wanted to write an opera. I answered without hesitation: "A death wish." Then he asked if I would ever compose another; again without hesitation I said: "Of course." All of us who compose know the combination of self-emptying and exhilaration that can lead to these two answers, but their significance is grossly amplified when one comes to a work on the scale of an opera—always assuming, of course, that a certain fastidiousness of detail and assurance that things will be theatrically *apropos* are major concerns. An opera is not a piece of music theater.

When I first saw the film version of *Brokeback Mountain* I had not yet encountered the short story which underlay it, but even in the over-long and rather sentimental treatment that the film presented, I knew there was operatic material at hand. But on opening the first of Annie Proulx' superb three-volume collection of *Wyoming Stories* to read the original, I was astonished at the differences between the famous story (which rather few people know) and the more famous film version. Granted, the film adaptation presented some interesting fleshing-out of subsidiary characters, but basic distortions had insinuated themselves as well. One of the worst of these is the failure of the film to project the lethality of the landscape in which most of the story unfolds, and which grinds down those who lived in it during the time of the action.

When to my great joy Annie Proulx agreed to write the libretto herself for my proposed opera, therefore, I told her that my mission in composing it would be to restore and project this and other meanings of a story that may have become world famous, but (as happens so often) has been completely hidden in the process.

Around this time, the New York City Opera was installing Gerard

Mortier as its new director. He had become aware of my interest in *Brokeback,* and offered to commission the work through the New York City Opera. The sad travails of that institution have been told in other places, but among other results of their crisis was the departure of Mortier for the Teatro Real in Madrid, and the subsequent transfer of the commission to that house, with the first performances now scheduled for January of 2014.

Annie Proulx and I began consultations on the work in 2008 with a week spent at the excellent Ucross Foundation (an artists' retreat) near Sheridan, Wyoming. There I had the chance to go into the mountains that provide the model for *Brokeback*, and to spend several delightfully libacious (on my part anyway) evenings with Annie Proulx, viewing the Great Sky of Wyoming and contemplating various possible natural disasters which might end human life on the planet, or perhaps the planet itself.

The result of this and many subsequent exchanges was a splendidly concise and apposite libretto, in which Proulx, through her characteristically laconic style, conveys character and scene with great efficiency. An essential property of any libretto which aspires to project cognitive content is this kind of efficiency, since sung language greatly slows the delivery of words. I count myself very lucky to have been given such an excellent exemplar.

When I began to assemble musical materials for the opera, the idea of fixing two special pitch-classes for the two principals suggested itself immediately. In the event these are C-sharp (for Ennis, a bass-baritone) and B-natural (for Jack, a tenor), and most especially the actual notes common to their two ranges: C4-sharp and B3-natural. (I picked the "higher" note for Ennis notwithstanding his lower voice-range because I always thought him—despite his fatal hang-ups—the sexually dominant of the pair.) Between these two (whether as equivalence classes or real notes) of course lies C-natural. Now C, in its embodiment as the root of the traditional C-minor, was associated in older times with sleep or death. (Think of the final entombment choruses of the two surviving Bach *Passions,* among countless other examples.) Since things do not end well for our two characters, the intervallic convergence of their special notes on the Note of Death seems appropriate. Indeed this simple relationship lies at the fundamental generative level of the opera's structure.

After this, all that remained was to compose the music.

ABOUT THE CONTRIBUTORS

RICHARD "DUCK" BAKER occupies a unique niche among contemporary guitarists. In terms of his instrumental style he fits squarely in the tradition of American folk, blues, and country fingerpicking, but his musical interests extend both into more modern styles (jazz and free improvisation) as well as older traditions (Irish and Scottish music). He has worked mostly as a soloist but has also adapted his finger-style approach to a variety of group situations. Baker is also known for his many tutorial books and videos, as well as his contributions to such magazines as *Coda* and *Jazz Times*. Shortly after moving from his native Virginia to San Francisco in 1973, Baker signed with Kicking Mule Records. His reputation in the acoustic guitar world is based on the five solo LPs he made for that label, which include the first solo guitar record devoted to traditional Irish tunes, and an interesting finger-style jazz album. It was also in the late seventies that Baker became associated with the free music scene, appearing with musicians like Eugene Chadbourne and John Zorn in New York and Bruce Ackley and Henry Kaiser in San Francisco. More recent associations include duos with trombone master Roswell Rudd, clarinetist/saxophonist Michael Moore and guitarist Jamie Findlay. Since transferring to London in 2005, Baker has formed a trio dedicated primarily to his own tunes and those of Thelonious Monk and Herbie Nichols, with clarinetist Alex Ward and bassist Joe Williamson. Though Baker has continued his involvement with traditional styles, his recordings since the mid-'80s tend to be more focused on his own compositions, which reflect the influence of jazz pianist/composers like Thelonious Monk, Herbie Nichols, Randy Weston, etc. His solo recording of Nichols tunes, *Spinning Song*, helped establish Baker as an important voice in the world of fingerstyle jazz guitar.

Richard "Duck" Baker

EVE BEGLARIAN's chamber, choral and orchestral music has been commissioned and widely performed by the Los Angeles Master Chorale, the American Composers Orchestra, the Bang on a Can All-Stars, the Chamber Music Society of Lincoln Center, the California EAR Unit, the Orchestra of St. Luke's, Relâche, the Paul Dresher Ensemble, Sequitur, Dither, Ekmeles, Loadbang, the Guidonian Hand and Newspeak. She has also worked extensively in theater, with directors Lee Breuer (Mabou Mines) and Chen Shi Zheng; in dance, with Ann Carlson, Victoria Marks, Susan Marshall, and David Neumann, and with visual and video artists Cory Arcangel, Anne Bray, Barbara

Eve Beglarian

Hammer, and Shirin Neshat. Her most recent work grows out of a journey she made by kayak and bicycle down the length of the Mississippi River in 2009. BRIM, her band with violinist Mary Rowell, is the core ensemble performing the music from the RiverProject. Recordings of Eve's music are available on labels including Koch, New World, Cantaloupe, Innova, Naxos, and Kill Rock Stars. For more information, please see www.evbvd.com

KARL BERGER is internationally active as a composer, performer (piano, vibraphone), conductor of improvising orchestras, and leader of soloists' ensembles, with vocalist/poet Ingrid Sertso. He also conducts development sessions with ensembles and individuals, coaching instrumentalists in finding a wider and deeper range of expression and perspective through his "Music Mind" approach. With Ornette Coleman and Ingrid Sertso Karl Berger founded the now legendary Creative Music Studio In Woodstock NY in 1972, with the overriding goal of developing concepts and practices highlighting the common elements of music beyond styles and categories as tools for intensifying personal expression in improvisation, interpretation and composition. Under Karl Berger's direction, and in collaboration with the Columbia University Library, the Creative Music Foundation is presently re-mastering its archive of ground-breaking live-recordings of the '70s and '80s, featuring a who-is-who of composers/performers of new music, the jazz avant-garde, and of world-musical traditions, in experimental settings. He recorded and performed with many international artists in jazz, world music, and new music, after arriving in New York from Paris with Don Cherry's group in 1966. He composed and arranged for classical ensembles, jazz groups, fusion groups, big band, symphony, and for special project recordings, featuring solo artists and producers such as Jeff Buckley, Angelique Kidjo, Bill Laswell and others. Presently, he releases recordings through Tzadik Records: *Strangely Familiar* piano music (2010) and a box-set of archived and new works (2012). Karl is a 6-time Downbeat Critics Poll Winner. He received grants and commissions by the National Endowment for the Arts, the New York State Council on the Arts, Rockefeller Foundation, German Radio: WDR, NDR, SWF, Radio France, Rai Italy. He was Professor of Composition at Frankfurt Hochschule, Germany from 1990 till 2000, and Chair of the Music Department at the University of Massachussetts in Darmouth, Mass until 2005.

Karl Berger

Claire Chase

Flutist CLAIRE CHASE is active as a soloist, collaborative artist and activist for new music. Over the past decade Claire has given the world premieres of more than 100 works for solo flute, many of them tailor-made for her, and she has played, produced and curated more than 500 concerts of contemporary music. First Prize Winner of the 2008 Concert Artists Guild International Competition, Chase has given solo recitals recently at Weill Recital Hall at Carnegie Hall, Avery Fisher Hall, and throughout the US. Upcoming engagements will take her to China, Japan, throughout Europe and Latin America. Chase's newest solo album, *Terrestre*, featuring works by Saariaho, Boulez, Carter, Donatoni and Fujikura, was released in January 2012 to critical acclaim. She released her debut solo album, *Aliento*, in October 2009 featuring six world premiere recordings by emerging composers, which was named one of the Top Ten Releases of the Year by *Time Out Chicago*. Chase is featured on over a dozen collaborative recordings on such labels as Tzadik, Bridge, Kairos, Mode, New Focus, and Samadhisound. In 2001, Chase founded the International Contemporary Ensemble (ICE), a nonprofit organization dedicated to reshaping the way new music is created and experienced. She has served as executive director of ICE since its inception. The ICE musicians currently serve as Artists in Residence at the Mostly Mozart Festival of Lincoln Center, and as Ensemble-in-Residence at the Museum of Contemporary Art Chicago. Under Chase's leadership, ICE was awarded the 2010 Trailblazer Award from the American Music Center. She lives in Brooklyn.

Currently the Chicago Symphony's Mead Composer-in-Residence, Music Director Riccardo Muti lauded ANNA CLYNE as "an artist who writes from the heart, who defies categorization and who reaches across all barriers and boundaries. Her compositions are meant to be played by great musicians and listened to by enthusiastic audiences no matter what their background." An avid advocate for music education, Clyne teaches composition workshops for local young composers and incarcerated youths as part of her residency with the CSO, and served as the Director of the New York Youth Symphony's award-winning program for young composers "Making Score" from 2008 to 2010. London-born Anna Clyne is a composer of acoustic and electro-acoustic music, combining resonant soundscapes with propelling textures that weave, morph, and collide in dramatic explosions. Her work, described as "dazzlingly inventive" by *Time Out New York*, often includes collaborations with cutting edge choreographers, visual artists, film-makers, and musicians worldwide. Her work has been championed by some of the world's finest conductors, including Pablo Heras-Casado, George Manahan, Jeffrey Milarsky, Riccardo Muti, Alan Pierson, Andre de Ridder, and Esa-Pekka Salonen. Recent commissions include the Los Angeles Philharmonic, Carnegie Hall, Chicago Symphony Orchestra, American Composers Orchestra, London Sinfonietta, Southbank Center, and the Houston Symphony with the Houston Ballet. Clyne has received numerous accolades, including a Charles Ives Fellowship from the American Academy of Arts and Letters. Her music is published by Boosey & Hawkes and her debut CD, *Blue Moth*, will be released by Tzadik.

Anna Clyne

John Corigliano

The American JOHN CORIGLIANO continues to add to one of the richest, most unusual, and most widely celebrated bodies of work any composer has created over the last forty years. Corigliano's numerous scores—including three symphonies and eight concerti among over one hundred chamber, vocal, choral, and orchestral works—have been performed and recorded by many of the most prominent orchestras, soloists, and chamber musicians in the world. Recent scores include *Conjurer* (2008), for percussion and string orchestra, commissioned for and introduced by Dame Evelyn Glennie; *Concerto for Violin and Orchestra: The Red Violin* (2005), developed from the themes of

285

the score to the François Girard's film of the same name, which won Corigliano the Oscar in 1999; *Mr. Tambourine Man: Seven Poems of Bob Dylan* (2000) for orchestra and amplified soprano, the recording which won the Grammy for Best Contemporary Composition in 2008; *Symphony No. 3: Circus Maximus* (2004), scored simultaneously for wind orchestra and a multitude of wind ensembles; and *Symphony No. 2* (2001: Pulitzer Prize in Music). Other important scores include *String Quartet* (1995: Grammy Award, Best Contemporary Composition); *Symphony No. 1* (1991: Grawemeyer and Grammy Awards); the opera *The Ghosts of Versailles* (Metropolitan Opera commission, 1991, International Classical Music Award 1992); and the *Clarinet Concerto* (1977). One of the few living composers to have a string quartet named for him, Corigliano serves on the composition faculty at the Juilliard School of Music and holds the position of Distinguished Professor of Music at Lehman College, City University of New York, which has established a scholarship in his name; for the past fourteen years he and his partner, the composer-librettist Mark Adamo, have divided their time between Manhattan and Kent Cliffs, New York. More information is available at www.johncorigliano.com

JEREMIAH CYMERMAN is a composer and clarinetist based in New York City since 2002. An active participant in several different scenes, Cymerman's work reflects an interest in improvisation, electronic manipulation and production, traditional, studio and graphic composition and solo performance. Cymerman has worked or performed with a broad range of contemporary artists and frequent collaborators include Toby Driver, Nate Wooley, Brian Chase, Mario Diaz de Leon, Christopher Hoffman, Jessica Pavone and Matthew Welch. Cymerman has toured internationally, received numerous commissions and published several articles on music and music production. He has released several recordings of his own music and his recorded output has been documented on the

Jeremiah Cymerman Tzadik and Porter record labels.

David Fulmer Still in his twenties, composer, violinist, and conductor DAVID FULMER is quickly emerging as one of the most unique musicians of his generation. His bold compositional aesthetic combined with his thrilling performing abilities have garnered numerous international accolades. The success of his *Violin Concerto* at Lincoln Center in 2010 earned international attention and resulted in immediate engagement to perform the work with major orchestras and at festivals in the United Kingdom, Europe, North America, Scandinavia, and Australia. Fulmer made his European debut performing and recording the *Violin Concerto* with the BBC Scottish Symphony Orchestra under the direction of Matthias Pintscher in February 2011. A surge in Fulmer's compositional activity has resulted from a series of distinctive commissions from major international orchestras, a new violin concerto for virtuoso Stefan Jackiw, and several new works for notable contemporary ensembles throughout Europe, China, Japan, and North America. His hour-long cycle, *On Night,* composed for saxophonist Eliot Gattegno and ensemble, was featured this season by the Argento New Music Project and conducted by the composer. The work will be commercially released on the Tzadik label in 2012. Fulmer is the first American ever to receive the International Edvard Grieg Competition for Composers. He also has received the ASCAP Morton Gould Young Composer Award, the BMI Composer Award, and the Charles Ives Award of the American Academy of Arts and Letters. Other honors and awards include a special citation from the Minister of Education of Brazil for Fulmer's series of lectures on music, the Hannah Komanoff Scholarship in Composition, the Dorothy Hill Klotzman Grant from The Juilliard School, and the highly coveted George Whitefield Chadwick Gold Medal from the New England Conservatory. Fulmer recently graduated from The Juilliard School where he received his doctorate, having studied composition with Milton Babbitt and violin with Robert Mann.

Violinist, composer, producer, label owner and concert presenter JEFF GAUTHIER has worked with many prominent musicians in a variety of creative contexts during a career that has spanned over thirty years. As an improvising violinist he has performed and recorded with Yusef Lateef and Adam Rudolph for Meta Records, The Alex Cline Ensemble for ECM, Nine Winds & Cryptogramophone Records, the Cline Gauthier Stinson trio for Cryptogramophone and Nine Winds Records, and The Vinny Golia Large Ensemble and Nels Cline for Cryptogramophone Records. His own ensemble, The Jeff Gauthier Goatette has recorded six CDs including *Internal Memo* and *The Present* for Nine Winds and *Mask, One and the Same, House of Return,* and *Open Source* for Cryptogramophone. He is currently Executive Director of The Jazz Bakery, and co-producer of The Angel City Jazz Festival in Los Angeles. Well known as a producer of jazz and new music recordings, Gauthier has worked with such luminaries as Alan Broadbent, Nels Cline, Mark Dresser, Peter Erskine, Bill Frisell Bennie Maupin, Myra Melford, Jimmy Rowles, Alan Pasqua, Don Preston, Jenny Scheinman, Scott Amendola, Ben Goldberg, Eclipse Quartet, and many others, having produced CDs for Bridge, Cryptogramophone, Delos, and Nine Winds Records. In 1998 Gauthier founded Cryptogramophone Records, which has since become a premiere West Coast record label for cutting-edge jazz artists. In a former life as a classical violinist, Gauthier performed regularly with the Los Angeles Chamber Orchestra, Los Angeles Music Center Opera, Los Angeles Master Chorale, Long Beach Symphony, the Oregon Bach Festival and the Carmel Bach Festival, and also performed on numerous film scores. He performed on the 2000 Grammy Award winning CD *Credo,* by Krzysztof Penderecki with the Oregon Bach Festival Orchestra and Chorus, as well as numerous recordings of classical and baroque music. Gauthier is a graduate of California Institute of the Arts.　**Jeff Gauthier**

Music Director ALAN GILBERT, The Yoko Nagae Ceschina Chair,　**Alan Gilbert**
began his tenure at the New York Philharmonic in September 2009,
launching what *New York* magazine called "a fresh future for the Philharmonic." The first native New Yorker in the post, he has introduced the positions of The Marie-Josée Kravis Composer-in-Residence and The Mary and James G. Wallach Artist-in-Residence, an annual three-week festival, and *CONTACT!,* the new-

music series, and has sought to make the Orchestra a point of civic pride for the city as well as for the country. Mr. Gilbert's 2011–12 Philharmonic season comprises world premieres and pillars of the repertoire to shed fresh perspectives on both the new and the established. It also includes tours to Europe and California, appearances at Carnegie Hall, and a program at the Park Avenue Armory featuring Stockhausen's *Gruppen*. Mr. Gilbert also made his Philharmonic debut as soloist when he joined Frank Peter Zimmermann in J.S. Bach's *Concerto for Two Violins* in October 2011. Last season's highlights included celebrated tours of European music capitals, Carnegie Hall's 120th Anniversary Concert, and the acclaimed performances of Janácek's *The Cunning Little Vixen*. Mr. Gilbert is Director of Conducting and Orchestral Studies and holds the William Schuman Chair in Musical Studies at The Juilliard School. Conductor Laureate of the Royal Stockholm Philharmonic Orchestra and Principal Guest Conductor of Hamburg's NDR Symphony Orchestra, he regularly conducts leading orchestras around the world. He made his acclaimed Metropolitan Opera debut conducting John Adams's *Doctor Atomic* in 2008. His recordings have received Grammy Award nominations and top honors from the *Chicago Tribune* and *Gramophone* magazine. In May 2010 Mr. Gilbert received an Honorary Doctor of Music degree from The Curtis Institute of Music, and in December 2011, Columbia University's Ditson Conductor's Award for his "exceptional commitment to the performance of works by American composers and to contemporary music."

Judd Greenstein   JUDD GREENSTEIN is a Brooklyn-based composer of structurally complex, viscerally engaging works for varied instrumentation. A passionate advocate for the "indie classical" community in New York and beyond, much of Judd's work is written for the virtuosic performers who make up that community, and is tailored to their specific talents and abilities. His work has been heard at venues such as the Tanglewood Festival of Contemporary Music, Amsterdam's Musiekgebouw, the Bang on a Can Marathon, and the MusicNOW festival; major recent commissions include those from Carnegie Hall, Present Music, ETHEL, the Seattle Chamber Players, yMusic, and Roomful of Teeth, as well as a 30-minute work for the Minnesota Orchestra's Inside the Classics series. His work, *Change*, for NOW Ensemble, was recently chosen as one of NPR Music's *100 Favorite Songs of 2011*. In addition to his work as a composer, Judd is active as a promoter of new music in New York and around the country. He is the co-director of New Amsterdam Records/New Amsterdam Presents, an artists' service organization that supports composers and performers whose work is open to all influence, regardless of genre. He is the curator of the Ecstatic Music Festival in New York's Merkin Hall, an annual showcase of new collaborative concerts between artists from different musical worlds, and he is a founding member of NOW Ensemble, a performer/composer collective that develops new chamber music for their idiosyncratic instrumentation of flute, clarinet, electric guitar, double bass, and piano. Judd has studied at the Tanglewood Music Center and the Bang on a Can Summer Institute and holds degrees from Williams College, the Yale School of

Music, and Princeton University.

Violinist HILARY HAHN's probing interpretations, technical brilliance, and commitment to new music and the commissioning process have not only made her one of the most sought-after artists of our time, but also brought her love of classical music to a diverse audience. At 32 years of age, her international fame and recognition, including two Grammys, multiple Diapason "d'Or of the Year" and "Preis der deutschen Schallplattenkritik" prizes, and the 2008 *Classic FM/Gramophone* Artist of the Year, are a testament to her talent and drive. Hahn appears regularly with the world's elite orchestras and on the most prestigious recital series. In the fifteen years since she began recording, Hahn has released fourteen feature albums on the Deutsche Grammophon and Sony labels, in addition to three DVDs, an Oscar-nominated movie soundtrack, an award-winning recording for children, and various compilations. Her recordings have received every critical prize in the international press, and have met with equal popular success. All have spent weeks on Billboard's Classical Top Ten list. In a special project in 2009, Hahn's former teacher, composer Jennifer Higdon, wrote a Pulitzer Prize-winning concerto for her. In October 2011, to great critical acclaim, Hahn released her newest album, *Charles Ives: Four Sonatas*. Hahn shows her ongoing commitment to contemporary music with her *In 27 Pieces: The Hilary Hahn Encores*. For this project, she has commissioned over two dozen composers to write short-form pieces for acoustic violin and piano. An engaging personality, Hahn is an avid writer and interviewer, posting journal entries and information for young musicians and concertgoers on her website, hilaryhahn.com. In video, she produces a YouTube channel, youtube.com/hilaryhahnvideos, and serves as guest host for the contemporary classical music blog *Sequenza21*. Elsewhere, her violin case comments on life as a traveling companion, on Twitter: twitter.com/violincase.

Hilary Hahn

Mary Halvorson

Jesse Harris

Guitarist/composer MARY HALVORSON has been active in New York since 2002, following jazz studies at Wesleyan University and the New School. Critics have called Ms. Halvorson "NYC's least-predictable improviser" (Howard Mandel, *City Arts*), "the most forward-thinking guitarist working right now" (Lars Gotrich, NPR.org) and "one of today's most formidable bandleaders" (Francis Davis, *Village Voice*). In addition to her long-standing trio, featuring bassist John Hébert and drummer Ches Smith, and her quintet, which adds trumpeter Jonathan Finlayson and alto saxophonist Jon Irabagon, Ms. Halvorson also co-leads a chamber-jazz duo with violist Jessica Pavone, the avant-rock band People and the collective ensembles Crackleknob, MAP and The Thirteenth Assembly. She is also an active member of bands led by Tim Berne, Anthony Braxton, Taylor Ho Bynum, Tomas Fujiwara, Curtis Hasselbring, Ingrid Laubrock, Myra Melford, Marc Ribot, Tom Rainey and Matthew Welch among others.

JESSE HARRIS is an accomplished singer, songwriter, guitarist and producer. Best known for having written and played guitar on Norah Jones' breakout hit *Don't Know Why* (for which he won the 2003 Grammy Award for Song of the Year), he has also had his songs recorded by numerous other artists, including Smokey Robinson, Willie Nelson, Cat Power, Solomon Burke and Emmylou Harris. As a solo artist, Jesse has released over ten albums.

DAVID LANG is the recipient of the 2008 Pulitzer Prize in Music for *the little match girl passion*, commissioned by Carnegie Hall for the vocal ensemble Theater of Voices, directed by Paul Hillier. In the words of *The New Yorker*, "With his winning of the Pulitzer Prize for *the little match girl passion* (one of the most original and moving scores of recent years), Lang, once a postminimalist enfant terrible, has solidified his standing as an American master." One of America's most performed and honored composers, his recent works include *writing on water* for the London Sinfonietta, with libretto and visuals by English filmmaker Peter Greenaway; *the difficulty of crossing a field*—a fully staged opera for the Kronos Quartet; *loud love songs*, a concerto for the percussionist Evelyn Glennie, and the oratorio *Shelter*, with co-composers Michael Gordon and Julia Wolfe, at the Next Wave Festival of the Brooklyn Academy of Music, staged by Ridge Theater and featuring the Norwegian vocal ensemble Trio Mediaeval. The commercial recording of *the little match girl passion*, on Harmonia Mundi, won the 2010 Grammy Award for Best Small Ensemble Performance. Lang is co-founder and co-artistic director of New York's legendary music festival, Bang on a Can.

David Lang

Mary Jane Leach

MARY JANE LEACH is a composer/performer whose work reveals a fascination with the physicality of sound, its acoustic properties and how they interact with space. In many of her works Leach creates an otherworldly sound environment using difference, combination, and interference tones; these are tones not actually sounded by the performers, but acoustic phenomena arising from Leach's deft manipulation of intonation and timbral qualities. The result is striking music which has a powerful effect on listeners. Critics have commented on her ability to "offer a spiritual recharge without the banalities of the new mysticism" (*Detroit Free Press*), evoking "a visionary quest for inner peace" (*Vice Versa Magazine*), and "an irridescent lingering sense of suspended time." (*Musicworks Magazine*) Leach's music has been performed throughout the world in a variety of settings, from the concert stage to experimental music forums, and in collaboration with dance and theater artists. She is an accomplished performer in her own right who has been presented across the United States and Europe, and her works have been performed by many eminent soloists and chamber ensembles, most recently in Europe by Manuel Zurria, Emanuele Arciulli and the Orchestra Sinfonica di Lecce, György Lakatos and Trio Lignum in Hungary, the Flemish Radio Choir, La Gioia, the London Concord Singers, and Vox Feminae (Switzerland). In recent years Leach has received considerable acclaim for her choral music, which is featured on two CD releases on the XI and New World labels. Drawing on inspirations as diverse as Monteverdi, Bruckner, and 14th century Ars Nova, these pieces "enliven a choral repertoire starved for good contemporary work." (*Village*

Voice). Several are published by C.F. Peters. In 1995 Leach was selected for a prestigious grant from the Foundation for Contemporary Performance Arts, which was established by Jasper Johns and John Cage to support innovative artists in the performing arts.

STEPHEN LEHMAN (b. 1978) is a composer, performer, educator, and scholar who works across a broad spectrum of experimental musical idioms. Lehman's pieces for large orchestra and chamber ensembles have been performed by the International Contemporary Ensemble (ICE), So Percussion, Kammerensemble Neue Musik Berlin, The JACK Quartet, and by members of the Argento and Wet Ink Ensembles. An alto saxophonist, Lehman has performed and recorded nationally and internationally with his own ensembles and with those led by Anthony Braxton, Dave Burrell, Mark Dresser, Vijay Iyer, Oliver Lake, Meshell Ndegeocello, and High Priest of Anti-Pop Consortium. Lehman received his B.A. (2000) and M.A. in Composition (2002) from Wesleyan University where he studied under Anthony Braxton and Alvin Lucier, while concurrently working with Jackie McLean at the Hartt School of Music. He received his doctorate (2012) in Music Composition at Columbia University, where his principal teachers were Tristan Murail and George Lewis. His recent recording, *Travail, Transformation & Flow* (Pi 2009), was chosen as the #1 Jazz Album of the Year by *The New York Times*. **Stephen Lehman**

Steven Mackey

STEVEN MACKEY was born in 1956, to American parents stationed in Frankfurt, Germany. His first musical passion was playing the electric guitar, in rock bands based in northern California. He later discovered concert music and has composed for orchestras, chamber ensembles, dance, and opera. He regularly performs his own work, including two electric guitar concertos and numerous solo and chamber works, and is also active as an improvising musician and performs with his band Big Farm. Among his commissions are works for the Chicago, St. Louis, New World, San Francisco Symphonies, and Dutch Radio, symphonies, the Los Angeles Philharmonic, the BBC Philharmonic, The Scottish and Swedish Chamber Orchestras, the Kronos Quartet, the Koussevitzky Music Foundation in the Library of Congress, Fromm Music Foundation, Brentano String Quartet, Borromeo String Quartet, Fred Sherry, Dawn Upshaw, PRISM Saxophone Quartet, Scottish Chamber Orchestra, and many others. As a guitarist, Mackey has performed his chamber music with the Kronos Quartet, Arditti Quartet, London Sinfonietta, Nexttime Ensemble (Parma), Psappha (Manchester), and Joey Baron. As a concerto soloist he has performed with many conductors including David Robertson, Michael Tilson Thomas, Peter Etvos, Dennis Russell Davies, and many others. There are a dozen CDs of Mackey's music and many other CDs that contain individual works. *Dreamhouse* (2010) and *Lonely Motel: Music From Slide* (2011), were both nominated for four Grammy awards. Mackey is currently Professor of Music and Chair of the Music Department at Princeton University where he has been on the faculty since 1985. His music is published by Boosey and Hawkes. For more information please see www.stevenmackey.com

Guggenheim fellow and Downbeat International Critics Poll Winner RUDRESH MAHANTHAPPA is considered one of the most innovative young musicians and composers in jazz today. Named Alto Saxophonist of the Year for 2011, 2010 and 2009 by the Jazz Journalist Association, Rudresh has incorporated the culture of his Indian ancestry and has fused myriad influences to create a truly groundbreaking artistic vision. As a performer, he leads/co-leads seven groups to critical acclaim and has achieved international recognition performing regularly at jazz festivals and clubs worldwide. As a composer, Rudresh has received commission grants from the Rockefeller Foundation MAP Fund, American Composers Forum, Chamber Music America, and the New York State Council on the Arts to develop new work. Mahanthappa holds a Bachelors of Music Degree in jazz performance from Berklee College of Music and a Masters of Music degree in jazz composition from Chicago's DePaul University. Mahanthappa currently lives in New York where he is clearly regarded as an important and influential voice in the jazz world.

Rudresh Mahanthappa

Rudresh K. Mahanthappa is a Yamaha Artist and uses Vandoren reeds exclusively. Mahanthappa is also a New York Foundation for the Arts Fellow.

Denman Maroney

Brad Mehldau

DENMAN MARONEY is known for his "hyperpiano" technique (playing the keys with one hand and the strings with other using slides and bows of metal, plastic, rubber, and wood) and his "temporal harmonies" (composing and improvising in multiple tempos). He has recorded for Porter, Innova, Clean Feed, Nuscope, Kadima, Cryptogramophone, New World, Mutable, Victo, CIMP, and Erstwhile among others with Dave Ballou, Theo Bleckmann, Robert Dick, Dave Douglas, Mark Dresser, Miguel Frasconi, Gamelan Son of Lion, Phil Haynes, Gerry Hemingway, Shelley Hirsch, Earl Howard, Leroy Jenkins, Lisa Karrer, Arthur Kell, Dominic Lash, Mat Maneri, Min Xiao-Fen, Alexandra Montano, Kevin Norton, Rich O'Donnell, Reuben Radding, Herb Robertson, Ned Rothenberg, Mary Rowell, Michael Sarin, Sheila Schonbrun, David Simons, Carl Stone, Hans Tammen, and Matthias Ziegler among others. He has received grants and commissions from Chamber Music America, the National Endowment for the Arts, the New York Foundation for the Arts, the New York State Council on the Arts, the Arts Council of Rockland County (NY), the Arts Council of Michigan, the Jerome Robbins Foundation, and the Mary Flagler Cary Charitable Trust among others. He has been in residence at Music Omi and the Yale Summer School of Music and Art. He was educated at Cal. Arts (MFA '74) and Williams (BA '71). He teaches at Fairleigh Dickinson University. In 2010 he was nominated for an Alpert Award. For more information please see www.denmanmaroney.com

One of the most lyrical and intimate voices of contemporary jazz piano, BRAD MEHLDAU has forged a unique path, which embodies the essence of jazz exploration, classical romanticism and pop allure. From critical acclaim as a bandleader to major international exposure in collaborations with Pat Metheny, Renee Fleming, and Joshua Redman, Mehldau continues to garner numerous awards and admiration from both jazz purists and music enthusiasts alike. His forays into melding musical idioms, in both trio (with Larry Grenadier on bass and Jeff Ballard on drums) and solo settings, has seen brilliant re-workings of songs by contemporary songwriters like The Beatles, Cole Porter, Radiohead, Paul Simon, Gershwin and Nick Drake; alongside the ever evolving breath of his own significant catalogue of original compositions. With his self proclaimed affection for popular music and classical training, Mehldau has become "universally admired as one of the most adventurous pianists to arrive on the jazz scene in years." (*Los Angeles Times*)

String instrumentalist, JESSICA PAVONE has led her own bands; Army of Strangers and The Pavones, has performed in ensembles led by Anthony Braxton, Jason Cady, Jeremiah Cymerman, Matana Roberts, Aaron Siegel, Henry Threadgill, and Matthew Welch, as well as such collective groups as the Mary Halvorson/Jessica Pavone Duo, Normal Love, and The Thirteenth Assembly. As a composer, Pavone has earned grants and commissions from the Aaron Copland Recording Fund, the American Music Center, The Kitchen, MATA, The Jerome Foundation, and the group, Till By Turning, which recently presented the European premiere of her piece *Quotidian* at Klangbad Festival in Germany. Jessica's music has been released by the Tzadik, Thirsty Ear, Skirl and Porter record labels.

Jessica Pavone

Tobias Picker

TOBIAS PICKER (b. Manhattan, 1954) is known as "a genuine creator with a fertile unforced vein of invention" (*The New Yorker*), "displaying a distinctively soulful style that is one of the glories of the current musical scene" (*BBC Music Magazine*) and "our finest composer for the lyric stage" (*Wall Street Journal*). His music has been performed and commissioned by the New York Philharmonic, Philadelphia Orchestra, Cleveland Orchestra, Chicago Symphony Orchestra, San Francisco Symphony, Minnesota Orchestra, BBC Proms, Munich, Helsinki and Strasbourg Philharmonics, numerous leading international festivals, chamber ensembles and soloists. Picker's first opera, *Emmeline* (1996) premiered at the Santa Fe Opera, telecast nationally by PBS Great Performances, led to commissions by LA Opera (*Fantastic Mr. Fox*), The Dallas Opera, San Diego Opera and L'Opera de Montreal (*Therese Raquin*), The San Francisco Opera (Dolores Claiborne), and The Metropolitan Opera (*An American Tragedy*). New productions have appeared at New York City Opera, Covent Garden and throughout Europe. *Awakenings*, commissioned by Rambert Dance Company, was performed eighty times with live orchestra during Rambert's 2010–11 UK and European tours. By age twenty-six, Picker received the Bearns Prize (Columbia University), BMI Award, Charles Ives Scholarship, and two fellowships from NEA and a Guggenheim Foundation Fellowship. Later he received the Award in Music from the American Academy of Arts and Letters. Picker's piano concerto *Keys to the City* (1983) was commissioned by the City of New York for the centenary of Brooklyn Bridge and described as "an exuberant, brassy, celebratory evocation, 18 minutes of irrepressible energy and a cosmopolitan eclecticism" (*The New York Times*). Tobias Picker studied composition with

Charles Wuorinen, Milton Babbitt and Elliott Carter and holds degrees from the Manhattan School of Music, the Juilliard School and Princeton University. In 2012, Picker was elected into the membership of The American Academy of Arts and Letters. His music is published exclusively by Schott.

GYAN RILEY won his first guitar in a raffle when he was 12 years old. After learning all of the songs in his cassette collection by ear, he began his life-long adventure in music, becoming the first full-scholarship graduate guitar student at the San Francisco Conservatory. He then spent fifteen years living in the Bay Area, touring as a classical guitar soloist and in various ensembles, including performances with Zakir Hussain, Michael Manring, Mike Marshall, Dawn Upshaw, the San Francisco Symphony, the Falla Guitar Trio, the World Guitar Ensemble and his father, the composer/pianist/vocalist Terry Riley. Along the way, he completed various compositional projects, including those commissioned by the Carnegie Hall Corporation, the American Composers Forum, and the New York Guitar Festival. Gyan's diverse work now focuses on his own compositions, improvisation, and contemporary classical repertoire. Recent performance highlights include Carnegie Hall, London's Barbican Theatre, the All Tomorrow's Parties Festival, the Big Ears Festival, and soloing with the Philadelphia Chamber Orchestra at Kimmel Center. Over the years, Riley has performed throughout Europe, Canada, Latin America and the US, both as a soloist and in various all-star ensembles. Having recently relocated to Brooklyn, NY, Gyan can be frequently heard performing at such local venues as Le Poisson Rouge and Barbès, either in solo form or with various

Gyan Riley

collaborators. In January 2011, Gyan's fourth recording of original compositions, entitled *Stream of Gratitude*, was released on Tzadik.

Jon Rose

For forty years, JON ROSE has been at the sharp end of experimental, new and improvised music on the global stage. Central to that practice has been "The Relative Violin" project, a unique output, rich in content, realising almost everything on, with, and about the violin—and string music in general. In the area of interactive electronics, he pioneered the use of the MIDI bow in the 1980s with the Steim Institute, Amsterdam—and with whom he continues to collaborate often in interactive projects involving sport, games, or the environment. Jon Rose has appeared on more than sixty albums and collaborated with many of the mavericks of new music including Derek Bailey, Butch Morris, Alvin Curran, Fred Frith, Chris Cutler, Otomo Yoshihide, Eugene Chadbourne, Veryan Western, Shelley Hirsch, Jim Denley, etc. at festivals of New Music, Jazz, and Sound Art world wide such as Ars Elektronica, Festival D'Automne, Maerzmusik, Dokumenta, North Sea Jazz Fest, Leipzig Jazz Fest, European Media, New Music America, the Vienna Festival, the Berlin Jazz Festival, etc. Recently Jon Rose was commissioned by the Kronos String Quartet to write and build *Music from 4 Fences* for the Sydney Opera House; realised his bicycle powered *Pursuit* project at Carriage Works (Sydney) and The Mona Foma Festival; performed a completely new and improvised solo part for the Tchaikovsky *Violin Concerto* with the BBC Scottish Symphony Orchestra; created two major radiophonic works for the BBC, on the first Aboriginal string orchestra, and the history of the piano in 19th century Australia; toured in Europe with his current improvisation groups Futch and Strike; produced his interactive Ball project at The Melbourne Festival; performed his interactive multi-media composition *Internal Combustion* for violin and orchestra at The Philharmonic, Berlin; and been apprehended by the Israeli Defence Forces at the Separation Fence near Ramallah in the occupied territories.

Percussionist, conductor, and author STEVEN SCHICK was born in Iowa and raised in a farming family. For the past thirty years he has championed contemporary percussion music as a performer and teacher, by commissioning and premiering more than one hundred new works for percussion. He was the percussionist of the Bang on a Can All-Stars of New York City from 1992–2002, and from 2000–2004 served as Artistic Director of the Centre International de Percussion de Genève in Geneva, Switzerland. Schick is founder and Artistic Director of the percussion group, "red fish blue fish." In 2007 he was named Music Director and conductor of the La Jolla Symphony and Chorus, and is currently a regular guest conductor of the International Contemporary Ensemble (ICE). Schick founded and is currently artistic director of "Roots and Rhizomes," an annual summer course on contemporary percussion music held at the Banff Centre for the Arts. In 2011 he was named the Artistic Director of the San Francisco Contemporary Music Players. Recent publications include a book on solo percussion music, *The Percussionist's Art: Same Bed, Different Dreams*, a 3 CD set of the complete percussion music of Iannis Xenakis (Mode) and a 2012 DVD release of the early percussion music of Karlheinz Stockhausen. Steven Schick is Distinguished Professor of Music at the University of California, San Diego.

Steven Schick

Jen Shyu

Known mostly for her singing with saxophonist Steve Coleman & Five Elements since 2003, vocalist/composer/multi-instrumentalist/dancer JEN SHYU currently performs solo in a convergence of ancestral and original songs which unfold into improvised ritual. Among her tools of expression are the voice, body, piano, erhu, audience, found objects that sing and ring, the two-stringed Taiwanese *gatkim* or moon lute, and the East Timorese *lakadou*. She sings in her own language, floating between her own lyrics and words of poets past and present in English, Portuguese, Spanish, Mandarin, Taiwanese, Tetum, Korean, Javanese, and Pinuyumayan (spoken by a Taiwanese indigenous group also known as "Puyuma"), in an effort to transport and transform the listener. Born in Illinois from Taiwanese and East Timorese parents, Shyu has performed and recorded as a soloist, bandleader, and sidewoman throughout the US, Europe, Asia, and Africa. Performing her original music in such venues as Lincoln Center, Brooklyn Academy of Music, Blue Note, Merkin Hall, and Amsterdam's Bimhuis, Shyu has collaborated with innovators Anthony Braxton, Mark Dresser, Bobby Previte, Dave Burrell, Mat Maneri, Chris Potter, and Michael Formanek to name a few. Since graduating from Stanford University, she has been awarded

MacDowell and Yaddo residencies as well as fellowships to travel and do research in Cuba, Brazil, Taiwan, China, East Timor from the Asian Cultural Council, Jerome Foundation, and Bronx Council on the Arts. She is currently a Fulbright scholar, based in Surakarta, Indonesia, researching Javanese music and dance while developing a new solo opera with filmmaker-director Garin Nugroho. She has produced five albums as a leader: *For Now, Jade Tongue, Inner Chapters, Raging Waters, Red Sands*, as well as being the first female artist and vocalist as a leader on Pi Recordings with her critically acclaimed duo album *Synastry* with bassist Mark Dresser.

DAVID TAYLOR performs recitals and concerti around the world, from Lincoln Center in New York with the Chamber Music Society of Lincoln Center, the New York Chamber Symphony and the St Luke's Chamber Orchestra to Switzerland's Basel Sinfonietta, Australia's Adelaide Symphony, and to the Niederösterreich Tonkünstler Orchestra at the Musikverein in Vienna. He has been involved in dozens of commissioning projects for the bass trombone in solo and concerto idioms; collaborating with composers including Alan Hovhaness, Charles Wuorinen, George Perle, Frederic Rzewski, Lucia Dlugoszchewski, Eric Ewazen, David Liebman, and Daniel Schnyder. He has appeared and recorded chamber music with Yo-Yo Ma, Itzhak Perlman, and Wynton Marsalis and performs with the Mostly Mozart Festival Orchestra, Orpheus, and the St. Luke's Chamber Orchestra. Throughout his career, Taylor has appeared and recorded with major jazz and popular artists including Barbara Streisand, Miles Davis, Quincy Jones, Frank Sinatra, and Aretha Franklin. Mr. Taylor has won the National Academy of Recording Arts and Sciences Most Valuable Player Award for five consecutive years, the most it could be awarded and has been awarded the NARAS Most Valuable Player Virtuoso Award, an honor accorded no other bass trombonist. He has been a member of the bands of Gil Evans, Thad Jones-Mel Lewis, George Russell, Jaco Pastorius, Charles Mingus, Michelle Camillo, Bob Mintzer, Dave Matthews, and the Words Within Music Trio (Daniel Schnyder, David Taylor, Kenny Drew Jr.). Although he has performed on numerous GRAMMY award winning recordings, 1998 was special. In 1998 Taylor performed on four GRAMMY nominated CDs: The J.J. Johnson Big Band, Dave Grusin's *West Side Story*, the Joe Henderson Big Band, and the Randy Brecker Band. The latter two CDs were chosen for GRAMMYs. David Taylor is also on the faculties of the Manhattan School of Music and Mannes College. He plays Edwards bass trombones exclusively.

David Taylor

Richard Teitelbaum

RICHARD TEITELBAUM has been active as a composer and performer for more than four decades, performing throughout world. His music includes notated compositions and free and structured improvisations in acoustic, electronic and electroacoustic media, often combining traditional western and non-western instruments with electronics. After receiving his Master of Music degree from Yale in 1964 he spent two years on a Fulbright in Italy where he studied with Luigi Nono. While there he co-founded the pioneering live electronic music group Musica Elettronica Viva with Frederic Rzewski and Alvin Curran in Rome. In 1970 he formed one of the first intercultural improvisation groups, the World Band, at Wesleyan University and has continued to work with traditional musicians from many non-western cultures. In 1976–77 he spent a year in Tokyo on a Fulbright, studying shakuhachi with the great late master Katsuya Yokoyama, while composing *Blends*, for shakuhachi, Moog synthesizers and percussion. A recording of it was released in 2002 by New Albion and named one of the ten Best Classical Albums of the Year by *The Wire* magazine in London. He has worked with many jazz and improvising musicians such as Steve Lacy, Anthony Braxton, George Lewis, Derek Bailey, Evan Parker, Carlos Zingaro, and many others. In the 1970s he began composing live, interactive computer music. He performed his digital piano system in the Berlin's Philharmonic Hall, the Concertgebouw in Amsterdam, the Pompidou Center in Paris, and many other prestigious venues. While on a DAAD residency in Berlin, a commission from the West German Radio in Cologne enabled him to compose his *Concerto Grosso* (1985). The piece was awarded a prize from the Austrian Radio and the Ars Electronica Festival. Teitelbaum has created two operas dealing with Jewish mystical expressions of redemptive hopes: *Golem*, An interactive Opera (1989) and *Z'vi*, (2001–). He received a Guggenheim Fellowship to create this piece, which has since been performed at Bard College's Fisher Center, the Venice Biennale and in New York City. He has also composed works for pianists Aki Takahashi and Ursula Oppens, and *SoundPaths* for chamber group and computer which was commissioned by the Fromm Music Foundation and the Da Capo Chamber players and premiered in New York City in 2009. A new recording of a recent live solo concert will be released on the Mutable Music label in 2012. Teitelbaum is a Professor of Music at Bard College, where he has taught in the undergraduate and graduate programs since 1988.

Drawing inspiration from folk, classical, and rock genres, JULIA **Julia Wolfe**
WOLFE's music brings a modern sensibility to each while simultaneously tearing down the walls between them. Her music is distinguished by an intense physicality and a relentless power that pushes performers to extremes and demands attention from the audience. Her string quartets, as described by the *New Yorker* "combine the violent forward drive of rock music with an aura of minimalist serenity [using] the four instruments as a big guitar, whipping psychedelic states of mind into frenzied and ecstatic climaxes." Wolfe's *Cruel Sister* for string orchestra was commissioned by the Munich Chamber Orchestra, received its US premiere at the Spoleto Festival, and was recently released with Ensemble Resonanz (along with her other string orchestra work, *Fuel*) on Cantaloupe Records. Written shortly after September 11, 2001, her string quartet concerto *My Beautiful Scream*, written for Kronos Quartet and the Orchestre National de France was inspired by the idea of a slow motion scream. Upcoming projects include a new work for the string quartet Ethel, a percussion concerto for Colin Currie and the BBC, and a theatrical chamber concerto cellist Johannes Moser.

Wolfe has collaborated with Anna Deveare Smith, architects DillerScofidio+ Renfro, filmmaker Bill Morrison, Ridge Theater, director Francois Girard, Jim Findlay, and choreographer Susan Marshall among others. Her music has been heard at BAM, the Sydney Olympic Arts Festival, Settembre Musica (Italy), Theatre de la Ville (Paris), Lincoln Center and Carnegie Hall, and has been recorded on Cantaloupe, Teldec, Point/Universal, Sony Classical, and Argo/Decca. In 2009 Wolfe joined the NYU Steinhardt School composition faculty. She is co-founder of New York's music collective Bang on a Can. Wolfe's music is published by Red Poppy Music (ASCAP) and is distributed worldwide by G. Schirmer, Inc.

A ubiquitous presence on the New York downtown scene, KENNY WOLLESEN's latest projects include playing vibes in John Zorn's Dreamers and Nova Quartet, playing drums with Sex Mob, Love Trio, Electric Masada, Aleph Trio, Butch Morris' Phantom Station and Bill Frisell, playing bass drum with the street bands Himalayas and Lesser Panda, building a musical mini-parade float for the International Toy Theater Festival and delivering Sonic Massages with an array of one-of-kind hand made Wollesonic instruments. Always interested in theater, Kenny has done several sound designs for Great Small Works, Puppeteers Cooperative, Imagination Explosion, Robert Wilson and Tom Waits and recently composed and designed an all-percussion score for Teller's (of Penn & Teller) stage production of *Macbeth* at the Folger Theater. For the premiere of one of John Zorn's classical works for bass flute and two foley artists *The Prophetic Mysteries of Angels, Witches and Demons* at the Miller Theater, Kenny designed and built three new instruments especially for the night. Kenny has directed musical instrument making workshops at MASS MoCA, Bonn Art Museum, Roulette, 52nd Street Project, Brook Park in the South Bronx, Fluxus Ministry in Lithuania, Bilgi University in Istanbul and is currently working with master percussionist Cryo Baptista on the Sound of Community project.

Kenny Wollesen

Nate Wooley

Charles Wuorinen

NATE WOOLEY (b. 1974) was raised in Clatskanie, Oregon, a small fishing and lumber town on the Columbia River. He began playing trumpet professionally with his father at age twelve. After college in Eugene, Oregon and Denver, Colorado he moved to Jersey City, New Jersey, where he currently resides. Since 2001 he has become a much sought after performer, composer, and improviser, working with Anthony Braxton, Evan Parker, John Zorn, Christian Marclay, C. Spencer Yeh, and David Grubbs, among others. His trumpet playing has been called "exquisitely hostile" by Italy's *Touching Extremes Magazine*, and his solo performances and recordings have been numbered amongst a privileged handful that have helped to shape a new approach to the instrument.

CHARLES WUORINEN (b. 1938, New York) is one of the world's leading composers. His many honors include a MacArthur Foundation Fellowship and the Pulitzer Prize (the youngest composer to receive the award). His compositions encompass every form and medium, including works for orchestra, chamber ensemble, soloists, ballet, and stage. Wuorinen has written more than 265 compositions to date. His newest works include *Time Regained*, a fantasy for piano and orchestra for Peter Serkin, James Levine and the MET Opera Orchestra, *Eighth Symphony* for the Boston Symphony Orchestra, and *Metagong* for two pianos and two percussion. He is currently (2012) at work on an operatic treatment of Annie Proulx's *Brokeback Mountain* to a libretto by the author. Wuorinen's *Haroun and the Sea of Stories* based on the novel of Salman Rushdie was premiered by the New York City Opera in Fall 2004. Wuorinen has been described as a "maximalist," writing music luxuriant with events, lyrical and expressive, strikingly dramatic. His works are characterized by powerful harmonies and elegant craftsmanship, offering at once a link to the music of the past and a vision of a rich musical future. Both as composer and performer (conductor and pianist) Wuorinen has worked with some of the finest performers of the current time and his works reflect the great virtuosity of his collaborators. Wuorinen is a member of the American Academy of Arts and Letters and the American Academy of Arts and Sciences.

John Zorn

Drawing on his experience in a variety of genres, including jazz, rock, hardcore punk, classical, klezmer, film, cartoon, popular, and improvised music, JOHN ZORN has created an influential body of work that defies academic categories. A native of New York City, he has been a central figure in the downtown scene since 1975, incorporating a wide range of musicians in various compositional formats. He learned alchemical synthesis from Harry Smith, structural ontology with Richard Foreman, how to make art out of garbage with Jack Smith, cathartic expression at Sluggs, and hermetic intuition from Joseph Cornell. Early inspirations include American innovators Ives, Varèse, Cage, Carter, and Partch, the European tradition of Berg, Stravinsky, Ligeti, and Kagel, soundtrack composers Herrmann, Morricone, and Stalling, as well as avant-garde theater, film, art and literature.

RECOMMENDED LISTENING

Richard "Duck" Baker

The Salutation Day Job Records

The Kid on the Mountain
  Kicking Mule

The Clear Blue Sky Acoustic Music

Spinning Song Avant

Everything That Rises Must Converge
  The Mighty Quinn

Ducks Palace Incus

The Waltz Lesson Les Cousins

Amnesia in Trastevere Les Cousins

Out of the Past Day Job

The Expatriate Game Day Job

Eve Beglarian

BRIM: Songs from the River Project
  EVBVD Music

Tell the Birds New World Records

Almost Human Koch

Hildegurls' Ordo Virtutum Innova

Twisted Tutu: Play Nice OO Discs

Overstepping OO Discs

Karl Berger

From Now On ESP

Tune In Milestone

We Are You Calig

Woodstock Workshop Orchestra MPS

Transit Black Saint

Crystal Fire Enja

Around Black Saint

Moondance Suite Bellaphon

No Man Is An Island Knitting Factory

Stillpoint Double Moon

Strangely Familiar Tzadik

Claire Chase

Terrestre New Focus Recordings/
  Naxos

Aliento New Focus Recordings/
  Albany

The Bright and Hollow Sky
  New Focus Recordings

Abandoned Time
  New Focus Recordings

Enter Houses Of Tzadik

Complete Crumb Edition, Vol. 12
  Bridge Records

Sonic Eclipse Kairos

Undersong Mode Records

Died in the Wool Samadhisound

Anna Clyne

Blue Moth Tzadik

John Corigliano

*Mr. Tambourine Man: Seven Poems
  of Bob Dylan* Naxos

Circus Maximus (Symphony No.3)
  Naxos

*Concerto for Violin and Orchestra
  ("The Red Violin")* Sony BMG

*Winging It: Piano Music of John
  Corigliano* Cedille

Of Rage and Remembrance:
   Symphony No. 1 BMG
Corigliano: Music for String Quartet
   Naxos
A Dylan Thomas Trilogy Naxos
John Corigliano: Phantasmagoria;
   To Music; Fantasia on an Ostinato,
   Three Hallucinations Ondine
John Corigliano: Symphony No. 2, etc.
   Chandos
Revolution Varèse Sarabande

Jeremiah Cymerman
Purification/Dissolution 5049 Records
Fire Sign Tzadik
Polyimage of Known Exits
   Ice Level Music
Under a Blue Grey Sky Porter Records
In Memory of the Labyrinth System
   Tzadik
Big Exploitation Solponticello Records

David Fulmer
Schoenberg Volume 10 Naxos
Wuorinen: Ashberyana/Fenton Songs I
   and II/Josquiniana Naxos
Webern Volume 2 Naxos
Stravinsky Volume 9 Naxos
Bugaboo Albany
Spins Neuma Records

Jeff Gauthier
Open Source Cryptogramophone
House of Return Cryptogramophone
One and the Same Cryptogramophone
Mask Cryptogramophone
Rite of Violet The Present Nine Winds
Internal Memo Nine Winds
Summer Night Delos
Window on the Lake Nine Winds
Ocean Park Nine Winds

Alan Gilbert
Ravel, Dutilleux, Messiaen Decca
A Concert for New York: In Remem-
   brance and Renewal Accentus
John Adams: Doctor Atomic Sony
Bach, Berg, Brahms New York
   Philharmonic Download
Rihm, Penderecki, Currier DGG
Anders Hillborg: Eleven Gates Bis
Mahler: Symphony No. 9 Bis
Mozart Koch International
Sergei Prokofiev: Scythian Suite
   CSO Resound
Christopher Rouse: Symphony No. 2-
   Flute Concerto-Phaethon Bis

Judd Greenstein
Beautiful Mechanical New Amsterdam
   Records
Awake New Amsterdam Records
first things first New Amsterdam
   Records
NOW New Amsterdam Records

Hilary Hahn
Hilary Hahn Plays Bach Sony
Beethoven: Violin Concerto, Bernstein:
   Serenade Sony
Barber & Meyer: Violin Concertos
   Sony
Brahms/Stravinsky Sony
Mozart: Violin Sonatas, K. 301, 304, 376
   & 526 Deutsche Grammophon
Elgar: Violin Concerto, Vaughan
   Williams: The Lark Ascending
   Deutsche Grammophon
Schoenberg & Sibelius: Violin Concertos
   Deutsche Grammophon
Bach: Violin and Voice Deutsche
   Grammophon
Higdon & Tchaikovsky: Violin Concertos

Deutsche Grammophon
Charles Ives: Four Sonatas Deutsche
Grammophon

Mary Halvorson
Bending Bridges Firehouse 12 Records
Saturn Sings Firehouse 12 Records
Dragon's Head Firehouse 12 Records
Departure of Reason Thirsty Ear
On and Off Skirl Records
Station Direct Important Records
Electric Fruit Thirsty Ear
Fever Dream Taiga
Crackleknob HatHut
Misbegotten Man I & Ear

Jesse Harris
Crooked Lines Bean
Without You Bean
The Secret Sun Verve/Blue Thumb
While The Music Lasts Verve Forecast
Mineral Secret Sun
Feel Velour/Secret Sun
Watching The Sky Mercer Street/
Secret Sun
Through The Night Mercer Street/
Secret Sun
Cosmos Tzadik
Sub Rosa Dangerbird/Secret Sun

David Lang
Are You Experienced? CRI
Lost Objects Teldec
The Passing Measures Cantaloupe
Child Cantaloupe
Elevated Cantaloupe
Pierced Naxos
The Little Match Girl Passion
Harmonia Mundi
(Untitled) Music from the Film
Cantaloupe

This Was Written By Hand Cantaloupe
The Woodmans—Music from the Film
Cantaloupe

Mary Jane Leach
*The NYFA Collection: 25 Years of
New York New Music* Innova
60 X 60 Capstone
Downtown Only Lovely Music
Ariadne's Lament New World
Aerial, Issue #6 AER
Celestial Fires XI
¿Who Stole the Polka? Wave/Eva

Stephen Lehman
Dialect Fluorescent Pi
Travail, Transformation & Flow Pi
On Meaning Pi
Demian as Posthuman Pi
Interface Clean Feed
Artificial Light Fresh Sound
New Talent
Door Pi
Simulated Progress Pi
Dual Identity Clean Feed

Steven Mackey
Lonely Motel: Music From Slide
Cedille
It Is Time Cantaloupe
Steven Mackey: Dreamhouse
BMOP Sound
*Speak Like the People, Write Like the
King* Bridge Records
Interior Design Bridge Records
Heavy Light New World Records
Banana/Dump Truck Albany Records
String Theory Albany Records
Tuck and Roll RCA Red Seal
Lost and Found Bridge Records

Rudresh Mahanthappa

Samdhi   ACT Music + Vision
Apex   Pi
Dual Identity   Clean Feed
Apti   Innova
Kinsmen   Pi
The Beautiful Enabler   Clean Feed
codebook   Pi
Mother Tongue   Pi
Black Water   Red Giant Records
Yatra   AEMMP Records

Denman Maroney

Double Zero   Porter
Gleam   Porter
Music for Words, Perhaps   Innova
Mark Dresser and Denman Maroney
   "Live in Concert"   Kadima Collective
Udentity   Clean Feed
Gaga   Nuscope
Distich   Nuscope
Time Changes   Cryptogramophone
Fluxations   New World
Duologues   Victo

Jessica Pavone

Hope Dawson is Missing   Tzadik
Army of Strangers, Cast of Characters
   Porter
Songs of Synastry and Solitude   Tzadik
Quotidian   Peacock Recordings
27 Epigrams   Peacock Recordings
Departure of Reason   Thirsty Ear
On and Off   Skirl
Under a Blue Grey Sky   Porter
Anthony Braxton Sextet, Victoriaville
   2005   Victo
Anthony Braxton 12+1tet, Victoriaville
   2007   Victo

Double Sunrise Over Neptune
   Aum Fidelity

Tobias Picker

Keys to the City   Wergo
Keys to the City   Chandos
Tobias Picker   Nonesuch
The Encantadas   Virgin Classics
Old and Lost Rivers   Virgin Classics
Sacred Trees   Sony Classical
Emmeline   Albany Records
Therese Raquin   Chandos
Songs and Encores   Bridge Records
American Music of the XXth Century
   Virgin Classics

Gyan Riley

Stream of Gratitude   Tzadik
New York Sessions
   Agyanamus Music
Melismantra   Agyanamus Music
Food for the Bearded   New Albion
   Records

Jon Rose

Rosin   ReR
Futch   Jazzwerkstatt
Great Fences   Dynamo House
Violin Factory   Hermes Discorbie
The Hyperstring Project   ReR
Fringe Benefits   Entropy
China Copy   Cream Gardens
Temperament   Emanen
Violin Music in the Age of Shopping
   Intakt
Violin Music for Restaurants   ReR

Steven Schick

Born to be Wild   Newport Classics
Cheating, Lying, Stealing   Sony Classics
Caught by the Sky with Wire   oo-discs

The Mathematics of Resonant Bodies
  Canteloupe
The Percussion Music of Xenakis
  Mode
Sanctuary Mode
The Chamber Music of Xenakis Mode
The Early Percussion Music of
  Stockhausen Mode

Jen Shyu
Synastry Pi
Inner Chapters Chiuyen Music
Raging Waters, Red Sands
  Chiuyen Music
Jade Tongue + bonus tracks
  Chiuyen Music
For Now 4am Music

David Taylor
Past Tells (or Orals) New World
David Taylor Bass Trombone
  New World
Hymns, Hums, Hiss, and Herz PAU
Red Sea Tzadik
Doppelganger CIMP
Pugh Taylor Project DMP
Pugh Taylor II PughTaylor.com
Morning Moon CIMP
Not Just CIMP
Worlds Beyond Faust Col Legno

Richard Teitelbaum
Richard Teitelbaum Solo Mutable
MEV 40 New World Records
Blends New Albion
Golem Tzadik
Double Clutch Silkheart
The Sea Between Victo Records
Live at Merkin Music and Art
The Sun Emanem
Run Some By You Wergo
AMM/MEV Apogee, Matchless

Julia Wolfe
Cruel Sister Cantaloupe
Dark Full Ride Cantaloupe
Julia Wolfe—The String Quartets
  Cantaloupe
Arsenal of Democracy Point Music
Bang on a Can Classics Cantaloupe
Renegade Heaven Cantaloupe
The Carbon Copy Building
  Cantaloupe
Lost Objects Teldec
Bang on a Can Live Vol. 1 CRI

Kenny Wollesen
Dictée Tzadik
Mount Analogue Tzadik
Dreamers Tzadik
Nova Express Tzadik
Overseas IV Loyal Label
All We Are Saying Savoy Jazz
Everything Is Alive Winter and Winter
Cosmo Tzadik
Lovers Rock Nublu
Graylen Epicenter Mythology Records

Nate Wooley
The Almond Pogus Recordings
High Society Carrier Records
[8] Syllables Peira
Seven Storey Mountain
  Important Records
Seven Storey MountainII
  Important Records
(Put Your) Hands Together
  Clean Feed Recordings
Trumpet/Amplifier Smeraldina-Rima
Creak Above 33 Psi Recordings
Wrong Shape to be a Storyteller
  Creative Sources)

Charles Wuorinen
On Alligators Tzadik

Lepton Tzadik
The Golden Dance Albany
Genesis Albany
Chamber Music Naxos
Ashberyana Naxos
Tashi Naxos
Cyclops 2000 London Sinfonietta
String Sextet Naxos
Piano Works Col Legno

John Zorn

In Search of the Miraculous Tzadik
Dictée/Liber Novus Tzadik
The Goddess Tzadik
Interzone Tzadik
The Satyr's Play Tzadik
Mount Analogue Tzadik
The Gnostic Preludes Tzadik
Nosferatu Tzadik
Templars Tzadik
The Hermetic Organ Tzadik